INTERACTING STORIES

Other titles in the
Systemic Thinking and Practice Series
edited by David Campbell & Ros Draper
published and distributed by Karnac Books

Credit Card orders, Tel: 0171-584-3303; Fax: 0171-823-7743;
Email: books@karnac.demon.co.uk

INTERACTING STORIES
Narratives, family beliefs, and therapy

Rudi Dallos

Foreword by
Arlene Vetere

Systemic Thinking and Practice Series

Series Editors
David Campbell & Ros Draper

London
KARNAC BOOKS

First published in 1997 by
H. Karnac (Books) Ltd.
58 Gloucester Road
London SW7 4QY

British Library Cataloguing in Publication Data

Dallos, Rudi
    Interacting stories : narratives, family beliefs, & therapy
    1. Family psychotherapy
    I. Title
    616.8'9156

    ISBN 1 85575 095 3

Edited, designed, and produced by Communication Crafts

10 9 8 7 6 5 4 3 2 1

To Eva and Rudi and our families
and their never-ending stories

ACKNOWLEDGEMENTS

I would like to thank Ros Draper and David Campbell for their invaluable support, advice, and enthusiasm for this project. Working under their editorship has been not only creatively stimulating but also great fun. My deepest thanks also go to Harry Proctor, whose quixotic mind and seminal ideas first inspired and continue to provoke my work in this area.

CONTENTS

EDITORS' FOREWORD

As the field of systemic and family therapy grows and new ideas come and go, it is important to have the opportunity to pause and reflect on ideas that appear to stand the test of time and scrutiny of practice in the field. We are pleased, therefore, to be able to include this book in our Series, as Rudi Dallos offers the reader just that opportunity to reflect critically on ideas in the field of systemic and family therapy.

The reader is challenged to engage with the author's arguments that some "fashionable" ideas may well not stand the test of time and is asked to re-evaluate some "older" ideas, in the light of experience, that are grounded in the everyday reality of professional life and offer more useful concepts for the systemic practitioner and family therapist.

Rudi's interest in the social and political contexts of emerging ideas means that the reader is treated to a review or genealogy of some of the most influential theoretical positions influencing our thinking and practice. Criticizing any attempts to swallow a constructivist epistemology naively when dealing with families who are victims of social, economic, or political oppression, Rudi urges readers to consider their own political position in order to minimize the risk of inadvertently adopting oppressive labelling of clients.

In addition to ideas about the political aspects of social constructionism, the reader is able to see throughout the book an unfolding debate between the author and his ideas. We believe that this kind of self-reflexivity can only stimulate the reader to think more critically about her/his own practice. Another feature of this text is that it provides an opportunity for both more, or less, experienced systemic and family therapists to clarify some theoretical issues and to take stock of their own repertoire of ideas.

Rudi has a particular interest in the narrative approach and offers the reader ways of looking at patterns of prevalent discourses using the still useful ideas of pattern, escalation, and feedback to promote greater understanding of how family therapists work effectively.

The broad spectrum of ideas portrayed in this one book is well documented and researched and will, we believe, be a good resource for trainees and experienced therapists alike.

David Campbell
Ros Draper
London, February 1997

FOREWORD

Arlene Vetere

I was unsure how a Foreword to Rudi Dallos' latest book might begin, for it seems to me that this book is more about the integration of major systems of thought and the practice that flows from such integration than it is about beginnings. Except that this book *is* about beginnings too. So I shall begin where he does, in our shared theoretical heritage.

Rudi reviews the development of family systems ideas and practices from a sound scholarly base, carefully following early sources. I not only enjoyed his review of the development of the field, I also enjoyed his accompanying commentary in which he discusses the enduring utility of many family systems concepts, such as feedback, patterning, circular processes, and so on. I found his commentary particularly well argued, with an attention to detail, such as challenging the premise that early family systems thinkers ignored emotions in their conversations with family members.

He builds on this review to elaborate, develop, and integrate the systems literature with the emerging constructivist and social constructionist writings in the field. Rudi acknowledges his "ancestors" in the development of his integration of ideas and approach to working with family members therapeutically. Such scholarship is important in acknowledging the social history of the development of ideas and is respectful to the contribution of those who have gone before. I miss this scholarship in some current writing in "postmodern" approaches to therapy. By reminding us of some of our theoretical roots, in my view he counters some of the recent fragmenting seen in this postmodern rush to throw the baby out with the bath water.

Rudi Dallos complements his review of the family systems literature with a detailed and wide-ranging review of constructivist and social constructionist traditions, including the personal construct theory of George Kelly. He integrates these diverse and overlapping ideas into a view of family members as actively engaged in formulating meaning, which is seen as a socially constructed and mediated activity. Many of the interpersonal dilemmas experienced by family members are seen, within this approach, as both inevitable and posed by the culture in which the family is embedded. The integrated approach advocated is careful to eschew a position that is seen to blame families for the individual's distress rather than recognizing the existence of structural inequalities in our society and their iterative influence on both the social construction of reality and on the life events experienced by family members. He devotes much attention in the book to a consideration of power, personal resources, and relative influence, weaving-in the interplay between multiple perspectives and power politics throughout the discussion. This is best seen in the many extracts and examples from therapeutic practice found in the book. In my view, it is in the practical applications of his integrative view that we find another strength of his approach, in the deconstruction of therapeutic processes and consideration and interpretation of dominant narratives and themes in peoples' lives.

I think the timing is right for the publication of this book. Rudi Dallos has written extensively in previous publications about the therapeutic potential of integrating systems ideas with personal construct theory and the ensuing analysis of constructs in action. It was always a puzzle to me why his unique contribution was not more widely acknowledged; perhaps it is a matter of timing and the acceptability of integrative approaches to theory and practice. The unique contribution of this book, I believe, lies in the quality of Rudi's scholarship and his commitment to rigour, which provide, on the one hand, a unifying framework for thinking about family members' dilemmas and, on the other hand, both a grounding in and possibilities for future practice.

February 1997

INTERACTING STORIES

INTRODUCTION

Frog:	Help, croak . . .
Princess:	What's the matter?
Frog:	I'm a prince under a spell.
Princess:	What do you want me to do?
Frog:	Kiss me.
Princess:	Will that break the spell, and turn you back into a prince?
Frog:	Who cares?

I remember once getting a message at a child clinic. The receptionist came to me with a bemused expression and said: "Mrs White just called to say she is sorry but they can't come for their family therapy session today because they have some family problems." What understandings had this family derived from their previous sessions with us? How did Mrs White see what we were offering if she thought that having problems precluded them as a family from coming for therapy? Was this predominantly her view or one that they shared as a family? Who made the decisions in the family? Did they as a family think therapy was about talking about your problems and feelings after you had sorted some things out so that you were calm enough to discuss them? Was the message mainly a polite way of saying that they did not like what had happened in the last session or felt that such family sessions were a waste of time? The more I thought about it, the more I realized that I knew very little about what was in their minds. Our predominant focus on their interactional patterns had not encouraged a detailed exploration of their beliefs, especially about how they saw therapy.

Questions about how people in families and other relationships see each other, themselves, their lives together, and the stories they tell have become of great interest to systemic therapists. However, an approach to family therapy which concentrates on stories and narratives also immediately presents us with a dilemma: how do we reconcile a view of families as composed of people acting on the basis of their individual stories with an emphasis on pattern and connection? As in the example above, whose story are we referring to—Mrs White's or the family's?

One of the aims of this book is to consider this issue in some detail and to consider how family members can be seen to hold stories in common and in opposition to each other—the differences between them. In fact, we might argue that the concept of difference—of competing, interacting stories—is necessary to capture the dynamics and tensions fuelling the evolving nature of family life. Any given event in family life is open to multiple interpretations, and it is just these differences, the dialectical tension between stories, that it is important to consider. As an example, one couple, Brian and Helen, had different stories about the periods of silences in their relationship. Brian, who said that he felt less intelligent and articulate than Helen, read into the silences a story of Helen's contempt for him, that he wasn't even worth talking to. Helen, in contrast, said that she perceived the silences as an imminent sign that Brian would explode into violent anger. They both agreed that the silences were dangerous and filled them with negative feelings, but it was precisely the differences in their stories that appeared to maintain this volatile and unpleasant pattern in their relationship.

The above brief examples also highlight how people are trying to predict not only each other's actions, but each other's thoughts and feelings—each other's stories. George Kelly (1955) has suggested that we are all rather like "scientists". Ordinary life involves trying to understand what is going on—trying to work out how others will act, how they are feeling, and what they might be thinking in different situations. The other aspect to this is the ideas that we hold about how others see us and what they think we are feeling and thinking. Circular questions such as "How do you think Mary sees the relationship between you two?" explore this web of mutual understandings. Though family members may not agree about each other's positions, they do seem to hold some shared or joint understandings. These understandings include not only the ability to predict each other's actions but also the stories that other members of a family hold and will articulate in different situations. It is through these interwoven mutual understandings that we are in various ways attempting to influence each other—at times benignly, at other times less so, perhaps sometimes feeling that we are justified in attacking and criticizing to repay old scores and grudges. In other words, family life appears to be made up of a number of people trying to get along with each other as best they can, trying to work out what the others are up to, all with their own beliefs, emotions, motivations, plans, strategies, and aims. The term "narrative", or "story", perhaps best captures these various elements in that a narrative connects events over time—the past, present, and future. How we view what has happened in the past contains the seeds of future action.

How do the various family therapy models relate to this view of people actively constructing explanations, predicting and trying out ways of influencing each other? We sometimes have to read between the lines to find these connections. For example, brief therapy approaches suggest a view of people as forming solutions, basing their attempted solutions—their choices of actions—upon their beliefs. Strategic approaches suggest that not only therapists but family members may act in a strategic, tactical manner—attempting to predict and antici- pate the consequences that various actions and statements will have. The Milan models suggest that people's beliefs are cen- tral, that these underlie what kind of relationships people want and hope for; consequently, how they act and communicate, consciously and unconsciously, is shaped by these beliefs. More recently, narrative approaches have emphasized how it is the meanings that people give to their actions and situations which shape how they act in families. These narratives shape the na- ture of conversations and interactions in which family members engage, and "problems" arise when they become fixed on see- ing events and forms of experiences as problems (Hoffman, 1993; White, 1995).

Questions about meanings, purposeful action, and conscious and unconscious communication have been at the core of sys- temic therapy. However, some of these appear to have been put aside for a while when some exciting discoveries were made about the pragmatic nature of relationships. Many individual therapies and psychological models have been concerned with questions about people's beliefs, motivations, and strategic actions. However, systemic theory revealed that what actually happens in families cannot simply be explained in terms of individuals' beliefs, motivations, and intentions. Whenever we attempt to influence another person, we cannot be sure how it will turn out. The other person may not respond quite as we expected, which in turn may shape our response, her or his response, and so on. Before we know it, the relationship may be proceeding along a path we had not—nor could ever have— totally predicted or planned. This idea of uncertainty, and the need to look at whole systems of interacting people rather than trying to build up explanations of relationships from the sum of individual actions, encapsulates one of the major contributions of systemic thinking.

This move to an interactional understanding was an exciting development, with a promise of a leap in our understanding of the human condition—life and its inevitable problems. The family therapy movement owes a great deal to ideas derived from systems theory or cybernetics. When applied in the context of therapy, these ideas were liberating and proved to be a radical departure from individual models of problems that pathologized people or implied faulty processes of learning, inherited defects, or irreparable damage of various sorts. Looking at problems as evolving from—and maintained by—current family dynamics laid less blame on individuals and seemed to offer hope that, by helping interacting systems to change, individuals and their families could be freed from their distress.

An intention of this book is to reconsider the heritage of ideas from systems theory and try to integrate these with constructivist and social constructionist ideas which emphasize families as linguistic systems, narratives, and the impact of culturally constructed discourses. This is not to minimize some of the significant criticisms of systems theory that have been voiced: that it can appear to be an excessively mechanistic theory that conceptualizes families like machines or simple biological systems so that family members become depersonalized and are seen not as autonomous persons, but as parts of an interacting system. Systems theory has also been seen to have some difficulty in accounting for adaptability and change, especially in explaining the role of language and the influence on families of the history of ideas in any given culture. However, it may be very regressive to abandon systemic ideas, especially in a rush towards constructivist and potentially individualistic ideas. It may be helpful to extend the systemic focus on jointly constructed, shared, patterned action to a similar analysis of narratives: how stories interact.

Though now much influenced by constructivist thinking, the family therapy movement has been less influenced by the seminal ideas of George Kelly (1955). The connection between systemic theories and Kelly's personal construct theory has been imaginatively developed and articulated by Harry Procter (1981). The present book attempts to continue this pioneering approach by examining the cross-fertilization of ideas that can result from an integration of systemic theory, personal construct theory, and the rapidly expanding and influential work on the analysis of conversations and narratives. These combine to offer a view of people as active, autonomous makers of narratives who, through intimate exchanges with others, evolve systems of *interacting stories*.

STORYLINE

The book starts with a brief historical review in chapter one of some of what I perceive to be the most significant concepts from the heritage of ideas bequeathed by systems theory. As a movement progresses, it become increasingly difficult to present the guiding ideas in an unambiguous way, since the original models have been followed by critiques, counter-critiques, and a second generation of revised models. The exposition can therefore become lost in a fog of rarefied and jargon-filled debate. The dilemma is how to present some of these core ideas without immediately undermining and obscuring them. The solution adopted in the first chapter is to present summaries of some of these pioneering ideas, followed by a review—a set of personal commentaries and reflections which offers some contrasts to currently dominant versions of these original ideas. This also starts to illustrate one of the core themes in the book— namely, that our views, including our views of theories, consist of a range of alternatives or narratives. At any given time, some may be dominant and others subjugated, the truth lying somewhere between the two.

Chapter two then attempts to trace the roots of constructivist thinking in early systemic theory and practice. This is followed by an outline in chapter three of some of the current constructivist theories that are influential in, for example, social psychology and have as yet made little impact on systemic theory and practice; included here are overviews of personal construct theory, attribution theory, and narrative- and accounts-based approaches. Chapter four offers an integration of these constructivist ideas with systemic perspectives, especially strategic approaches. Chapter five extends this analysis by embracing ideas from social constructionism to consider the wider sources of influence on the beliefs and explanations that constitute the stories that shape family life. In chapter six this perspective is extended to consider the important issue of power and the problems that may result due to internalization of societally constructed inequalities of power and related distortions of ideas and experiences. Finally, in chapter seven these ideas are synthesized and illustrated through extracts from research interviews and clinical case material.

CHAPTER ONE

Cybernetics
and family therapy

"We presume that the universe is really existing and that man
is gradually coming to understand it. By taking this position
we attempt to make clear from the outset that it is a real
world we shall be talking about, not a world composed solely
of the flittering shadows of people's thoughts . . . people's
thoughts also really exist, though the correspondence between
what people really think exists and what does really exist is a
continually changing one."

George Kelly, 1963, p. 6

Theories, like children in families, sometimes turn out to
be clearly visible continuations of their parents and at
other times to appear radically different or even contrary. Systems theory is no exception. At its inception, psychoanalytic thinking was the dominant force in psychotherapy,
and subsequent systems theorists both connected to these ideas
and also adopted positions that became increasingly more
opposed to it. My intention in this chapter is to consider both

what appear to me to have emerged as some of the dominant concepts within a systems theory framework and also what aspects seem to have been relatively ignored or subjugated. This also captures the fundamental approach of this book, which is the idea that there are, inevitably, different versions or stories available of events in families, as there are of theoretical frameworks. So, systems theory does not exist in any definitive sense but lives as different versions in our personal interpretations—the varied ways that each of us connects with these ideas. Whilst supporting this personal view, it may also be fair to suggest that, over time, some versions of a theory become more accepted, more dominant, than others and coalesce together to form a version that starts to take on the status of being the "real" or "correct" version.

This process may be necessary to help us to organize and clarify important aspects and differences between theories, but it may also blinker us and even lead us to reject ideas that are useful. There is some danger that this is happening with system theory. One influence of the powerful emergence of constructivist and social constructionist ideas appears to be a rejection of systems theory, in some cases almost wholesale. This may be unfortunate and a case of "throwing the baby out with the bath water" or what Jacoby (1975) referred to as a "social amnesia" —a consumerism of ideas: "Within psychology new theories and therapies replace old ones at an accelerating rate ... the application of planned obsolescence to thought" (p. xxviii).

This is not to argue that theories should not be criticized and rejected in part or whole when necessary, but that we should be careful that the grounds on which we reject a theory are valid rather than fuelled by fashion and shining newness. An amusing example of such processes can be seen in currently popular critiques of psychoanalytic theory—e.g. that Freud was simply a product of his time, and that even his "genius" could not rise above his cultural conditioning. But, as early as 1914, Freud wrote:

> We have all heard the interesting attempt to explain psycho-analysis as a product of the peculiar character of Vienna as a city ... that neuroses are traceable to disturbances in the

sexual life, could only have come to birth in a town like Vienna. . . . Now honestly I am no local patriot; but this theory about psychoanalysis always seems to me quite exceptionally stupid. [Freud, 1914, p. 325]

He also stated dryly: ". . . First they call me a genius and then they proceed to reject all my views" (p. 142; Wortis, 1974). To realize that he was aware of such possible criticisms (early in his career) and to read what he thought of them perhaps prompts us to think a little further. Likewise, with systems theory it is fashionable to offer sweeping criticisms—e.g. that early theorists paid little attention to emotions, families' beliefs, the meanings they gave to events and societal factors—yet a reading of the early literature shows this to be eminently untrue. At the same time, I cannot claim to offer any definitive account of what some of the influential thinkers in the systemic movement *did* think. It is fashionable—or postmodernist—to say that there can only be competing narratives or stories, and so my interpretation of systems theory is no more valid than any other—just my own view. This is, of course, partly true, but at the same time there may be some versions (mine included) that ignore, distort, or have never encountered some important aspects: "All ideas are not equally true, and hence not all are equally tolerable. To tolerate them all is to degrade each one" (Jacoby, 1975, p. xviii).

More practically, I frequently meet academics and practitioners who explain that they have some knowledge and experience of family therapy but now do not find much use for systems theory. They often go on to say things about it such as:

1. It is pathologizing and normative, in making assumptions about "healthy" families. In so doing, it also simply moves the level of blame or attribution of responsibility from individuals to the family, so that families are the new scapegoats. Hence, its claims to be a radically new way of looking at problems is a bit of a sham.

2. Likewise, that it accepts the "nuclear", conventional family model as the norm ignores the rich diversity of modern

family life and casts blame on alternative forms, such as single-parent families or families from diverse cultures.

3. That it is mechanistic and deterministic in viewing people as parts of interacting systems, like a central-heating system. It ignores people's potential for autonomy, choice, and taking control of their own lives.

4. It is cold and non-emotional in having little to say about the complex feelings, joys, sorrows, anguish, and satisfactions that are a fundamental part of relationships.

5. In contrast to point (1), systems theory is seen, in its claim to be neutral and to view all problems as arising from inter-actions, implicitly to condone abuse and oppression in fami-lies—e.g. in cases of abuse or violence, sometimes one or more members of a family are to blame and should be held responsible for their actions.

Apart from a touch of sadness, one of my responses has been to defend systems theory by saying something along the lines of, "Ah, well, it's changed quite a bit, they don't assume that any more . . .". But, in fact, it never was like this for me. These were not the stories or narratives that I heard when I first came across systems theory, first in a theoretical context and, five years later, in a therapeutic one. In both it appeared as an elegant, ecological, realistic, and intelligent theory, contrary to the above criticisms, which presented a different version or interpretation to mine. Within the systemic movement, there are also debates, and some appear likewise to be so different from my view that it is almost as if we are talking about a different theory altogether. At first, I thought that it was simply my misunderstanding of some fundamental shifts in thinking that had taken place. But then I started to realize that I was not alone. Many therapists and researchers still felt that aspects of systems theory are useful and should not so readily be dis-carded. What follows in the remainder of this chapter is an attempt to outline some of what I see as the core ideas that underpin systems theory. In addition, I offer some reflections on these ideas—in particular, observations about some of the subjugated aspects of these ideas, aspects that offer some important connections with current thinking but have been for-gotten, neglected, or relegated out of our consciousness. These reflections are presented in italics.

SYSTEMS THEORY AND FEEDBACK

From the 1950s onwards, a number of theorists (Ashby, 1956; Bateson, 1972; von Bertalanffy, 1962) developed ideas that came to be known as the field of cybernetics. Some of the impe-tus for these ideas came from the biological sciences, where it was observed that an analysis of an organism, such as the hu-man body, into its component parts and specific functions could not adequately explain the ability to maintain stability and form in the face of varying demands for change. It was suggested that the body could be seen as a set of components that operated together in an integrated and coordinated way to maintain stability. The coordination was seen to be achieved through *communication* between the components or parts of the system. Bateson (1958) was one of the first to suggest that a variety of social relationships—rituals, ceremonies, family life—could be seen as patterns of interactions developed and maintained through the process of *feedback*:

> Feedback is a method of controlling a system by re-inserting into it the results of its past performance. If these results are merely used as numerical data for the criticism of the system and its regulation, we have the simple feedback of the control engineers. If, however, the information which proceeds back-wards from the performance is able to change the general method and pattern of performance, we have a process which may be called learning. [Wiener, 1954, p. 84]

This became a key concept in family therapy—namely, that some *information* about the effects or consequences of actions returns to alter subsequent action. Rather than focusing on how one event or action causes another, it was suggested that it is more appropriate to think of people as mutually generating jointly constructed patterns of actions based on continual proc-esses of change.

Jackson (1957) went on to propose that a symptom in one or more of the family members develops as a response to the actions of the others in the family and becomes in some way part of the patterning of the system. Attempts to change the symptom or other parts of the system were seen to encounter "resistance", since the system operated as an integrated whole. By "resistance", Jackson implied not a conscious but a largely unconscious pattern of emotional responses to change in one or other family member: "A husband urged his wife into psychotherapy because of her frigidity. After several months of therapy she felt less sexually inhibited, whereupon the husband became impotent" (Jackson, 1957, p. 88). In social interaction, the functioning of groups of people made up a pattern, a meaningful whole that was greater than the sum of its individual parts. By analogy, family dynamics are like a piece of music or a melody that we hear as the *combination* of the notes, but each individual note gains its meaning in the context of the others—the total *gestalt* or whole. The concept of homeostasis was employed to describe the tendencies of systems to preserve a balance or stability in its functioning in the face of changing circumstances and demands. A system was seen to display homeostasis when it appeared to be organized in a rule-bound, predictable, and apparently stable manner. As an example, Hoffman cites a triadic family process:

> The triangle consists of an ineffectively domineering father, a mildly rebellious son and a mother, who sides with the son. Father keeps getting into an argument with son over smoking, which both mother and father say they disapprove of. However, mother will break into these escalating arguments to agree with son, after which father will back down. Eventually father does not even wait for her to come in; he backs down anyway. [Hoffman, 1976, pp. 503–504]

We can see here a pattern of actions, but how do we draw this as a system? One version might be to focus on the smoking as the trigger, which, when it is perceived, leads to the activation of a set of beliefs and rules leading to further actions (see Figure 1.1). However, potentially there are an infinite number

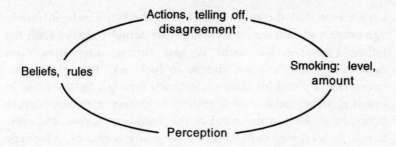

Figure 1.1. A simple cybernetic system

of other ways we could describe this system: for example, focusing on father's level of dominance, or the level of collusion between mother and son, or even on the son as a system—his nicotine intake, arousal level, level of addiction, and so on. A system is not static but always in motion, ever changing. In the example above, arguably what we in fact are seeing as homeostasis is patterning over time. We can even call this a narrative or story about how these people interact over a period of time. However, during this period the system will look different at any given point: for example, the son does not always have a cigarette in his hand; at times they are not discussing his smoking but doing something totally different and unconnected to it, like going to work or making love; and so forth:

> No behaviour, interaction, or system . . . is ever constantly the same. Families, for example, are perpetual climates of change —each individual varies his behaviour in a whirlwind of interactional permutations . . . a "homeostatic cycle" is a cycle that maintains constancy of relations among interactants through fluctuations of their behaviour. [Keeney, 1983, pp. 68 and 119]

Families do, of course, have explicit rules, such as the children's bedtimes, manners at the dinner table, and so on, but the more interesting rules were seen to be the implicit ones that we as therapists could infer, e.g. that when mother scolds her son, the father usually pretends to go along with it but subtly takes the boy's side. The smoking example can be seen to contain a covert rule that the mother will take the boy's side in family agreements even over issues where she actually agrees with the father. However, we could suggest various alternative rules depending on where we choose to look, e.g. that contact between the boy and his father is initiated through his smoking. In practice, what constitutes a system is always a construction, a belief, or an idea in the mind of the observer: "Cybernetic epistemology suggests that there are as many forms of cybernetic systems as there are of drawing distinctions" (Keeney, 1983). Which view we adopt is partly a question of choice and usefulness. However, some versions may certainly appear to make more obvious sense than others.

Critics of early systems theory formulations argued (Dell, 1982; Keeney, 1983) that Jackson's model of families displaying pathology as operating like closed homeostatic systems promoted a vision of families as mechanical (not even biological) systems, with little awareness, insight, or capacity for change or evolution. Yet Jackson (1957) had suggested that family homeostasis should be seen as the operation of a set of propositions about rules governing their interactions. He emphasized that these rules should be regarded as if: "the rule is an inference, an abstraction ... a metaphor coined by the observer to cover the redundancy he observes" (Jackson, 1957, p. 11). In other words, they existed in our minds as observers, not "really" in the families "out there". Jackson also made clear in his writings that he regarded people in relationships as capable of voluntary and deliberate action. It is interesting to realize that a view of a system as a hypothetical abstraction that was more or less useful was fundamental to systems theory.

COMMUNICATION, EMOTIONS, AND SYMPTOMS

Keeney (1983) points out that the early pioneers of cybernetics approaches were aware that a system was not simply composed of components that engaged in behaviours. The fundamental aspect of a system was that the parts were in communication with each other. Most importantly, communication between the parts of a system—the members of a family—was not necessarily, or even predominantly, conscious. By analogy to biological systems, communication can occur through electrical impulses, chemical secretions, and so on. In human systems, communication can occur at a variety of levels, such as gestures, proximity, voice tone, posture, breathing rate, smell, touch, and so on. Watzlawick, Beavin, and Jackson (1967) had suggested that any action can potentially count as a communication and, further, that any communication is multi-faceted, so when we speak we are also emitting a variety of non-verbal messages.

What is predominantly communicated non-verbally is emotion—how people feel in relation to each other, how they feel about what has just been said or done. Emotional processes were absolutely central in Jackson's (1957) original formulations of families as homeostatic systems:

> The paternal uncle of a woman patient had lived with her parents until she was 10 when he married. Her mother's hatred of him was partially overt; however, his presence seemed to deflect some of her mother's hostility toward her husband away from the husband, and the brother gave moral support to the father. Following this uncle's departure, four events occurred that seemed hardly coincidental: The parents began openly quarrelling, the mother made a potentially serious suicide attempt, the father took a travelling job, and the patient quietly broke out in a rash of phobias. [Jackson, 1957, p. 82]

The "constancies" proposed to be operating in families were seen to be related to deep-seated, often unconscious fears associated with changes in the satisfactions of needs and dependencies. Furthermore, Jackson emphasized that the emotional balances operating were a result of selection of our partners: "... the particular dramatis personae with whom each of us plays out his life are as rarely chosen by accident as the cast of a Broadway production" (Jackson, 1957, p. 3).

Likewise, such emotional processes were emphasized by Ferreira (1963) in his concept of "family myths":

The family myth functions like the thermostat that is kicked into action by the "temperature" in the family. Like other homeostatic mechanisms, the myth prevents the family system from damaging, perhaps destroying itself. It has therefore the quality of a "safety valve", that is, a survival value. [p. 462]

"Temperature" appears to mean emotional atmosphere or tensions. Family members were seen as able to perceive at an unconscious level that there are dangerous feelings around and in turn unconsciously communicate with each other that these are to be avoided and, further, that they should be ignored or disguised as something else. The original basis of the concept of homeostasis was centrally concerned with the interplay of unconscious fears, anxieties, and attachments in families. Much of the discussion of homeostatic processes in families, therefore, also assumed such semi-conscious or non-conscious communicational processes, so that family members sensed and responded to emotional changes in the others (Wile, 1981)

Also, it is useful to consider that unconscious communication of feelings can be seen to serve a much more benign and positive function in relationships, e.g. in providing a fund of warmth, motivation, and sense of connection (Bruner, 1977; Shotter, 1987). This has been confirmed by a considerable amount of research on early relationships between babies and their mothers (Brazelton & Cramer, 1991; Trevarthen, 1992). Babies, for example, appear to show considerable distress when they are unable to exert any control or influence in their interactions with their mothers. Generally, unless some unfortunate events have occurred (such as recent distress or trauma for the mother, a context that is unsupportive for her, or a history of emotional distress), there is a mutually satisfying, emotionally pleasant, and reciprocal pattern of influence. An exchange of pleasurable feelings through smiles, eye contact, shared games, and activities appears to occur spontaneously and functions to foster attachment.

The place of emotionality therefore appears to have been central in systems theory from the outset, certainly in Jackson's initial formula-

tions. Others, like Haley, likewise suggested that feelings were central and were essentially centred around the struggle for control—attempts to gain control of the relationships, to assert influence, and above all to define its nature. Similarly, Bateson considered that a variety of emotional processes underlay relationships and in particular the double-bind processes (see chapter two):

Generally, Bateson preferred to assume that people were motivated as had been traditionally assumed: by fear, hate, love, threats of punishment, and avoidance of pain (Haley, 1976a, p. 91).

Perhaps part of the subsequent lack of attention to feelings in some of the literature was encapsulated in Haley's (1976a) point that to focus on a discussion of feelings could be counterproductive in therapy and gave little information about actual actions, attempted solutions, and explanations. More broadly, as the early Milan team indicated (Palazzoli, Cecchin, Prata, & Boscolo, 1978), there is a tendency (the tyranny of linguistic conditioning) in many languages to equate feelings—and a discussion of them—with individual experience, which distracts from a systemic or interpersonal analysis of problems.

SYMPTOMS
AS UNCONSCIOUS COMMUNICATIONS

Systems theory has emphasized the idea that symptoms can, in a perverse way, serve to stabilize a family or a relationship. Haley (1963) in particular has argued that despite the obvious pain, distress, anxiety, and negative feelings that people may have, the presence of a symptom can perversely play an important *function* in ensuring that a system does not radically change. For example, symptoms of depression may mean that the sufferer becomes increasingly helpless and therefore in need of the support of the others. This may make it harder for a partner who would like to leave the relationship to depart, because of various practical dependencies and feelings of guilt generated. The symptom may at the same time distract attention away from the core relational conflicts, and so on. More contentiously, it was argued that the symptom bearer may even experience some satisfaction, perhaps unconsciously, at seeing the others inconvenienced by having to give some sympathy, having to do more around the house, and so on.

Communication in systems theory has been seen not simply as transmission of information but as an action in itself. Again, Haley (1963, 1976b) had been most emphatic in declaring that any act of communication inevitably involved, often unconsciously, an attempt to exert influence, define the relationship, and above all negotiate power. An example of how symptoms can be seen to function as communications embodying aspects of a power struggle in a relationship is given by Haley (1963):

> A patient with an alcoholic wife once said that he was a man who liked to have his own way but his wife always won by getting drunk. His wife, who was present in the therapy session, became indignant and said she won nothing but unhappiness by her involuntary drinking. Yet obviously she did win something by it. In this case she won almost total control of the relationship with her husband. He could not go where he wanted because she might drink; he could not antagonise her or upset her because she might drink; he could not leave her ... she could bring him to heel merely by picking up a glass. She might suffer distress and humiliation ... but she controlled those situations and thereby controlled what was to happen. Similarly, her husband could provoke her to drink at any time, either by exhibiting some anxiety himself or forbidding her drinking. Each partner must make a contribution perpetuating the symptom and each has needs satisfied by it. [pp. 15–16]

The link between attempts to exert control, unconscious communication, and symptoms is fairly clear and explicit here. The system is the way it is because it functions so that each partner has "needs satisfied by it". Haley's analysis here may appear rather bleak, perhaps because the focus is on pathology and on attempts to gain power in negative, destructive ways. Madanes (1981) made an important contribution in linking symptoms to issues of power in her concept of "hierarchical incongruity". This proposed that a symptom places both partners in a relationship simultaneously in a position of power and also powerlessness: the symptom bearer gains power through exerting *some* influence on the other, e.g. making their life inconvenient and forcing them to carry out more domestic duties. However, they also lose power in that they may be stigmatized as "sick", gain a "spoilt" identity, and associated with this have their freedom curtailed, rights taken away from them, and various forms of humiliating treatments applied, even against their will. On the other hand, the other partner (or family members) loses power in becoming impotent in the face of the "uncontrollable" symptoms, which, despite their efforts, they fail in overcoming. They gain power by virtue of being the "well" one, designated as competent and healthy and needing to be in charge.

This functionalist view has been highly criticized, not least on the grounds that a view of symptoms as having a purpose or function ascribes a form of intention and can end with blaming the symptom bearer (Dell, 1982). There can also be the fatal trap of assuming that the symptom bearer therefore gains *equal* power. This may be patently untrue in many family situations, especially those involving various forms of abuse (James & McIntyre, 1983)

The view of symptoms as communications of unconscious feelings can be seen to have played a central part in the development of systems theory. The emphasis in systems theory that feelings were not simply located as historical unconscious residues inside people, but as flowing continually between people in their moment-to-moment interactions, is an important contribution and adds to an understanding of unconscious processes. Psychoanalytic approaches have similarly come to emphasize processes such as transference as forms of ongoing unconscious communications between people (Sandler, 1993). Functionalist approaches stressing that symptoms serve to stabilize a system have been severely criticized. Nevertheless, the idea of symptoms as a form of unconscious communication can offer some insights:

(i) The idea of symptoms as unconscious communications that can have an effect on the power relationships in a family was a valuable contribution. However, this influence, and the power gained by the symptom bearer, needs to be seen as marginal in the face of the position of relative powerlessness that he or she is likely to be in, and

which is likely to become increasingly more extreme as a consequence of the symptom,

(ii) Symptoms are not tactics as such but are borne out of desperation and distress. They may at times embody elements of communicating a wish for change, including some anger or resentment regarding the powerless situation the person is likely to be in.

(iii) The system with a symptomatic member may be better described as an open, complementary one, with the power differential between the symptom bearer and the other(s) escalating over time. A symptom can be seen as giving the symptom bearer some temporary token of power or influence on other family members. In the long term, the effect may be the reverse so that they become increasingly more powerless as a pathological identity and its many negative consequences are established.

An awareness of the inequalities of power in families need not be inconsistent with an analysis of the systemic nature of symptoms. They can be seen as "attempts at resistance" as long as we acknowledge that resistance fighters do sometimes gain greater freedom and glory—but perhaps more frequently they are humiliated, tortured, or shot!

Circular causation and "neutrality"

Perhaps one of the most controversial aspects of systems theory was the fundamental proposition that interaction is explained not simply in causal chains of events—what one person does to another, their internal dispositions, and so on—but in terms of recursive spirals of mutual influence over time. When two or more people interact, each person's actions are seen as both a stimulus and a response to the other(s). Each person is both simultaneously reacting to the other(s) and proactive in stimulating the other(s) to react to them. We are seen as continually involved in a flow of interactions over time. *Circular* explanations emphasize that causes reside in the interactional processes between two or more people. In contrast, within a *linear* causal model the assumption is that experiences are caused by internal factors, such as personality, and that one person simply causes an effect in another. Alternatively, within a circular/ interactional model it is the recursive interplay of actions, feelings, thoughts, and *intentions* that is seen to shape an interactional pattern that constructs and maintains feelings and actions.

Related to this is the proposition that it is impossible to exert *unilateral control*. It is certainly the case that we often appear to take it upon ourselves to achieve certain ends, to adopt particular roles—e.g. as the "peacemaker" or the "provocateur". It is also apparent that we often explain our actions in terms such as, "Joan *made* me angry", or "He can get people to do what he wants". A circular explanation, however, suggests that since interactions and relationships can be regarded as mutually constructed, it is therefore not seen to be possible to exert unilateral control. It might be possible, to take an extreme case, to coerce or bully someone into compliance, but we might never be sure of their motives for complying, of our relationship with them, whether they would want to get back at us in the future, and so on. However, when I say "Someone made me do something", in fact it may be more accurate to see this as an interactional process, e.g. to say that I decided to react in certain ways towards Joan, perhaps unconsciously, despite my conscious intentions.

It is arguable whether and to what extent a circular epistemology led systems theorists to adopt a totally neutral view that no one was to blame or that all family members were equally responsible regarding problems. Various systems theorists viewed families as hierarchically organized, e.g. Minuchin's (1974) concept of executive sub-systems and Haley's (1976b) proposal that systems have ascending levels of control. Hence, child abuse, for example, cannot be seen to be equally the "child's fault" but due to the operation of the parental sub-system and the relationships of this system to others that can exert control over it, such as work, the police, neighbours, and so on. Neutrality is therefore not simply about how all members of a family equally influence each other, but that a family is inevitably connected to other systems in complex ways that makes it dangerous to make simplistic ascriptions about causes.

Moreover, neutrality was seen (e.g. by Haley, 1963, 1976b) as a pragmatic therapeutic position that offered a better chance that people could change. It was not intended to be a moral position, though it is perhaps inevitable that all theories of therapy will be taken as such since they deal with profound issues of human experience. Perhaps a failure to engage with these issues of morality was a weakness of systems theory. In its defence this may have been due in part to the excitement promoted by the possibility of helping people to escape the shackles of individualistic and pathologizing therapies. Interestingly, the non-neutral aspects of systems theory (e.g. the double bind as mother-blaming) were a great source of criticism. On the other hand, the blaming of fathers in families has been less contentious. In retrospect, it is possible that Bateson recognized the importance of power and abuse in families, but unfortunately there was less evidence available at the time about the prevalence of women's oppression in families, which subsequently has helped to contextualize mother–child relationships.

HEALTHY FAMILIES?

A significant critique of systems theory has been that it makes assumptions about what counts as "healthy" family life and is prescriptive about how families should be. In particular this has been associated with two strands of systems theory: structural approaches to family therapy (Minuchin, 1974) and the concept of the family life cycle (Carter & McGoldrick, 1988; Haley, 1981). It is possible that uncritical use of concepts such as boundaries, enmeshment, power, coalitions, and sub-systems may appear to be prescriptive. However, it is also clear that Minuchin (1974) and other structural therapists employed these concepts in a sophisticated manner, in the spirit of Jackson's (1957, 1965) notion of rules—"as if"—as hypothetical constructs.

However, systems are inevitably connected to other systems: a family is connected to the extended family, the work system, the school, friendship systems, and so on. Arguably these systems can be seen as layered hierarchically so that higher-order systems have more power to influence those lower in the order. For example, any given society lays down structures, ideologies, and so on that constrain families, which in turn constrain individuals. The concept of the family life cycle (Carter & McGoldrick, 1988; Haley, 1976b, 1981) suggests that family systems need to evolve continually and change in order to deal with varying internal and external demands for change. Internally, the demands for change include biological changes, development, and maturation, leading to different needs appearing. Family life also requires continual readjustments to changes and fluctuations in people's moods, interests, and so on. Externally, the family can be seen as located within the wider ecology of the extended family, neighbourhood, locality, and the wider society or culture. These have a variety of influences, some of which are practical but also ideological. We inherit from our culture ideas about what is appropriate "family life", what roles people should play, what responsibilities we hold towards each other, and also when and how things should change—e.g. the appropriate time for children to leave home, get married, start a family, and so on. In order for society to stay balanced and stable, families are regarded as needing to progress appropriately through these stages, e.g. to prepare children adequately to leave home, set up their own families, and make their due contribution to society.

Interestingly, in his paper, "The Study of the Family", Jackson (1965) drew attention to some of the ways that family dynamics and rules are connected to the wider ecology or society:

> ... values in this theory of the family are one kind of homeostatic mechanism. ... Because values represent an extra-familial coalition (with religion, society, culture, etc.) they exert leverage on relationships within the family ... values are used as interpersonal tactics which affirm or enforce a norm ... values have recognisable origins in the culture, subculture, ethnic background, or social group, but there are idiosyncratic values as well. [p.15]

Here he suggested that family members may in a sense make reference to or use such norms or values tactically, e.g. when a wife reminds her partner that "most men do more around the house nowadays". The wider culture therefore plays a significant part in shaping the nature of the internal world of a family.

Various criticism have been levelled at the concept of the family life cycle. Chief amongst these was that it was excessively normative and prescriptive in suggesting that there was a "normal" and inevitable pathway through family life. Many families diverge from this: there are, for example, single-parent families, some couples divorce and re-marry, some people do not have children, and so on. In effect, the societal level of analysis, along with the family life-cycle model, could be seen as imposing a set of norms that people were expected to follow instead of focusing, as second-order cybernetics might suggest, on the unique patterns of meanings that evolve in families and the futility of attempting to make any kinds of simple generalizations. More specifically, even the observation that a family is struggling with a particular transition, such as leaving home, is an inference. The family might not see things in such a way, and even if they do, we cannot be sure what other implications this holds for them, or how it fits with their wider system of beliefs.

One of the important contributions of family life-cycle theories (which are pursued in chapter six) is that they did point to the powerful influence of societally shared expectations, norms, and discourses about when and how things should develop in families. More specifically, they also reveal the powerful assumptions that exist in any society about gender roles and intergenerational roles and the expectations and the sanctions that may result if a family diverges from what is perceived to be "normal" and acceptable development. Rather than being seen as simply prescriptive, family life cycle theory points to, or can be employed to consider, how a variety of factors influence families and enable a more sympathetic view of people as subject to various outside pressures and strains that are beyond their control— the common "slings and arrows" of the society that they inhabit. Jackson's early observations also point to some fascinating connections between these societally shared beliefs (norms and values) and family members' personal beliefs, choices, and strategies of influence.

CHOICE VS. PATTERNS

Arguably, people in families are being faced with an increasing diversity of choices: should they marry or cohabit? what sexual attitudes shall they adopt? should they both work? how will they divide up the housework? when to have children? who will take the burden of responsibility for child care? and so on. Such broad questions, apart from the more detailed day-to-day—even minute-to-minute—decisions that face family members, suggest that we need to incorporate within systemic approaches an analysis of people as potentially autonomous, capable of reflecting on their circumstances, and continually making choices and decisions (Dallos, 1991). However, a dilemma is apparent in that despite our capacity to reflect on our actions and make our own choices, despite our best intention not to repeat certain behaviours in our relationships, we may find ourselves acting in the "same old ways". People frequently explain this in terms of how they are reacting to the other, or how they were "made to feel in a certain way". As Bateson (1972) suggested, perhaps it is not just that others do have the power to make us do things, but also our belief that they can, that shapes our actions.

The view of the person as self-determined is emphasized in studies of early relationships between babies and their carers. Infants as young as a few day's old can not only respond to their mothers, but are able to initiate interaction and influence her actions, feelings, and thoughts (Bruner, 1977; Trevarthen, 1992). Patterns of joint action, such as favourite games and mealtime routines, appear to be fundamental to human development; episodes of joint activity appear to act as reference points for current and future actions, and it is through the mutual recognition and ability to play out joint, predictable sequences that infants develop complex human abilities, especially language. Through early conversations with adults centred around such games and activities, infants apparently develop the ability to internalize conversations and thereby take control and direct their actions through inner dialogues (Bruner, 1977; Penn & Frankfurt, 1994; Vygotsky, 1978a). What is more, it is possible to observe these patterns of joint action both from the inside and from the outside—e.g. when a mother and child jointly build a house from toy bricks and can mutually refer to this game, engage in it, and act out their corresponding parts. Much of the interest in family therapy has been on sequences of joint actions that appear to surround pathology, but clearly joint actions can also be extremely pleasurable and are, in fact, a vital component of family life and an essential part of intellectual and emotional development.

Contingent choice

Vygotsky (1978a) suggests that choice and autonomy develops in a child through the internalization of conversations with others. These become established as "inner dialogues", which serve to enable the child symbolically to represent and plan actions over time. Through internalizing conversations, we also become able to hold others' voices and therefore able to predict how they will act and think. This process continues into later relationships and is facilitated by our increasing sophistication with language and ability to hold internally the voices of others, including internalized images and sounds of our conversations and interactions with them. Importantly, we come to be able to see ourselves through others' eyes and, in turn, also to be able to predict their reactions to our actions. Since we can anticipate the consequences in this way, we may be constrained either to avoid certain actions or deliberately to engage in them "just to prove that we are free". Either way, it is likely that our choices are constrained either by avoidance or by a conscious choice to perform the actions that we believe will be sanctioned. In addition, the other person is likely to be able to anticipate both these (and other) responses on our part, which in turn further shapes the relationship into predictable patterns

---

Systems theory, in its emphasis on the intimate interconnection of the parts of a system, reveals that choice is inevitably contingent. Each person's actions have an influence on others', which in turn shapes

their subsequent actions. Feedback therefore partly serves to build a picture of how others will act in future, and this shapes further choices of actions. Apart from simplistic, mechanical versions of systems theory, this idea of a mutual construction of meanings and potential alternative courses of action was fundamental in the early writings of Bateson (1972) and Wiener (1954). A view of choice as inevitably contingent helps to move beyond a sterile debate based upon an unhelpful and false distinction between personal autonomy as opposed to systems determinism (people's actions being determined by the system).

SECOND-ORDER CYBERNETICS

Arguably, the picture of family life as rigid, rule-bound, and determined—which to some extent appears to have emerged—was in part due to a subjugation, or neglect, of some aspects of early systems theorists' writings. Second-order cybernetics can be seen to represent both an attempt to correct this picture and a new emphasis on the role of the observer and the potential multiple constructions of reality (Hoffman, 1993). This introduces a subjectivity, an awareness that what we call a family system and the perceived patterns of interactions are based on our personal descriptions. What is seen always involves an observer. In the case of family therapy, the latter can be seen as predominantly the therapist and his or her supervision team. Even basic issues, such as what we take to be the system or who is seen to be in the family, are perceptions. Even more radically, how we think this system is functioning—its patterns, coalitions, hierarchies, circularities—become hypotheses on the part of the observers. Different observers may hold different hypotheses, and quite likely these in turn may be different to the family members' own perceptions. Our description of a family is therefore to be considered as essentially a fluid set of inferences.

Keeney (1983) pointed out that each and every communication can be regarded as potentially containing a variety of intended and unintended meanings, which may in turn be perceived in a variety of ways. A family is therefore a system of communications, with subtle, complex, and varied meanings. By implication, it is therefore no longer possible to say objectively what is going on. The idea of families as composed of autonomous individuals, continually reflecting on their own actions and relationships and having views about the therapist, suggests the idea that the therapist her/himself views families from a personal position. Perhaps there can be no objective vantage point, and, instead, in describing a family and its functioning as a system, we are in fact also describing our interaction with it—i.e. our act of observing inevitably perturbs or changes what we are observing.

A further important emphasis of second-order cybernetics was that the process of therapy, the intrusion of the therapist, inevitably alters the family system. In other words, the family will behave in a particular way in the therapy context, but we cannot be sure that it behaves in the same way in other contexts, e.g. at home, in a supermarket, at a school meeting. More generally, this was stated as the idea that not just therapy, but even the process of observing a family system, inevitably alters or perturbs the system. Perhaps the only way to gain a "true" picture is to record a family secretly, "candid camera", without their knowledge. However, even here we are faced with interpreting their actions, and any two interpreters may generate conflicting, or at least partially conflicting, interpretations.

Second-order cybernetics therefore moved systems theory towards a view of families as composed not simply as systems of people's actions and emotions, but as systems of meanings. Arguably, second-order cybernetics was not predominantly a new and better version of systems theory, but it more accurately reflected some of the original core ideas. As Bateson suggested, a system was not simply a collection of behaviours, but a system of interconnected meanings: "No part of such an internally interactive system can have unilateral control over the remainder or over any other part. The *mental characteristics* are inherent or immanent in the ensemble as a whole" (Bateson, 1972, p. 315).

CONSTRUCTIVISM
AND SOCIAL CONSTRUCTIONISM

The discussion so far has attempted to lay down some of what I regard as the fundamental and continuingly useful ideas from systems theory. This hopefully helps to reveal some important connections with two currently influential theoretical positions and movements in family therapy and social sciences. The next two chapters explore these in turn, but a brief outline may help to establish connections:

• *Constructivism* assumes that individuals and families are a sort of self-contained organism that constructs private meanings about the world that it encounters.

• *Social constructionism,* in contrast, argues that meanings are socially constructed; they arise from interpersonal interactions and conversations, which in our use of language are shaped by, and in turn contribute to, maintaining the prevailing beliefs, ideologies, or discourses shared in any given culture.

This second position emphasizes considerably more the wider social and cultural context and how this potentially places constraints on the meanings, understandings, and beliefs that may evolve in any relationship or family. Both of these positions are considered in some detail, with an emphasis on how the construction of meanings takes place in families.

Both theories face the danger of underestimating the dynamic, negotiational, argumentative processes whereby meanings are created and maintained in families. When we talk about family stories, whose story do we mean? How are differences between stories resolved? Are there recurrent patterns of how stories are offered, considered, dismissed, ignored, and so on? Arguably, families do not simply absorb ideologies and discourses but translate them within their own "family culture" and the traditions and current dynamics in their own families. Between society and the individual, we can observe a set of shared premises, explanations, and expectations: in short, a family's own belief system. But this belief system may not be monolithic: there will be differences, and awareness of differences, and perhaps even an awareness of how the different interpretations are regularly and predictably discussed.

Metaphorically, what happens in families can be represented as a deck of cards offering a range of options or stories from which particular choices can be made. These "cards" or options are derived from family members' own personal experiences, family traditions, and societal discourses. Continuing the metaphor, each family can be seen as having its own unique set of "cards", which serves to constrain their perceived options and consequently the choices they make: family members make choices, but not simply in circumstances of their own choosing.

CHAPTER TWO

The roots of constructivist systemic therapy: nothing convinces like success

"All purposive human behaviour depends greatly on the views or premises people hold, which govern their interpretation of situations, events, and relationships. For . . . psychotherapy, this means the ideas or premises a person [therapist] holds concerning the nature of problems and treatment will strongly influence the kind of data he will focus attention on, whom he will see in treatment, what he will say and do—and equally, not say and do—with the patient and others involved, and, not least, how he will evaluate the results of such actions."

Weakland, 1982, p. 5

Reference to family members' beliefs, explanations, and premises appears to have been apparent in the thinking of many family therapists from the inception of the family therapy movement. This has been evident not only in the writings of the Mental Research Institute (MRI) team in Palo Alto, but also in those of the structural, Milan, and other schools. Minuchin, for example, starts his book *Families and Family Therapy* with the following example:

Minuchin: What is the problem? . . . So who wants to start?

Mr Smith: I think it's my problem. I'm the one that has the problem . . .

Minuchin: Don't be so sure. Never be so sure.

Mr Smith: Well . . . I'm the one that was in the hospital and everything.

Minuchin: Yeah, that doesn't, still, tell me it's your problem. Okay, go ahead: what is your problem?

[Minuchin, 1974, p. 1]

He goes on to explain that, from the outset of the therapeutic encounter, the therapist's statement, "Don't be so sure", challenges the dominant view of the problem as residing in Mr Smith.

Arguably, though, this analysis of beliefs was initially peripheral, and much of the literature shows an analysis only from the "outside", perhaps including some speculation about what family members might be thinking but without any concerted attempt to investigate their beliefs and explanations. Attempting to promote changes in how family members see their problems, however, has more typically been associated with what has come to be called a "constructivist" view or orientation to family therapy (Cecchin, 1987; De Shazer, 1982; Maturana & Varela, 1980; Watzlawick, Weakland, & Fisch, 1974; Weakland, 1982). There are major differences between these various therapists, but they do appear to share an emphasis on promoting change in families by encouraging some changes in how problems are perceived.

DOES REALITY EXIST?

One of the central propositions of a constructivist approach is that reality is relative. It does not make sense to talk about "facts" or objective realities. The world "out there" is always and inevitably a construction, one among many possible ways of seeing things:

Constructivism holds that the structure of the nervous system dictates that we can never know what is "really" out there. Therefore we have to change from an "observed system" reality (the notion that we can know the objective truth about others and the world) to an "observing system" reality (the notion that we can only know our own construction of others and the world). This view has a long and noble lineage, from Vico and Kant to Wittgenstein and Piaget. [Hoffman, 1988, p. 110]

So, more mundanely, when a member of a family slams the door, this action in itself does not have an unambiguous meaning: it might be taken to mean that the person is in a bad temper or has been upset by someone, teenage tantrums, inner sadness and hopelessness, and so on. The constructivist movement in family therapy has also usefully brought our attention to the question of the therapist's own perceptions and the futility of attempting to make objective statements about what is going on in families. What we perceive to be happening must, in a large part, be a function of our own perceptions. In some ways, this resembles psychoanalytic ideas, which emphasize that our perceptions are coloured by a variety of internal emotional and defensive processes, such as transference, projection, and identification.

Watzlawick (1984), in particular, has been influential in challenging the notion of the existence of an "objective reality" and—even presuming that there is one—whether we could ever come to know it. It is pointless to talk of reality, since the world is slippery, changing, and we cannot in any objective way say that a particular event, phenomenon, or action exists, except in terms of our personal perception and assumptions about it (Bogdan, 1984; Dell, 1982). This position resonates with much of the theoretical development in psychology and elsewhere, i.e. a move towards a relativistic view of the world. This has been called variously an ecology of ideas, family epistemology, or family belief system (Dallos, 1991). The first wave of this approach in family therapy, however, despite such dismissals of an objective reality, appeared to make assumptions about the beliefs and perceptions of family members and did so without making a serious attempt at checking with family members what their ideas or beliefs actually were. For example, in Watzlawick et al.'s (1967) famous nagging–withdrawing example, there is very little reference to what the couple may have been thinking and what beliefs and attributions underlay their relationship; nor is there much reference to how they responded to or how they understood the reframe offered to them.

HYPOTHESIZING

Constructivist perspectives suggest that since we cannot be sure of reality, then what in effect we are doing is forming hypotheses about the world. Outside systemic theory, constructivist models have been developed largely in relation to explaining individual action and experience. George Kelly (1955) suggested that, metaphorically, we are all like scientists, in that we are attempting to explain and predict what is going on. Though we can argue that there is a real world of objects, actions, and even thoughts, nevertheless we can only know it through our construct or understandings of it. Similarly, Piaget (1955) suggested that children are like philosophers trying to puzzle out questions of causation, changes, and transformations of objects, concepts of time, and agency. As the child's brain develops biologically in complexity, so the potential for increasingly sophisticated understandings and complex, symbolic representations, especially through language, increases. Our attempts to understand families can be seen to involve processes of inference about their actions, about their own internal representations and processes of inference. Keeney (1983) suggests that families are infinitely complex and ultimately unexplainable in an objective sense. He suggests that it is, perhaps, more appropriate to think about families and relationships not in terms of scientific, logical, and rational explanations, but in aesthetic terms of patterning and connections.

Our descriptions are seen not in terms of objective validity, but in terms of "fit":

> From a constructivist view, it is not possible to match our perceptions with items in the environment; what is important is that they fit sufficiently to ensure our on-going viability. A bricklayer might believe that all openings in walls require an arch. The truth

of this belief is neither decidable nor necessary. What matters is that, in a world where houses are made of bricks, that premise is part of the fit between the builder and his environment. [Hoffman, 1988, p. 113]

Interestingly, Hoffman (1988, 1990) appears to be implying that there is in fact a real world out there, i.e. "a world where houses are made of bricks". This suggests that we cannot therefore just develop any hypothesis or belief about the world: "In order to remain among the survivors, an organism has to 'get by' the constraints which the environment poses. It has to squeeze between the bars of the constraints" (Von Glasersfeld, 1979). Certainly, the physical world imposes a variety of real constraints—food, shelter, safety, and so on—but equally there is a wide range of socially constructed realities, such as gender expectations or the expectations mapping out changes and transitions in any given culture.

For the Milan team, the process of successive hypothesizing became a central tenet of their therapeutic approach. They helped to draw attention to forms of implicit or unconscious hypothesizing, such as our unspoken assumptions or prejudices that might be activated by fragments of information, e.g. in referral letters or chance remarks from colleagues. The initial hypotheses—rather like first impressions—guide our actions/ interventions, leading to the emergence of new information, which we employ to revise, extend, reformulate, and discard our hypotheses (Palazzoli, Boscolo, Cecchin, & Prata, 1980). However, in the examples the Milan Team present it is obvious that not just any hypothesis will do, but ones that fit with the reality of what is going on in families:

Our team formulated an hypothesis during our standard pre-session discussion: the behaviour of the boy could be a way of trying to get the father to come back to the family.... During the interview, this hypothesis was rapidly disproved, but we were able to formulate a second hypothesis: the mother was an attractive and charming woman and, perhaps, after all those years of maternal dedication, she had met "another man", and perhaps her son was jealous and angry and was showing it through his misbehaviour.

Our second hypothesis *hit the target*. This example demonstrates how the two hypotheses formulated by the therapists and
the questions asked in order to verify them led to the information
essential for a choice of therapeutic intervention. [Palazzoli et al.,
1980, pp. 4–5; italics added]

This example also illustrates that frequently the hypotheses
are about unconscious processes—in the above, what the boy
secretly feared and wanted. An emphasis on hypothesizing
helps us to see that it is not that forming inferences about
unobservable unconscious processes is incorrect, but that we
should treat these as tentative and be ready to revise them. As
Cecchin (1987) points out, we should try to maintain our curiosity. It is possible, however, that therapy becomes effective
when the hypotheses that are generated do, in fact, capture
the reality of the family dynamics (Speed, 1984, 1991). As in the
example above, families are likely to correct us when we appear
to them to hold inferences or hypotheses about them that are too
different from how they see things, or which fit with certain
facts (e.g. that the mother had found a boyfriend):

. . . there are only a limited number of hypotheses that can be
produced from a given set of family patterns. Moreover, . . . some
of them will be judged by the therapist to be more adequate than
others and potentially when used in an opinion to the family,
prove themselves to be sufficiently adequate by their usefulness. [Speed,
1984, pp. 515–516]

Kelly (1955) has similarly argued that our beliefs are continually and successively tested in our interactions with others.
Importantly, this can be seen to apply as much to the activity of
the family members as to the therapist. Above all, this "testing"
operates by means of processes of communication as we continually attempt to decode, or make sense of, others'—and even
our own—communications.

COMMUNICATION

A patient comes into the hospital canteen and the girl behind the
counter says, "What can I do for you?" The patient is in doubt as
to what sort of a message this is—is it a message about doing him

in? Is it an indication that she wants him to go to bed with her? Or is it an offer of a cup of coffee? He hears the message and does not know what sort or order of message it is. He is unable to pick up the more abstract labels which we are most of us able to use conventionally but are most of us unable to identify in the sense that we don't know what told us what sort of a message it was. It is as if we somehow make a correct guess. We are actually quite unconscious of receiving these messages which tell us what sorts of message we receive. [Bateson, 1972, p. 195]

The quote from Bateson illustrates how, even in apparently simple, mundane, and trivial moment-to-moment interactions, conversations proceed through such mutual processes of inference or hypothesizing about what is going on now. The early work at MRI, including that of some of the founding figures of family therapy—Watzlawick, Weakland, Jackson, and Haley —was rooted in a communicational approach. This work was inspired by Bateson's ideas on communication, which employed and extended Whitehead and Russell's (1910) theory of logical types. This proposed that confusions in our thinking could occur because meanings are hierarchically structured. Specifically, in relationships a communication was simultaneously an act and a message. For example, if I say "all generalizations are nonsense", my act of saying this is in itself a generalization and therefore invalidates itself. More generally, we have the capacity to engage in ever-higher schemes of reflections—I can act, think about my action, think about my thinking about my action, and so on. This is not merely a philosophical diversion since in relationships these processes can be seen to be very problematic. To take a simple example, when one partner says, "Oh, don't hassle me—you are always doing that", this communication contains a classification of the action: it labels it in a particular way—"hassling"—and, secondly, contains a general statement about the place of this in the relationship over time. The receiver of the message therefore has a complex task in responding, e.g. whether to dispute the classification of the act, or the generalization of how often it occurs, or both, or to treat and respond to the communication itself as an act of criticism, aggression, or attack. Whether it is treated as an attack is further indicated by the non-verbal features—the voice-tone, posture, and so on—and also the history or context of the relationship. This may be the immediate history, e.g. whether they have been in conflict or kidding, and/or the long-term history, e.g. what kind of a relationship they think they have. In addition, other contextual factors, such as where they are—before an important exam, in a supermarket, at an airport, in bed—may also influence how the communication is interpreted.

Communication is therefore viewed as simultaneously multi-faceted, i.e. that each and every communication contains a multiplicity of potential messages. In particular two aspects of communication are identified: the content, and the relational message. To take an example, a mother might say [content] to her teenage daughter that she should not speak to her father so rudely, but the way she says this—her non-verbal tone [relational]—might indicate that she sympathizes with the girl and is prepared to be her ally. This view of communication also resonates with a wider challenge to dominant theories of language, which stresses its abstract and semantic aspects. Austin (1962), for example, developed the concept of "speech acts" to emphasize that language is employed to do things like getting another person to do (or not do) something, or defining the nature of the relationship between people. Furthermore, the consequences of a speech act are not invariably predictable; the meaning in effect partly resides in how the receiver interprets what is said.

The systemic model of communication also contains the idea of levels of messages; in this instance, the relational level is the more important. Levels of communication are most clearly seen in meta-communications, i.e. communicating about communication; for example, a man might comment on his partner's compliment about a new recipe: "Do you really like it? You don't sound very sure . . . aren't you going to finish eating it?" One of the most central aspects of this communicational model was the proposition that it is impossible to not communicate. Watzlawick et al. (1967) pointed out that, in the presence of others, all and any actions could be taken as communication.

This dictum has been widely repeated, but it raises the question of intention, misunderstanding, and unconscious communication. It is perhaps possible that intentions may be attributed to us, e.g. when someone is intent on picking a fight by saying: "What are you looking at?" A paranoid and aggressive expectation can fabricate that a provocative message was being sent. To attribute some communication on the part of the "victim" in this situation is tantamount to ascribing some blame to him or her, which is not too dissimilar from ascribing blame to any victim, essentially just for being there. Perhaps Watzlawick's axiom should be redefined slightly as: "It is difficult to engage in action or non-action without this potentially being interpreted as a communication."

This emphasis on communication was central to the emergence of systems theory and cybernetics. A system was seen to operate on the basis of feedback, i.e. information about the consequences of action. The influence between the components of human systems such as families therefore occurs in terms of communications, not simply actions or the physical consequences of actions. Irrespective of what people do in relationships and families, their actions are seen as communications, i.e. these carry information or meanings. This idea is absolutely central to both systems theory and to constructivist approaches. What is happening in a family is not simply a pattern of actions, but a pattern of communications and hence meanings.

INFORMATION VS. MEANINGS

However, this communicational view has possibly paid inadequate attention to the complexity of meanings embedded in the content of communication. For example, "private" language that develops in families invariably contains personal nuances attached to certain words or phrases, which are given meanings by the shared history of the family. The reason that the complexity of talk in families has been relatively underemphasized may be due to a narrow definition of *information* in human systems:

Information is indifferent with respect to meaning. . . . The system is blind with respect to whether what is stored is words from Shakespeare's sonnets or numbers from a random number table. According to classic information theory, a message is informative if it reduces alternative choices. This implies a code of established choices. . . . Such a system cannot cope with vagueness, with poly-semy, with metaphoric or connotative connections. . . . It precludes such ill-formed questions as . . . "how does the concept of Self differ in Homeric Greece and in the post-industrial world?"And it favours questions like "What is the optimum strategy for providing control information to an operator to en-sure that a vehicle will be kept in a predetermined orbit?" [Bruner, 1990, pp. 4–5]

Systems theory and cybernetics gained wide application and produced significant technological innovations in control engi-neering and telecommunications. Here, the term "information" was used precisely to mean quantifiable bits (binary pieces) of information. This relates to statistical probabilities, so one bit represents an either/or level of uncertainty, analogous to the toss of a coin. In a simple central-heating system, this is the level of information needed: the room is either too hot or too cold. However, in human systems, uncertainties cannot be reduced to such quantifiable amounts. Communication can better be defined as conveying complex meanings, and this carries un-known uncertainties since people differ in the potential mean-ings they may give to a communication. When two people employ language to engage in a discussion, the concept of ex-changing information can only capture a small part of what is going on between them (Bruner, 1990). In fact, communication between people may frequently increase uncertainty by con-juring up new ideas, new metaphors, new images, new possi-bilities of action. Yet the confusion remains: for example, throughout his discussion of cybernetics and the aesthetics of change, Keeney (1983) alternates between the terms "mean-ings" and "information".

It is possible that this confusion, or perhaps variability in how the term information is used (though it was employed almost certainly more broadly by Bateson to include metaphor and levels of meanings), has handicapped the development of systemic theory. The problems arise throughout the discussions of the new systems theory and second-order cybernetics. Maturana and Varela (1980), for example, use ideas drawn from the biology of simple organisms to offer a cognitive model of how organisms process information about the world outside them. The suggestion made is that the processing in fact occurs internally and may be removed from any direct correspondence with the outside world. This is an important observation, but, nevertheless, one that offers a simplified and reductionist picture of the complexity of human processes of meaning construction. One key problem is to offer any account of how human beings exchange meaning—metaphors, images, stories, concepts, attributions—though language.

ACTION AND BELIEFS

Communication was seen by Watzlawick et al. (1967) as a seamless, flowing, never-ending, never-beginning process. Each communication, they suggested, can be seen as a response to a previous communication and as a stimulus for the next one. So there is no point, it is suggested, in arguing about who started a quarrel, since this "starting" point may well be a response to a previous episode. However, as they pointed out, that invariably is just what people do. Instead of viewing our relationships and communications in terms of a cycle of events, we segment or punctuate the cycle into chunks, frequently seeing just one arc of it—our action as an immediate response to the other person's. Watzlawick's well-known example was of a cycle of approach and avoidance in which each partner perceives her/his own actions as caused by the other's actions, leading them to do "more of the same"—withdraw or approach, or "nag" and "withdraw". Possibly this example has done more than any other to revolutionize our ideas about relationships and the development of problems. It indicates, for example, how the partners are acting on the basis of their own choices: they are autonomous, self-determined human beings, but their very ability to make choices tightens the rope that holds them in their positions. The example also offers an embryonic model of the links between patterns of actions and beliefs, which is central to an understanding of human relationships. However, in the original example it is not made clear whether the terms "nagging" and "withdrawing" are the partners' own terms and descriptions, or whether these are attributed to them from the "outside". Neither is it made clear how these perceptions fit with their wider system of beliefs or the historical context of the relationship.

The concept of punctuation was intimately linked to the development of the therapeutic technique of reframing:

> To reframe, . . . means to change the conceptual and/or emotional setting or viewpoint in relation to which a situation is experienced and to place it in another frame which fits the "facts" of the same concrete situation equally well or even better, and thereby changes its entire meaning. [Watzlawick et al., 1974, p. 95]

Watzlawick and his colleagues offered as an example, here, reframing the wife's "nagging" behaviour as being protective towards her withdrawn husband. By sacrificing her own image, she is helping him to "look good" in the presence of others. They suggested that, though inane, this redefinition of her behaviour might help to interrupt the repetitive pattern of behaviour/communication between them. However, even if the couple did themselves employ these terms, we do not know how they viewed these: for example, in some cases "nagging" can be seen as a benign, cosy sort of activity that men should expect or, alternatively, as an example of women's attempt to castrate and emasculate. Likewise, withdrawing can be seen benignly as "having his head in the clouds needing to be by himself" or as a cruel rejection. It is also not made clear why the focus of the reframe was on the wife and whether this might have led her to think, since the therapeutic directive was aimed at her, that the implied message was that she was in the wrong. Reframing therefore appeared to have a sense of playing with truth, concerned not so much with the therapist sharing with a family what she thought was going on but with what seemed to be helpful in changing patterns, even if sometimes the reframe seemed slightly absurd or provocative.

For constructivist approaches, meaning and action are inextricably interwoven: "How people view their situation is intimately connected with, in fact inseparable from, what they do about it" (Eron & Lund, 1993, p. 295). More radically, Goolishian and Anderson (1987) have stated that: "Problems are no more than a socially created reality that is sustained by behaviour and coordinated in language" (p. 534). These authors have argued that families should fundamentally be regarded as linguistic systems. Problems are thereby a result not of unconscious homeostatic processes but of ways of talking about or thinking about each others' actions and beliefs. The problems are seen to develop from and be maintained by ways of talking about people's actions, e.g. seeing certain actions as predominantly indicative of illness or pathology may lead to the problems being aggravated. As new ways of talking about their situation are introduced, the problems are seen to dissolve. This idea is also inherent in the "dialogic constructivist" views of Epstein and Loos (1989):

> Language is the vehicle for the development of meaning . . . and languaging entails, "not only the denotations of objects with linguistic symbols but also the action taken with respect to that notation". [p. 412]

Unfortunately, the move in constructivist approaches towards viewing language as central may also have served to obscure the links between meanings and action. Elsewhere, Goolishian (1988), for example, has stated: "Problems are in the intersubjective minds of all who are in active communicative exchange." This begins to sound as if what people do, other than talk, is either irrelevant or merely an aspect of their beliefs and meanings. But surely what people do, their actions—especially in more severe cases such as violence and abuse—is important, and their problems are not simply to do with how they talk about things? Part of the problem may arise from a potentially confusing and mistaken emphasis on language—as opposed to communication—in interpersonal relationships. Communication is a broader concept which allows a multi-levelled perspective wherein speech and actions are both forms of communication. Another way of looking at this is to ask, "Where does the meaning reside in a communication?" The sequences of actions, the behavioural patterns in varying situations, as well as the meaning of the words used convey important meanings. In fact it can be contradictions—ambiguities between an act and what is said—that can be a source of considerable confusion and problems. Family members frequently report that they experience such ambiguities or contradictory components in each others' messages.

The MRI communicational approach, and also Austin's idea of speech as itself an act, attempted to eliminate the false dichotomization of behaviour and meaning, but this has persisted perhaps to the point where therapy is seen as nothing but the exchange of words, narratives, or stories. Possibly each attempt at clarifying and expanding the MRI models has perpetuated the previous false duality between behaviour and meaning. Bogdan, for example, has referred to this as the difference between viewing and doing. He argues:

> . . . it cannot, strictly speaking, be the case that behaviours, problematic or otherwise, are maintained by other behaviours. I have no access to your behaviour per se, only to my representation or interpretation of it. Therefore, it must be my interpretation of your behaviour, not your behaviour per se, that maintains my own actions. [Bogdan, 1986, p. 35]

Problems were seen as resulting from competing definitions or struggles over the meaning of sequences of actions. In relationships this typically takes the form of justifications for one's own actions and of blame or accusations for the other's. Much of this interpreting process appeared to be seen to occur at an unconscious level. Furthermore, these unconscious processes are not capricious but are related to other people's actions. In fact, considerable research evidence suggests that, for example, in early relationships communication takes a relatively unmediated form. On the basis of detailed analysis of interactions between mothers and their young infants, Trevarthen (1992) argues that the emotional responses between them are relatively automatic and unmediated, e.g. responses to crying, smiles, and eye contact. Likewise, in families each member's behaviour is important and shapes or constrains the interpretations possible. A different array of interpretations is possible or *fits* the behaviour of someone smiling, as opposed to shouting at us. In cases of sexual abuse or violence in families, it may be unhelpful to suggest that it is merely a question of interpretation of these behaviours (McKinnon & Miller, 1987). There may be some dispute about what such actions mean, although even this may be within a narrow band of contention. Also, meanings can be seen to arise over time, and actions may predispose or tilt the balance of meaning in a particular direction over time. So, one incident of shouting may be multiply interpretable but, given continual repetitions of this over time, will start to constrain the meanings available (Pearce & Cronen, 1980).

Family therapists and theorists of various schools of therapy appear to accept that there is an intimate link between actions and meanings. Minuchin, for example, emphasizes that a most useful place to start is to attempt to enable changes to happen in the organization of the family, the patterns of actions: "When the structure of the family group is transformed, the positions of the members in that group are altered accordingly. As a result, each individual's experiences change" (Minuchin, 1974, p. 2).

Though the MRI team are perhaps best known for the development of brief and strategic therapy, their writing—particularly that of Watzlawick—sets out the basis for a constructivist position. The quote from Weakland (1982) at the beginning of this chapter suggests that a fundamental point is that life presents us with continual difficulties or tasks. How we perceive these is based on our beliefs or cognitions, and these guide what we try to do about our difficulties—we generate "attempted solutions". Our beliefs may lead us to see a problem when there is nothing but a minor difficulty, or not to see a problem when there is one, or continue to believe that what we are attempting to do about a problem is really working when it patently isn't. Though the concepts of punctuation and reframing indicate that an analysis of beliefs and understandings was central to the MRI approaches, nevertheless these seem to have occupied slightly ambiguous positions subsequently. For example, the brief therapy model developed from their work emphasized the elegant idea of problems as emerging and escalating from attempts to solve difficulties that may initially have only been ordinary difficulties. As an example, they offered the onset and escalation of a case of depression following illness. The wife and grown children of a man who had recently experienced a stroke attended for therapy. The man, from the family's description, prided himself on being the head of the household, until the stroke left him helpless. The family members tried hard to be helpful, cheer him up, and cater for his needs but found that he only became more withdrawn and despondent (see Figure 2.1). The example depicts a "more of the same" problem cycle, which emphasizes actions attempted as solutions to the difficulties and their effects: the more the stroke victim acts helpless, the more the family members do things for him. Both sets of actions maintain the problem.

The focus is on the "problem cycle": the therapist tries to figure out what the family members are doing about the problem that keeps it going. The next stage is to devise a strategy to persuade them to act differently in order to disrupt this pattern. One way of persuading families to act differently was to promote different dynamics by suggesting a "reframe" that helped to shift the meanings of their actions. In this case it was suggested that the man's depression was the "last refuge of his self-respect", and it is then suggested that the members should act more helpless in his presence. As the family takes on this new approach, they begin to report a positive change in the father's overall mood and activity level. The reframe in effect uses the family members' view of the man as proud and stubborn in order to convince them to act differently. However, it does not explicitly change their perceptions; in fact, in this case it is likely that their view might be reinforced. There is also a question here that the family are in a sense playing games with their father, not being honest with him, which perhaps further places him in a "helpless" role.

It seems clear that Watzlawick and many other founders of the family therapy field saw clearly the connection between action and constructs. The phrase "nothing convinces like success" captures the idea that "reframing" should perhaps be seen as the start of a chain of events leading to change. If it does not assist a family to develop some new patterns of actions,

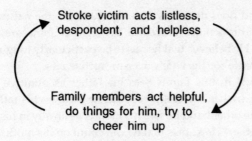

Figure 2.1.   A "more of the same" problem cycle.

then there will be "no success" to convince them, and the old patterns may remain or even deteriorate. Human experience involves behaviour—actions as well as talk, symbolization, and meanings.

FAMILY STRUCTURES

From a constructivist view, family structures are merely a construction, a chimera, in the mind of an observer. On the other hand, it can be argued that these patterns are the embodiment of the actions and beliefs in a family each maintaining each other in a dialectical way. The pattern and structure resulting can be detected with some degree of consensus between observers. The fundamental point is that the beliefs are maintained by the patterns of actions between family members and this idea appears to be implicit in much constructivist writing. Bogdan offers the following example to suggests that the concept of an "ecology of ideas" is a much more valid way of discussing family life than are ideas of structure or patterns:

A *mother* views her husband as excessively critical of their son. She regards the boy's behavioural problems as in part a result of the father's demeaning statements about the boy. She views her husband as having a "mean streak" that accounts for his behaviour toward the boy. Consistent with this view of the father and son, she feels the son must be protected from his father and compensated for the suffering induced by his father's remarks.

The *father* sees his wife as excessively tender-hearted and protective. From his point of view, she lets their son get away with

murder and does not allow him to experience the natural consequences of his actions. Therefore, the child is immature and irresponsible. He believes that he has to be particularly tough in order
to compensate for his wife's over-protectiveness.

The *child* in this family sees his father as punitive and uncaring. He wishes it were not so, but he believes his father hates
him. On the other hand he sees his mother as an ally in his struggle
with his father. He knows that he can count on his mother to stick
up for him when his father punishes him. This gives him the
courage to rebel openly against his father's authority. [Bogdan,
1984, p. 383]

This can readily be recognized as an example of a classic
pattern of family interaction, known as a cross-generational
coalition. It also encapsulates the idea of conflict detouring, in
which disagreements between the couple impact upon the son
and are displayed as his symptoms. The actions and beliefs in
this family are clearly interconnected, and it is almost certain
that the beliefs would change were the patterns of actions to
change. A set of beliefs that are unrelated to the "facts" of
behaviour is in effect a delusional system, which, unless maintained by other factors such as external labelling processes, will
fall into disuse.

This example raises two important questions:

1. How do the beliefs of each member of the family relate to
   the patterns that are established?
2. Why is it that these gender positions are so common, i.e. that
   women are more likely to be "soft" and men "hard"?

The first question has in effect been answered in various
ways: "punctuation organizes behavioural events and is therefore vital to ongoing interaction" (Watzlawick et al., 1967, p.
56). Campbell and Draper (1985) also clearly state the interconnection between action and beliefs more fully:

At some time in the life of every family, Johny will come down-
stairs to breakfast and announce, "I don't want to go to school
today". At the very moment anyone in the family replies to Johny,
an interacting system will be formed. Mother might say, "All right
dear, why don't you stay home", or she might say, "We all feel like

that at times, now run along and get dressed". These different types of feedback create different patterns and the patterns generate beliefs about how and why individuals should behave. [p. 2]

This statement of the inevitable link between beliefs and actions has much wider implications for research and theorizing in the area of relationships. Social constructionists (see chapter four) have likewise discussed the linkage between discourses, conversations, and *practices*, i.e. that regimes, structures, and organizations are set up as a result of the way we think about the world. As an example, beliefs about the organic basis of illness, including mental illness, have led to the construction of a variety of medical practices about how such problems should be treated. This includes the diagnosis by medically trained persons, such as doctors, the application of medication, confinement to hospitals, and so on. However, these practices and the structures (including buildings, equipment, etc.) associated with them ensure the maintenance or promotion of these medical beliefs.

Watzlawick has also hinted at these wider systems of beliefs or punctuations: "Culturally, we share many conventions of punctuation which, while no more accurate than other views of the same events, serve to organize common and important interactional sequences" (Watzlawick et al., 1967, p. 56). (The question of the wider cultural contexts from which common punctuations arise is pursued in chapter four in the discussion of social constructionist positions.)

CONTEXTS AND TIME

The picture emerging from early constructivist approaches of family relationships appears a little like "snapshots", e.g. the concept of punctuation mainly seems to capture the current "here and now" process in a couple. But relationships are characterized by the fact of having a shared history, a present, and an anticipation of future interaction. What is happening at any given moment will therefore be given meaning—contextualized—by what has happened, or what is believed to have happened previously. Time is a central dimension in systemic analyses of families and was emphasized as such by Bateson, e.g. in his account of the double-bind phenomenon:

> A young man who had fairly well recovered from his acute schizophrenic episode was visited in the hospital by his mother. He was glad to see her and impulsively put his arms around her shoulders, whereupon she stiffened. He withdrew his arm and she asked," Don't you love me any more?" He then blushed, and she said, "Dear, you must not be so easily embarrassed and afraid of your feelings." The patient was able to stay with her only a few minutes more and following her departure he assaulted an aide and was put in the tubs [restraining room]. [Bateson, 1972, p. 216]

Bateson makes clear that these contradictory meanings in the interaction between the mother and her son take place over time. There is a sequence of events or actions that are successively framed or given meanings. The mother appears ... the son puts his arms round her ... the mother stiffens ... he withdraws his arm. Each element in the interaction is accompanied by interpretations by mother and son and by an observer(s) (in this case, Bateson). Like Chinese boxes, each action and its interpretation can be seen to provide a meaning or context for the next action, e.g. the son is pleased to see his mother, but her action of stiffening suggests that she does not want him to touch her. She then asks, "Don't you love me any more", and the son blushes, apparently having interpreted the situation now as he having done something wrong and he shows his embarrassment, to which his mother next comments that he shouldn't be afraid of showing his feelings, and so on. Furthermore, this sequence has been repeated frequently and leads to an *expectation* that it will happen again: "We assume the double bind is a recurrent theme in the experience of the victim. Our hypothesis does not evoke a single traumatic experience, but such repeated experience that the double bind structure comes to be an habitual expectation" (Bateson, 1972, p. 206).

When people interact with each other over an extended period, as in families, friendships, and other long-term relationships, they can be seen to develop a shared history of experiences—a web of shared anticipations, not only about each other's behaviour, but about each other's feelings and thoughts:

"The individual, or the family [group], is fundamentally a linguistic system. . . . Through language individuals interact with and coordinate behaviour with others in a variety of ways" (Anderson, Goolishian, & Winderman, 1986, p. 6).

Included in this process of co-ordination is the development of meta-perspectives (Hoffman, 1993; Laing, Philipson, & Lee, 1966; Watzlawick et al., 1974) or ideas about how each person sees the others—their motives, their intentions, and how they see their relationships with each other. Through discussions, comments, and disclosures the people in a relationship may form a set of *shared beliefs*, assumptions, explanations, and concerns, which in turn come to regulate their interactions and produce predictable patterns of actions and also patterns of emotional responses and thoughts. Partners may hold competing explanations and stories about the meaning of what is going on between them or what should be going on. A system is, in this way, seen as a group of people engaged in struggles or negotiations over meaning. A number of writers, therapists, and researchers have argued that the conflicts in relationships are fundamentally "struggles over meaning" (Haley, 1963, 1976b; Watzlawick et al., 1967, 1974). Meanings, like actions, can be seen as interactional and potentially as escalating, e.g. an interaction that involves a negative frame of "blaming" can escalate to a dangerous degree, and so a more positive "frame" is introduced to protect the group from collapsing into bitter dispute.

Relationships are seen to proceed through successive attempts to make sense of what is happening. At times, people communicate directly about this using phrases such as "What do you mean", "You don't seem too happy about that", and so on. A feature of the double-bind phenomenon is that such meta-communication is not allowed, apparently because of unconscious fears of provoking anxiety: "According to our theory, the communication situation described is essential to the mother's security, and by inference to the family homeostasis" (Bateson, 1972, p. 221). These higher-order communications, or meta-communications, play a significant role in managing relationships (Watzlawick et al., 1967, 1974). In fact this multi-layered appraisal may be one of the distinguishing features of long-term relationships. The reflexivity or meta-communication in a relationships system can therefore be seen to be at ascending levels, with each higher level defining those below.

Bateson subsequently revised the double-bind theory to suggest that the process is a reciprocal one, with the child also engaged in double-binding communication. Even less attention appears to have been paid to Weakland's (1976) suggestion that it can in fact be seen as a three-person process: "The three-person situation has possibilities for a 'victim' to be faced with conflicting messages in ways that the inconsistency is most difficult to observe and comment on that are quite similar to the two-person case" (Weakland, 1976, p. 29).

At a verbal level, parents may express unity—"We want you to be independent"—but may negate this by how they individually express this message to the child or how they act, i.e. overt agreement and covert disagreement. For example, there may be an overt message from the father that he disapproves of hostility and that everyone in the family is happy. Though appearing superficially to support this, the mother frequently criticizes the father's dislike of physical activities. Furthermore, she may offer justification for holding different views to his, not in terms of her disagreement with him but in terms of a "benevolent" interest in the welfare of the children, thereby laying on them responsibility for parental differences in opinion. Weakland offers the following example of a family with a schizophrenic son:

> The father and mother insisted for some time that they were in agreement on all matters and that everything was right in their family—except, of course, the concern and worries caused by their son's schizophrenia. At this time he was almost mute, except for mumbling "I dunno" when asked questions. During several months of weekly family interviews, the therapist tried to get the parents to speak up more openly about some matters that were obviously family problems, such as the mother's heavy drinking. Both parents denied at some length that this was any problem. At last the father reversed himself and spoke out with only partially disguised anger, accusing his wife of drinking so much every afternoon with her friends that she offered no companionship to him in the evenings. She retaliated rather harshly, accusing him of

dominating and neglecting her, but in the course of this accusation she expressed some of her own feelings much more openly and also spoke out on the differences between them. . . . In the following session the son began to talk fairly coherently and at some length about his desire to get out of hospital and get a job, and thereafter he continued to improve markedly. [Weakland, 1976, p. 33]

MULTI-LAYERED MEANINGS

Family members' beliefs and consequently their communications incorporate meanings from a range of levels: societal beliefs or discourses as superordinate, and family traditions/scripts which may include a set of general ideas about relationships but are more specifically based on the intergenerational family histories and traditions. Relationships are, therefore, seen to be operating at several levels of meaning simultaneously: shared societal beliefs, family scripts, the formal definition of the relationship, and the interpretation of the current episode of interaction. Pearce and Cronen (1980) emphasize that at any particular point of time any action can be given meaning from these various levels. However, in addition Pearce and Cronen emphasize that communication derives its meaning not only from the content of the communication, but also from the context in which it occurs. In turn, the context is defined by the previous history of the relationship. Partners have available a repertoire of memories embodying a set of constructs that they employ to anticipate present and future interactions between them. These anticipations may be very influential: for example, a wife may anticipate that her husband will make sexual demands irrespective of her feelings, and this may set up a self-fulfilling prophecy whereby she responds in a cold and wary way to any signs of affection from him. Over time they may both come to anticipate this kind of interaction. Attempts to behave differently or suggest a different definition of each other's behaviour may be thwarted by this context. On the other hand, a warm, more positive context can serve to tolerate, or forgive, a certain amount of "bad" behaviour.

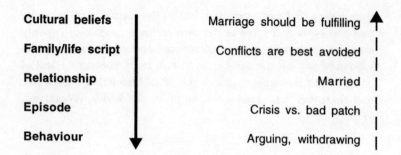

Cultural beliefs	Marriage should be fulfilling
Family/life script	Conflicts are best avoided
Relationship	Married
Episode	Crisis vs. bad patch
Behaviour	Arguing, withdrawing

Figure 2.2. Multi-layered meanings and relationships

Meanings in relationships are seen rather like Chinese boxes, with culturally shared meanings placed at the top in that they may shape more specific family and relationship beliefs (see Figure 2.2). Any particular action (behaviour) in a relationship derives its meaning from the context of the episode, which in turn derives its meaning from the overall meanings of the relationship; these in turn are defined by the family scripts and, finally, by the cultural context. For example, Stuart and Diane, a couple whose case is discussed further in chapter three, appeared to share a core cultural belief that that marriage should be fulfilling and relatively free from conflict. In turn, in both their families conflict had been seen as dangerous and to be avoided. Hence, when they experienced arguing or withdrawing this tended to be seen as a "crisis" and dangerous since at the higher levels it was given these negative meanings:

Crisis vs. bad patch

Arguing

Pearce and Cronen (1980) have suggest that there is a reciprocal relationship between the levels, so that the behaviour at the bottom of the hierarchy can also be employed to define the higher levels of meanings. The evidence of behaviour may have a cumulative effect over time, so that frequent rows tilt the definition of the episode towards a definition of a crisis, e.g. "We are having yet another argument, therefore we must be in crisis". The definitions at this level are, in turn, defined by the wider definition of the relationship: for example, if the couple are married, as opposed to co-habiting, this might provide a more tolerant context, i.e. that marriages are relatively perm- anent and are expected to have "ups and downs" (cultural constructs). However, there may be a family/life script, such as a previous broken relationship, that provides a context in which conflicts are seen as dangerous and to be avoided. The various levels of contexts may offer contradictory interpreta- tions, which may promote attempts at change to achieve con- sistency. There may also be contradictions between various competing cultural constructs: for example, more "modern" conceptions of marriage expect greater satisfaction and hold less tolerance for conflict, which may be seen as a sign that the relationship is not working and should be terminated.

AMBIGUITY AND RELATIONSHIP LOOPS

Pearce and Cronen's (1980) model emphasizes the history of a relationship, which is seen to provide a context within which current actions are interpreted. So the attempts by one partner to be "nice" may be distrusted if there has been a history of conflict. On the other hand, some unpleasant behaviour may be tolerated if the relationship is defined as "good". A problematic situation can occur when there is a fine balance between these definitions, as when there has been considerable conflict but also some satisfaction. An ambiguity may occur so that a par- ticular action, such as "teasing", can be defined as vindictive if the negative aspects are focused on, or alternatively can be seen as "fun". However, a couple may also attempt to use the cur- rent action to define the relationship—we are having "fun", so our relationship must be good, and so forth. Each person may also define the present action and the relationship differently. People seem to refer to such states as "not knowing where we're at", "being at a crossroads", and so on. The higher levels of contexts—the family and cultural scripts—can help stabilize such reverberations, but for people who have had contradic- tory and ambiguous experiences in previous relationships and in their families (life scripts), the reverberation may continue to the higher levels, so that problems in their relationship may imply that the world cannot be trusted. Possibly such reverberations represent an important factor in the deterioration of relationships and the production or maintenance of feelings of insecurity in the partners.

SUMMARY

This chapter has attempted to trace some of the roots of constructivist thinking in systemic family therapy and theory. The intention has been to outline constructivist ideas, especially the emphasis on the importance of meanings and on the recursive processes between actions and beliefs. One implication of this brief overview is to suggest that the emphasis on exploring a family's beliefs is an idea that unites the various forms of systemic therapies, even including structural family therapy, rather than one that divides them. How we make use of such explorations of family beliefs is an important but secondary point—some therapists have preferred to focus on the patterns of actions, some on the patterns of beliefs. But these are two sides of the same coin, and to ignore one at the expense of the other is seen here as potentially restricting to our therapeutic potential—drawing in our horizon of therapeutic possibilities. Above all, the intention of this chapter has been to highlight the point that families are composed of people who, like therapists, are actively engaged in trying to form understandings, theories of what is going on in their lives. Concepts such as punctuation and therapeutic techniques like reframing and positive connotation take this into account. However, it is important for us to develop ways of exploring a family's beliefs systematically, and in detail, in order to help us to understand how problems have arisen and, consequently, how to facilitate some changes.

The next chapters suggest that one of the developments in systemic therapy has been to look more closely at the content of family beliefs and to try to understand the processes whereby these have evolved and problems have arisen. The concept of narrative captures this sense of evolving beliefs over time and, coupled with the expanding interest in the studies of conversations, allows systemic therapy to connect more broadly with theoretical developments in the rapidly expanding area of research on relationships. We need a broader picture of how families interact, discuss issues, have conversations, and solve problems. How do "natural" processes of change, of revisions of beliefs, and of growth of narratives occur in relationships? Our increased understanding of these processes can help us to make therapy a more truly collaborative activity.

CHAPTER THREE

Beliefs, accounts,
and narratives

"The dialectical approach, while admitting the influence of
nature on man, asserts that man, in turn, affects nature and
creates through his changes in nature natural conditions for
his existence"

Vygotsky, 1978b, p. 60

This chapter outlines three perspectives: narrative
approaches, personal construct theory, and theories of
attributions and accounts which help to extend systemic
theory and practice. The contributions of these three are seen as
complementary: personal construct theory offers a comprehen-
sive account of how people actively develop systems of understandings based upon juxtapositions of alternative views of
events. Attribution and accounts perspectives emphasize how
understandings are embedded in attempts to formulate causal
explanations and consequently to assign blame and offer justifications for actions. Narrative approaches offer a broader picture of how our understandings and beliefs are embodied in a

story form that connects events over time. Most significantly, a narrative perspective emphasizes how stories connect individuals and families to a wider social context. Societally shared narratives, like the air that we breathe, are inevitably absorbed and, though transformed in personal ways, nevertheless shape personal and interpersonal experiences.

The chapter focuses on narrative approaches and personal construct theory and attributional perspectives are woven in to offer some suggestions for clarification and elaboration. The chapter revolves around the following questions:

1. Are narratives essentially personal or shared?
2. Do family members hold competing narratives?
3. What is the nature of narratives, and how do they differ?
4. What is the relationship between narratives and action?
5. How do narratives link with patterns of actions, with systemic processes?

The intention is to outline these perspectives in order to help us to consider further how narrative approaches can be integrated with systemic ideas. One potential problem is that these perspectives appear to be essentially individualistic. What may be needed is a new perspective—a systemic/narrative framework that can incorporate these into a view of beliefs and narratives in families as functioning in a dialectical, dynamic process. (Some attempts to achieve this are outlined further in chapter four.)

Systemic therapies have in various ways taken into account the beliefs and understandings held by family members. One problem to be faced in attempts to examine beliefs in families is how to distinguish between what is held individually and what is shared. A discussion of "family beliefs" can blur this distinction: are we talking about the separate beliefs of each member, or what beliefs are jointly held? Partly, this confusion may be a result of the legacy of the individualistic psychologies that have been dominant where processes such as attention, memory, perception, and problem-solving were conceptualized as individual processes. In contrast, it is becoming increasingly apparent that even such fundamental processes are basically social.

Vygotsky (1978b) has suggested that the internalization of dialogues is fundamental to the development of all forms of mental functioning: memory, learning, perception, attention, and problem-solving. Young children embark on attempts to solve problems by "doing" and, when they are unable to solve a problem, turn to others, usually asking a parent for assistance. The conversations that ensue from such enquiries become internalized so that children start to be able to plan solutions to problems internally. The most fundamental mental activities, such as attention and memory, are therefore seen as socially constructed, i.e. children learn from others how to develop and employ memory, to represent symbolically the external world internally. The child's social experiences are likewise seen to become represented within him or her as internalized conversations or dialogues. Our thoughts and plans are seen to be largely the internalization of the conversations we have been involved in. Signs, symbols, and images are woven into these inner conversations to help us to extend our ability to plan and create novel solutions.

This process centres around the internalization of conversations:

> . . . when children find they are unable to solve a problem by themselves, they turn to an adult, and verbally describe the method that they cannot carry out by themselves. The greatest change in children's capacity to use language as a problem-solving tool takes place . . . when socialised speech (which has previously been used to address an adult) is *turned inward*. Instead of appealing to the adult, children appeal to themselves; language thus takes on an intrapersonal function in addition to its *interpersonal use*. [Vygotsky, 1978b, p. 227]

Social interactions and conversations make up the child's inner world. Internalizing the use of speech and conversations with others allows the child to transcend the immediate situation by planning activities based on previous experiences. These are connected to the demands of the present situation to formulate a plan or story about future action. This weaving-together of actions over time has the form of a story or narrative. However, these are both personal and social in that a child internalizes conversations but weaves these, in a unique way, into his own history of experiences and development.

THE NATURE OF NARRATIVES

Bateson (1980) suggested that a fundamental feature of living organisms is patterning of their structure and the ability to discern patterns in the interaction with the environment. Likewise, what characterizes mind is the ability to identify and adapt in a patterned way. He went on to suggest that narratives or stories best encapsulate this idea of patterned, adaptive action over time. Narratives or stories serve to help us to connect, make sense of, and integrate events into meaningful sequences over time. It is increasingly suggested that narratives may be one of the fundamental features of the formation of meanings, of cognitive processes in human beings:

> Perhaps its principal property is its inherent sequentiality: a narrative is composed of a unique sequence of events, mental states, happenings involving human beings as characters or actors. . . . Their meaning is given by their place in the overall configuration of the sequence as a whole—its plot or fabula. . . . A second feature of narrative is that it can be "real" or "imaginary" without loss of its power . . . the sequence of its sentences rather than the truth or falsity of any of those sentences, is what determines its overall configuration or plot . . . indispensable to a story's significance and to the mode of mental organisation in terms of which it is grasped. [Bruner, 1990, p. 44]

Each of us can be seen as having a story about our life, an ongoing narrative that connects who we are today with who we were yesterday, a year ago, in childhood, and how we see ourselves as being in the future. Stories in this way plot our passage across time and enable us to offer to ourselves and to others some explanation of how we have become who we are. Events are thereby connected into a coherent, meaningful whole over time, to make sense of life's journey:

The advantage of a narrative perspective is that it takes into account the ebb and flow of family life, the highs and lows—the times when problems dominate and the times they retreat into the background. [Eron & Lund, 1993, p. 298]

Of course, some people see their lives as largely due to chance—things just happen, and you go along with them. For others, the story is much more purposeful and deliberate, an achievement of goals aimed for. A story may also have the power to present a version of events that may not be true to the facts but—because of its inherent qualities, consistency, vividness, and internal consistency and because it fits at least with some of the facts—may persevere.

Typically, we construct stories to make sense of events in our relationships after they have occurred, and in these stories we may see ourselves to varying degrees as having caused events. Dell (1982) has discussed how, from inside relationships, we may be tempted to employ linear punctuations or causal stories of who did what to whom, how one partner's actions was propelled or caused by the other partner's, and so on. However, use of narratives as person-centred explanations misses the potential contribution that narratives hold for systemic analysis. Relationships in families consist of sequences of joint activity, joint interactions, and jointly creating new patterns of actions and narratives. Shotter (1987, 1992) suggests that what is created has an unpredictable quality, that the joy and excitement of relationships is partly to do with the unpredictability of what will emerge. We have expectations and may deliberately attempt to ensure that certain outcomes will occur, but in our moment-to-moment exchanges we cannot deliberately plan our every action, gesture, or feeling, nor can we be continually aware or reflexive. Instead, we typically reflect later on what has happened and retrospectively assign meanings to it. Such reflection may also be an interpersonal activity, so as we reflect, discuss, and reminisce with others we thereby also interact, and this interaction influences the meanings—the narratives—that are generated, which influences our reminiscing, and so on.

VIEWS FROM INSIDE

Systemic therapies have typically been wary of offering "insights" or of sharing a systemic analysis with families. Related to this is the puzzle about whether it is possible to apply systemic thinking to our own lives. If I see my own relationship in systemic terms, as an emerging pattern of events, jointly constructed between myself and my partner but over which I have no unilateral control, then how do I act? By analogy, it is like the river trying to watch itself flow by from the river bank: in forming narratives/reflections about our relationship we are in the river, but simultaneously we are also trying to watch from the river bank. But perhaps this is a central task in relationships, i.e. to try to stand back and reflect but also be aware that this, in itself, contributes to or perturbs what we are reflecting on—the relationship. Therapy need not, therefore, try to remove this reflexive attempt or try to avoid occasionally offering and discussing insights. Family members know quite well that therapists, and others, have thoughts and views about their relationships. They, too, have ideas about their own relationships, and about those between them and the therapists, and possibly even about the relationships between the therapists and those in the therapists' own families. The therapeutic relationship can likewise be seen as a flowing narrative that therapists and family alike are simultaneously constructing and attempting to observe.

In summary, two features of narratives can usefully be distinguished and explored further:

1. as making sense of one's experiences, connecting past events into a coherent story, and serving to offer some predictions for how we expect the relationship to be—how it will evolve and develop in the future;

2. as emerging and evolving from the moment-to-moment interactions in relationships, mutually, jointly constructed, and at least partly unpredictable.

For systemic perspectives an exploration of narratives or stories is particularly essential because this is the manner in which people not only describe their relationships to professionals such as therapists and researchers, but also to each other and to themselves. Our personality, our sense of self is in a significant part the narratives that we hold about ourselves and discuss with others. The development of friendships, selection of sexual partners, and so on typically involves sequences of mutual disclosure that consist in the exchange of stories about ourselves, our past circumstances, how we see our history as making us who we are. Parts or sub-stories may be about how we have become who we are, what parts we are happy with, what we would like to change if only we could, and so on. The continuing flow and progression in our stories has a self-fulfilling quality, which reaches out into the future.

INTERNALIZED DIALOGUES

When we ask family members to tell us about their circumstances—their problems, what things are like in their family, what they have tried to do, who is the most concerned about the problems, how one member sees the relationship between another pair, and so on—what they frequently attempt to do is to try to tell us stories that feature dialogues: who said what to whom and what was said next (Penn & Frankfurt, 1994; White & Epston, 1990). Sometimes these supposedly verbatim extracts of dialogue may seem exasperating, especially since at times they do not appear to be going anywhere. Frequently, also, family members are likely to start to correct each others' versions of these dialogues, e.g. "No, I didn't say that I didn't care, I said I didn't think anyone could . . .", "I didn't say I was upset, I said I was concerned". These speeches can be seen as conversational enactments whereby each member reproduces the conversations that have previously taken place and have been internalized in various versions by each member of the family. Their accuracy is less important than the function they serve as a set of internal conversations that guide each person's feelings and actions in the family. Following on from this idea, we should expect that states of psychological distress feature us "hearing", or replaying in our minds, the conflicting conversations to which we have been exposed. Families are not simply responsible or to "blame" for these conflicting, contradictory, and destructive voices. Instead, these in turn are shaped by dominant cultural ways of thinking or discourses (see chapters six and seven).

The stories we tell may be informed or shaped by the wealth of stories that surround us and form an essential ingredient of all our lives, from childhood bedtime reading and family stories, to adult fiction and the wealth of media productions: films, theatre, television, and so on. The study of relationships therefore becomes an enterprise of trying to understand the unique creations, systems of meanings, and unfolding production of stories that make up a relationship instead of trying to form general models or make predictions. Shotter (1987) adds that these creations may at various times be seen by the partners or outsiders as closed, as opposed to open, stories. When we import common stories into our relationships, e.g. a story of a wicked stepparent, we impose a closed story onto a situation that is open, as yet unfinished. Relationships, Shotter argues, are invariably unfinished, since there is the potential in each new interaction or exchange to redefine, alter, re-negotiate, or reconstruct the relationship. However, our belief that it is closed, that the story is set, and that we know the ending may mean that we conspire, perhaps unwittingly, to produce just that ending. Of course, this makes it all sound a little too easy to "author our own texts". Other family members may act to maintain a particular story, and, most importantly, dominant stories may be imposed externally, e.g. through labelling processes in contact with mental health agencies.

Though there may be a variety of other sources of conversations, our own family is likely to be one of the most influential sources. Chances are, therefore, that we might find ourselves speaking, thinking, and using the same phrases, words, and stories that we have heard in our families. Also, the way that these conversations/dialogues have proceeded in our families —the ways topics are discussed and stages of meanings, agreements, or disagreements reached—forms the basis for an inherited and shared view bequeathed to us by the history of our experiences in our family. In interactions outside our families, with strangers, we may in effect recreate ourselves by enticing others to play parts in our internalized conversations, e.g. to take the part of mother's or father's voice (Penn & Frankfurt, 1994). Importantly, this recreating is not simply recreating ourselves but recreating the internalized relationships that are a significant part of our "self".

NARRATIVES
AND PERSONAL CONSTRUCT THEORY

George Kelly's' personal construct theory, which offered a systematic model of the processes whereby we actively develop constructions of events, has much to offer and can complement a narrative perspective. Kelly (1955) emphasized reflexivity, he regarded people as able to reflect, introspectively, not only on their external world but also on their inner world of thoughts, images, and feelings. Most importantly, he believed that we are capable of reflecting on our relationships, anticipating others' actions and the outcomes of our own actions. He emphasized that our understanding is fundamentally in the form of *alternative* hypotheses. We are seen to build theories about the world that are more or less useful to us in predicting what is likely to happen, and we may discard our theory for a new one in the light of new, or contradictory, evidence. Kelly saw stories, explanations, and constructs in terms of bipolar or contrasting choices: any given narrative implies and is given its meaning by a contrasting story. This contrast may be "submerged", i.e. unconscious or subconscious and only partly available to conscious awareness. The idea of "submerged" narratives offers an alternative way of discussing unconscious processes which avoids some of the tortuous hypothetical constructs embodied in psychoanalytic theory. For example, when we hear family members discussing their situation in terms of a narrative about depression, this implies a contrasting state. Not infrequently, this contrast is unelaborated or has fallen into disuse, so that the family can much more readily discuss the problems of depression than what being "not-depressed" might be like. Due to disuse, this path may have become subjugated, obscured, trivialized, and relegated to the side-lines (White & Epston, 1990)

This idea of contrast and opposition is important to help us to focus on the active, oppositional nature of narratives. Bateson (1972) has likewise emphasized that our mental processes of perception, attention, and memory are based on detecting "difference" or contrasts—news of difference. It is possible, of course, that there may appear to be various alternative stories, though it is likely that these could be grouped on some core opposing dimensions, e.g. stories relating to mental health problems which essentially fall into a contrast between organic and social explanations. Kelly argued that we can act only from a whole or meaningful picture of the world which we attempt to create as opposed to simply deducing or building up a picture of the world from isolated events and experiences. Once we have created a picture, we can then change, improve, extend, and elaborate it. The overall picture, though, is what guides our activity; it directs our attention and where we try to look for further evidence. People and circumstances are seen to be constantly changing, so we need to revise our understanding in order to be able to deal with such changes, especially in our relationships. People do not usually change unpredictably from moment to moment, but certainly they do change a "bit" most of the time, and sometimes "quite a lot". Even if we propose that people have stable personalities which change very little, we would have to admit that friendships change, people grow older and take up different interests, and relationships develop and disintegrate. Each of us, in a sense, also creates the people with whom we interact, especially in long-term relationships, such as families, by the way that we act towards our partners. In relationships, changes in people's beliefs about each other are required, e.g. due to changing roles such as becoming a parent, the transition from a "child" to "adult" status in families, changes in status at work, or changes in health.

CHOICES—BASES FOR ACTION

People are viewed as fundamentally autonomous and capable of actively making choices about events and relationships. Any relationship is seen as consisting of two or more potentially

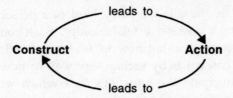

Belief—My partner will be angry when I walk in through the door . . .

Action—Enter the house and immediately apologise or start to criticize the state of the house etc.

Figure 3.1.   Mutually interdependent interaction.

free, independent, autonomous partners. We see the world through our personal narratives, and these offer us alternative ways of viewing people and events. This need not imply a "relativistic" position—that we simply "invent" reality and that any version is as good as any other. Events, including aspects of relationships, are seen as "real", but we can only know these through our own senses. Some interpretations are more adequate than others in a variety of ways, such as predicting the future actions of others and understanding how others see things. Since the world, especially our social world, is continually changing, so therefore has our understanding also to be able to adapt and change.

Choice of action is seen to be taken on the basis of personal beliefs, and these in turn start to construct the interaction that will follow—beliefs and actions are seen as mutually interdependent (see Figure 3.1).

TYPES OF BELIEFS AND CHANGE

When we listen to people's stories, we may note that these stories differ, e.g. some appear to be logical, clear, and unambiguous, whereas others may be rambling, vague, and disconnected. Some of our beliefs may be very general or loose, e.g. a belief that "Relationships require continual work, adjustment, and sacrifice". On the other hand, constructs may also be quite specific, such as "Jane is a homely kind of a person" or "Peter and Mary have a possessive relationship". Such constructs help us to make decisions about how to act towards others. We can then test our constructs by seeing how well or how badly they help us to anticipate the situations into which we enter. For example, if Jane decides to travel and expresses a lack of interest in household activities, we might revise our constructs about her or conclude that she has changed.

CONTINUITY AND ANTICIPATION

Our social worlds change continually and sometimes rapidly, so that we need to be able to revise our understanding to adapt to these changes. At the same time our narratives also provide us with a sense of continuity and predictability. We predict the future by expecting a measure of replication of past events, e.g. we probably expect our friends, our partner, and our children to be "pretty much" the same as when we last saw them, at least over relatively short periods of time—days or a few weeks. Probably most of us expect our interactions with others to be predictable in the sense of being "like" the interactions that we had had previously. Narratives therefore provide this bridge and continuity between the past, the present, and the future. Kelly (1955) referred to this process as *anticipation*— predicting what will happen in the future based on what we believe to have happened in the past—and *replication*—a belief that the future will be a repetition of the past, at least partly. As an example, couples in therapy frequently speak about wanting their relationship to be as it was in the courtship—to replicate that state of being together. Past events do not in themselves cause us to act in particular ways; rather, it is memories of these events—and our anticipation that these will cause events to be repeated—which may lead to or maintain our problems:

> Each adult carries within him, ready for awakening or even on the tip of his tongue, his own memories of childhood, and these in cooperation with the impulses of the child provide the dynamics for which each new generation must live. ... As the father watches his five-year-old son posturing with a spear, sending an

arrow straight to its mark, bidding for the mother's breast or being pushed away as too old for such indulgence, he lives again his own feelings when he at the same age was treated in the same way. [Mead, 1949, pp. 117 and 130]

Relationships would become extremely chaotic if we did not have any resistance to giving up our beliefs and narratives in the face of limited samples of evidence. For example, if we radically re-evaluate a relationship based upon each shift in a partner's mood, we might find it extremely stressful, if not impossible, to plan and organize any activities with that partner. We might also abandon too readily some useful ways of seeing things. Alternatively, there can be a danger that we become too resistant and try to ignore, discredit, or even falsify the evidence available to us. In relationships, a particularly pernicious process can occur (Bateson, 1972; Laing, 1966) when others falsify evidence, so that eventually the person may have difficulty in distinguishing "what is going on". Such inability to be able to anticipate, predict, and have a sense of control over events and relationships has been linked to serious mental illnesses (Bannister, 1960; Watzlawick et al., 1974; see also chapters five and six).

ATTRIBUTIONS:
INTERNAL AND EXTERNAL EXPLANATIONS

Attempts have been made to explore more specifically how people formulate explanations of their own and others' actions. Attribution theory and the analysis of accounts are two related approaches that attempt to investigate how people form explanations in terms of the causes of events. Heider (1946) proposed that people invariably make some attempt, consciously or unconsciously, to formulate theories or explanations about the causes of other people's actions. He argued that the need to find reasons or causes is extremely fundamental and illustrated this in a classic experiment in which people were shown a film of simple animated geometrical shapes (Heider & Simmel, 1944). The reports typically included interpretations such as that the circle was "following " the square, or in some instances that one triangle chased another because he was jealous of his relationship with the circle. (You can notice a similar effect if you watch your television without the sound: almost invariably you will find that you start to attribute feelings and intentions to the silent actions of the actors).

From these and other studies of interpersonal perception, Heider (1946) suggested that we form two contrasting forms of attributions of causes:

- internal/dispositional—explanations of causes in terms of peoples wants, needs, intentions, personalities;
- external/situational—explanations of causes in terms of environmental causes, circumstances, or situations in which an action is performed (time and place).

Any action can therefore be seen as having a number of potential explanations within these two categories. Kelley (1967) suggested that we should operate rather like detectives and try to summarize a range of information: for example, historical evidence, such as "Has Peter acted like this before?"; consistency across situations, such as "Has he always acted like this at home but not elsewhere?"; the possibility of some triggering event, such as "When did it start, how often does it happen?"; and so on. We try to predict how unusual or consistent a person's behaviour is, and whether other people see it in a similar way to us. These long-term predictions can also be seen to form the basis of a narrative about the other person, connecting a story of how the person acted previously in the relationship with what the future holds in store.

The distinction between internal and external attributions offers some important points of connection with White and Epston's (1990) concept of *externalizing* problems. They argue that dominant cultural narratives emphasize the cause of problems or distress as due to personal pathology. When people try to explain events in their lives, it is likely that these narratives will be seized on. In contrast, external attributions look for causes outside of the individual—relationships problems, financial problems, gender inequalities, stresses at work, and so on. However, these external attributions differ in that a focus on the problem as being in the relationship can be a step away from internal personal pathologizing, but only as far as moving the blame to the relationship. Looking more broadly at societal and cultural factors—such as inequalities, conflicts resulting from wider narratives, and structural aspects of gender and class— extends the range of the external attributions. Family members may negotiate or struggle over which type of attribution will prevail. This, in turn, may be linked to their relative positions of power and circumstances. For example, a woman who is extremely financially dependent on her partner and has few sources of validation outside the family may be more vulnerable to internal attributions of pathology than a woman who has a satisfying and rewarding job. Disempowered groups have similarly been found to be more prone to internal attributions, such as working-class blacks being labelled as schizophrenic (Littlewood & Lipsedge, 1989) or women being labelled as depressed (Brown & Harris, 1989). In effect, internal attributions often reflect social values about what constitutes a "real" person—how we "should" be—and defines what it is to be "deviant" or "aberrant". Rather than being a rather neutral or predominantly a rational cognitive process, attributions can be seen to be embedded in issues of power at the personal, interpersonal, and societal levels. The move towards external attributions of distress for individuals and families can be seen, therefore, as involving empowerment and a resisting of the dominant social tendencies to encourage internal, self-blaming attributions (White, 1995).

ACCOUNTS

The attributions we make, however, are influenced by the demands of the relationship we are in. In families and other relationships, our attempts at explanation tend to be in the form of accounts that we develop for ourselves and also for others. Accounts serve various purposes; in particular, they do important work in managing our relationships. Panalp and Surra (1992) suggested that the making of accounts involves a number of stages:

precipitating event — interpretation — response — change

The account we offer to others may frequently have a strategic component: to some extent, we develop an account according to how we think they will react and what consequences may follow. Personal accounts in relationships are defined as our attempts to justify, exonerate, protect, make excuses—in short, to ascribe blame or responsibility. The study of accounts also reveals that people are also called upon to justify their actions. The attempts at justification are evaluated and may or may not be accepted as credible or adequate (Heider & Simmel, 1944; Kelley, 1967). Failure to provide an account may in itself be seen as an admission of responsibility or "guilt". This situation is particularly significant in cases of abuse or violence in families; such cases understandably tend to involve attempts to apportion responsibility and blame. For example, if Peter has been violent towards Susan, he may try to defend himself by claiming that he could not help it, that she provoked him so much that he "lost control". Susan, on the other hand, may accuse him of using violence as a deliberate strategy to intimidate her. Peter may also attempt to block Susan's requests for an account of himself by refusing to speak or again becoming angry.

The accounts that are offered can contain within them attributions in terms of internal versus external causes. For example, Susan might formulate an account that features dispositional attributions, e.g. that Peter "lost control" because he is a violent person or because he wanted to "intimidate her". Likewise, Peter might try to suggest a dispositional account that Susan is a "provocative" sort of woman, or that she "exaggerates" his violence. External/situational accounts might feature external attributions, e.g. that the other person is overworked or that some external incident or trigger such as a problem at work or with his family has caused Peter's mood. An accounts perspective also emphasizes that accounts are not only offered but also requested—that we may be called to justify our actions. If an acceptable situational account cannot be offered, then there may an expectation that an apology is required, perhaps involving some dispositional factors and acceptance of responsibility.

The accounts that are offered are also evaluated in the context of time, so that, for example, if violence is repeated, Susan might conclude that Peter does not just "lose control" but is abusing her and that their relationship is no longer viable. External physical or medical causes may frequently be invoked if a situation has persisted, e.g. that the other is starting to suffer from some form of illness. However, the dominant attributions embedded in accounts can change from being predominantly external to internal, e.g. long-term illness can itself become seen as a dispositional feature and eventually as a part of the person's personality or character. Accounts are evaluated in terms of societal norms or discourses, e.g. an account in terms of losing one's temper may be more acceptable for a man than for a woman since men have commonly been seen as naturally more aggressive than women.

VANTAGE POINTS

People offer different explanations for their own as opposed to others' behaviour. In relationships, people are simultaneously both *actors* and *observers*, both inside the relationship and shaping it but also attempting to stand back and observe it—our partner's actions and even our own: "There is a pervasive tendency for actors to attribute their actions to situational requirements, whereas observers tend to attribute the same actions to stable personal dispositions" (Jones & Nisbett, 1972, p. 80). This effect may be particularly marked, for example, when people make excuses or self-justifications for something having gone wrong in terms of external events or chance. Alternatively, they may be more likely to want to claim the credit when things have gone well.

However, not all situations involve blame, and hence it is argued that this effect may also have a more general basis resting on differences between the information available to actors and observers. Specifically, actors will have greater access to their own covert thoughts and feelings, as well as knowledge about variations in their own behaviour at different times and places. We can know about our own intentions and feelings, but we may know much less about another's (though, in long-term relationships, partners are more likely to have beliefs about how the other typically sees things). Hence, if the present interaction appears to be different from what we have experienced before as actors, we are more likely to see it as due to factors outside ourselves, since we are likely to see ourselves as relatively stable. In addition, we cannot see ourselves in the same literal sense as an observer can see us.

We cannot be continually aware of what non-verbal signals we are sending that may be influencing the other person. Instead, we can see the other person's actions but may miss the point that these may, at least in part, be responses to our actions. When we are taking part in a relationship, it may be hard to see ourselves—our mannerisms, movements—but an observer can see all of this. However, as actors we need to note changes in our environment and especially changes in how other people act in order to synchronize our actions with theirs. It is easy in interactions to lose sight of how the other participant's actions may have, at least in part, been produced or influenced by our own input. When two video cameras were employed in an experimental study to record a piece of interaction, the partners made different attributions depending on whether they saw the replay from their own or the other person's perspective (Storms, 1973). Each participant initially said that the conversation was controlled more by the characteristic of the other person and the situation, and when they subsequently viewed the interaction from their own (actor) perspective, this bias continued, i.e. they saw themselves as reacting to the other. However, when shown the replay from the other person's point of view, they tended to see themselves as initiating and more in control, and much less determined by the situation or the characteristics of their partner.

An example of this process of formulating attributions and attempting to adopt different vantage points is offered in an extract from a therapeutic session with a couple, Tony and Dorothy. A significant part of the referring problem was that Dorothy was being continually unfaithful:

> Tony: I get very anxious, hot, and flustered in some situations; when I went shopping the other day . . .

Dorothy: I think, too, in a way I am like him. Though on the outside I look like an extrovert, I like attention. I think what niggles me is 'cos he's like he is ... it takes some of the attention away from me because if he was good-looking and hunky and I was with him, people would look at me and think, "Isn't she lucky". But because he is like he is it makes me angry, that he is dragging me down ... I mean that in the nicest possible way. That's why I get angry with him, because I want him to be stronger and more macho, more dominant.

Therapist: Was your first husband dominant?

Dorothy: He couldn't care less what anyone thought. No, not very with me. Again, I felt so conscious with him because he was so short. I used to think that people are thinking the same as what I think what other people are thinking about Tony. ... It just comes out in anger ... not how I want to be.

Therapist: Was your father dominant?

Dorothy: No, my mother ruled the roost.

In this extract Dorothy offers an account of how she feels about Tony's anxiety and shyness in public and how this makes her feel. However, an important component of how she feels is an attempt take the vantage point of others who might be looking at their relationship and possibly not being impressed by Tony. This appears to affect her sense of identity and evaluation of self-worth. Underlying this is her first statement that she, despite appearances, is "really" like Tony in being anxious and she resents the attention that he draws by his problems since this takes away attention and the possibility of being taken care of herself. This, however, is a hypothetical outside vantage point, since she cannot objectively see what they look like together or be sure that others do not admire Tony. Furthermore, the vantage point is clouded by the fact that she is attempting to look outside while being in the relationship; also, her perceptions have an effect on Tony, which may partly erode his confidence, thus further fuelling the perception from the inside that from the outside people might feel sorry for her, or even contempt.

ACCOUNTS AND EMOTIONS

As we have seen, accounts are not neutral but do important "work" in managing the relationship. They function to ascribe blame and responsibility but also, on the other hand, praise and credit. They are intimately tied in with how we feel about ourselves and others. The relationship between George and Helen provides an example:

George discovered that his wife, Helen, had had an affair. Their sexual relations have been very unsatisfactory for some time, with his wife expressing reluctance and lack of enjoyment of sexual intimacy. George had previously accepted Helen's explanation that her lack of interest was mainly due to her "frigidity", that she was just not a very sexual person. The affair therefore felt like a heavy blow. He couldn't believe it at first and felt betrayed, inadequate, unloved, numb, and depressed. His first attempts at dealing with it were to try to minimize it, e.g. that it had been a one-off, did not mean anything, that she had not enjoyed it, that she had been seduced, even that it had not really happened, she was just telling him it had to get back at him. He found thoughts about the affair intruding in his mind continually—where they did it, what sexual positions, what she was wearing, and so on. He just could not seem to get it out of his mind. At times he would get angry or cry and would end up feeling drained, depressed, and tired. He tried to talk about it with his wife and attempted to develop some accounts with her. These alternated between various explanations and implications for the future—that it meant it was all over so they should split up ... it was just a one-off and perhaps now their sexual life could be better ... this was part of the conflict, the power struggle between them, and he should now do the same to her ... the affair was a sign that the marriage was on the rocks, and they needed to work on it together, it was not too late ..., and so forth. Eventually, he started to confide in some of his friends, and they responded in various ways and with varying degrees of sympathy, some taking his side, others trying to see both points of view.

The input of others, their reactions to the account-making, whether they are sympathetic, uninterested, or critical, is crucial. George's friends were sympathetic and generally advised him to have an affair as well. Eventually, however, they became less sympathetic and somewhat impatient, especially when he revealed that he had previously had an affair but complained that this had not really helped to resolve matters since he still loved and desired his wife but she was still cold and unresponsive towards him sexually. This did not seem to fit with his friends' ideas of fairness, equality, and reasonableness, i.e. George perceived that some negative ideas were being formed about him—perhaps that he was being a bit "neurotic" or displaying a bit of a "male chauvinist double standard". Over time, the dominant account that started to emerge was that his wife had enjoyed the sexual encounter but "not that much" and that she still loved him, but more as a brother than a sexual partner. This account was partly acceptable to George, at least to the point that he could function again, manage at work, and was not continually obsessed by the affair. However, the reactions to his attempts to explain and account for the affair appeared to be blocked from further resolution.

Accompanying the attempts at forming accounts or interpretations there are a variety of possible emotional reactions, such as numbness, panic, and despair or, alternatively, hope, relief, and excitement. Mixed up with these feelings will be efforts to try to formulate some accounts that frequently involve attempts to deny or escape from the reality of the events. Often this period appears to be accompanied by confusion, with disturbing intrusions of thoughts and feelings and ruminations. These interpretations can help to make sense of difficulties, and even to transcend them. The interpretations also start to form the process of change, which will involve moulding these interpretations into an account that helps us to think about the precipitating events in a more positive or longer-term way and/or to develop alternative avenues of action.

Harvey, Orbuch, and Weber (1992) stress that the development of an account is an especially important component in dealing with problematic or traumatic events, resolving crises in a relationship, and so on. They suggest that successful accounts typically involve a new way of seeing things and accompanying new ways of acting. As an example, a couple may be distressed by their continual conflict and arguments but start to construct an account of this as "going through a bad patch" and subsequently as "having grown from the experience" (Veroff, Sutherland, Chadrha, & Ortega, 1993). It is interesting to note that this kind of spontaneous reinterpretation has also been found to be an effective therapeutic intervention, referred to as "reframing" (Dallos, 1991; Watzlawick et al., 1974) and "restorying "(Anderson et al., 1986; Cronen, Pearce, & Tomm, 1985; White & Epston, 1990) with people in distressed relationships. In Helen and George's case, the affair was not seen in such a constructive way, but an account of it as having been damaging persisted, as did the fundamental interactional pattern of sexual demand–rejection. Also, as will be explored in chapters five and six, the account-making processes have to fit within the wider societal expectations, ideologies, and norms—what is seen to be acceptable or reasonable. However, this evaluation does not always take account of personal circumstances—in George's case, the loss of his mother when he was very young, which he (and Helen) felt made him emotionally vulnerable and insecure.

Obviously such account-making does not occur in isolation, and the reactions of others to our attempted accounts is crucial in how effective the process can be. Harvey et al. (1992) stress that attempted accounts are "tried out" on others (e.g. friends and relatives), and their positive or affirmative reactions are of central importance. A tolerant, non-judgmental approach to people's attempts, for example, to account for relationship difficulties such as separations, losses, or divorces, helped people to formulate effective new ways of making sense of and "coming to terms" with these changes. Importantly, this also illustrates how account-making can become wrapped up in layers of needs, ambiguities, and interdependencies. The main recipient of George's attempted account formation was Helen. But she, of course, was the very person whom he perceived as having "inflicted" the pain on him in the first place. In this entangled context, it becomes extremely hard to gain or to perceive an "honest" response to his accounts. He may think, for example, that she is accepting a particular version just to placate him or alternatively to hurt him further. Likewise, Helen may experience alternating feelings of guilt that she has upset him and anger that he does not stop punishing her.

At such points of crisis, we might wonder, in fact, not why some relationships or families become problematic, but why many more do not become so. One possibility relates to the discussion of action and beliefs in the previous chapter. Actions in such situations of crisis and emotional upheaval may appear less ambiguous than words and be more convincing. For George and Helen, two possibilities for action would have been to change the patterns of actions, e.g. by separating or by becoming closer physically. But as neither of these behavioural changes occurred, neither did changes in their accounts and feelings.

STRATEGIC ASPECTS OF ACCOUNTS

When people offer an account, offer a story in their relationships, there may be various underlying strategies—what they hope the story will do, whether it will put them in a good light, appease, enable them to get their way. People may therefore engage in either positive or negative distortions, and explanations given can serve both as justification and as strategies for influencing the other person. A study by Lavin (1987), which explored couples' negotiational processes, revealed that partners could employ their explanations in a strategic manner:

- *Men* tended to attribute their own behaviour as due to stable internal factors whether it was seen to be positive or negative. This allowed a "no-lose" position for them, so they could take credit for perceived positive behaviour and defend against negative—"I can't help it, that's the way I am". Conversely, they tended to attribute more of their wives' behaviour to variable factors—"They were good this time, but you can't count on that". Lavin suggested that this offered them a strategic leverage to push for change, e.g. "You can do better next time".

- *Women* tended to make very similar attributions for their own and their partner's actions. They assigned similar levels of responsibility for their own and their husband's actions. The main differences between the men and the women, however, were found in couples who had stated that they were experiencing some difficulties in their relationship.

In families, people are likely to have a rich base of knowledge about each other and, importantly, may have ideas about each other's explanations and attributions—meta-perceptions, e.g. "I know you think I did it deliberately, but actually I broke it accidentally". Explanations and understandings may fit events and actions into accounts that have a narrative or story form: "I might have been awkward about helping out around the house, but not anything like as much as she accused me of. I think she used to say those things just to make me feel bad, so she could play the 'martyr'" (Foreman, 1995).

CO-CONSTRUCTION OF NARRATIVES

Personal construct theory and attributional/accounts perspectives help show how narratives contain a variety of components—they can be seen as alternative representations of events, as serving to predict and anticipate other's actions, as having a strategic quality in attempting to exert influence and control by offering justifications and apportioning blame, and they are shifting and changing and differ in their nature. In relationships, they can also be seen to have an evolving interpersonal nature that does not simply reside in either person and to have an unfinished quality. In this section, an attempt is made to explore some of the ways that integrating the three perspectives with a systemic analysis raises some further questions.

The following is an extract from a conversation between a couple, Stuart and Diane, in therapy, taken from a piece of clinical research with couples (Foreman, 1995). In the interview, Diane and Stuart describe a typical interaction between them when they go out together as a family with their two young children:

Case study: the walk

Stuart: I enjoy going for walks, but Diane doesn't seem to. ... We were out for a walk the other day, and she said "I want to go back now", not "shall we go back", and I know if I say I'd like to go a bit further it would aggravate the situation, no reason for it . . . . I wonder if you really like doing it, or are you kidding me? I'm happy to admit I like doing things by myself, but also as a family. ... I would like to know. ... Do you enjoy going for walks?

Diane: You never ask ... you were furious about it.

Stuart: No I wasn't furious, I thought you were angry ...

Diane: No I wasn't ...

Interviewer: Would you like to ask her now?

Diane: Do you want to know? Because we were walking along the cliff. ... I'm petrified of heights and our two boys were running around, but you are never very attentive, we have different standards of safety, and I couldn't wait to get down ... I get very anxious. ... I didn't tell him because I knew it would really annoy him..

Interviewer: Did it?

Stuart: Uhhhmn. ... I think it does. I've become more aware of her problems ... doesn't like heights, etc. ... but it's a threat to my great love of life, open spaces, climbing. ... She thinks I'm irresponsible, makes me feel mad. I feel perfectly confident. I've been mountaineering, etc.

Diane and Stuart explained that this pattern had occurred many times and with slight variations had represented some fundamental patterning of their relationship for several years. There are various themes running through it: misunderstandings, inferences about intentions and feelings, different interests, trust, and so on. The couple appear to have quite different interpretations of the situation described, especially their ideas about each other's motives, intentions, thoughts, and feelings. But, at the same time, their interaction also demonstrates some predictable patterns. The couple described how the above interaction had been frequently repeated on previous walks and other activities:

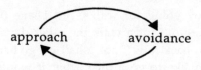

approach   avoidance

Diane—complains about Stuart being away so much, not doing things together, and initiates some joint activity.

Stuart—somewhat reluctantly agrees but picks an activity that suits him, harbours some resentment, but avoids confronting the issue.

Diane—joins in the activity though she does not feel happy with it, because at least it is time together. As the activity progresses, she feels dissatisfied with it and eventually complains.

Stuart—complies with ending the activity but then feels annoyed and feels less inclined to spend such time together again and he withdraws, avoids contact.

Diane—feels frustrated that her attempt has failed and has not helped to make them closer, and she is likely to complain again . . .

This account also suggests an example of an escalating cycle: both of them became increasingly unhappy with the walk, Diane becoming increasingly worried and Stuart increasingly annoyed at being prevented from carrying on. The interactional cycle might have continued to escalate (e.g. leading to a "row"); as it was, this escalation was avoided by Diane indicating that she wanted to go back and Stuart reluctantly complying. However, the negative feelings appeared to have stayed unresolved. Diane and Stuart each have their story of what is happening in this incident, and the stories are located in the wider history of their relationship, how they see each other as individuals, what each other's intentions are, and so on. Perhaps most importantly, the stories are not static but may become increasingly more *polarized* as they each try to assert their version.

The ingredients of narratives

Stuart and Diane's account illustrates many of the aspects of narratives discussed so far and raises some further issues:

1. Validation of narratives or of one's "preferred" view of self is central.

2. Emotionality and narratives—as we become aroused, angry, tense, or anxious, a form of "tunnel visions" may develop (Gottman, 1982): at such emotionally charged periods, such as life-cycle transitional stages, there can be a dysjunction between our preferred narratives and how others see us. The question therefore arises that there is an important interaction between emotionality and construing processes—what kinds of narratives are formed.

3. Rigid vs. loose narratives—narratives may differ in the extent to which they are flexible and open to revisions and elaborations, as opposed to being rigid, static, and unyielding.

4. Polarization of narratives—each partner's version of events may become more extreme as they attempt to assert their version or definition.

5. Power—the dynamics of the narratives are related to issues of power, so that the most powerful person may be able to impose his or her version or definition of the relationship on the other.

Interacting narratives—building realities

When family members engage in conversations and actions, they can be seen as actively constructing versions of reality—their social, interpersonal world. Earlier, we considered that the process of making accounts can be seen as serving a variety of purposes: to explain events, resolve conflicts, forge a coherent and acceptable sense of self-identity, and so on. In relationships, the stories and accounts that people offer can be seen to fulfil these aspects, but in addition they can be seen to have effects on the others. As Watzlawick et al. (1974) have suggested, any action/communication can be seen as having an effect that may be intentional but, even if not, may be taken by others to be intentional, e.g. forgetting to do something may be construed by others (depending on how familiar they are with Freudian theory) as an act of unconscious rejection or hostility.

Power and escalations

In families, conversations and interactions can be seen as consisting of exchanges of narratives, accounts, and stories, and one of the intentions behind these is to promote the person's version of events. Successfully gaining acceptance of one's version of events may be associated with a variety of desired actions—getting one's way, e.g. performing a particular desired activity or more broadly gaining a sense of recognition or acceptance. In the case of Diane and Stuart, there appears to be a contest over the meanings of their actions around "going for a walk". Part of this consists of mutual attributions for each other's actions and requests for justifications or explanations.

- Accusations or seeking explanations
  Diane:
    accuses Stuart of not consulting her—"you never ask"
    accuses Stuart of not caring enough about the children's safety—"you are never very attentive"
    accuses Stuart of having negative feelings—"you were furious"
  Stuart:
    accuses Diane of deceiving him about whether she really wants to go on walks with him or not
    accuses Diane of depriving him of his interests—"great love of life, open spaces, climbing"

accuses Diane of unfairly labelling him as "irresponsible"

accuses Diane of not trusting him

accuses Diane of having problems—"I've become more aware of her problems"

accuses Diane of not wanting to go for walks

- Self-accusations

Diane:

admits she is petrified of heights—"I get very anxious"

Stuart:

admits he likes doing things on his own

- Justifications

Diane:

by implication she is a good parent who cares about the children's safety

Stuart:

refers to his experience of and competence at climbing, etc.

In describing this sequence, the couple can be seen as actively recreating their typical interaction process, which appears to be imbued with a struggle for a definition of the relationship. The process of remembering the event, though roughly agreeing in the physical details, differs radically in the meanings given to it.

The issue of power is profound. Stuart arguably had more sources of power than Diane: he had a career, controlled the finances, was away from the home more, and so on. One of the consequences of such an imbalance can be that the less powerful person is more liable to be seen in terms of pathologizing narratives and accounts. This was apparent in this case: Diane was seen by Stuart, and saw herself, as having "problems"— phobias about heights, anxieties about Stuart going away, and reluctance to engage in sexual intimacy. Validation in contexts outside the home can encourage alternative narratives featuring competence and mental health rather than ill health. In short, the less powerful and more socially isolated partner or member of a family may be more prone to have attributions of internal and pathologizing narratives ascribed to him or her. Attempts to resist these can, unfortunately, lead in some cases to increasingly negative narratives that the person is over-emotional, aggressive, difficult, ambivalent, and so on.

These escalating sequences of alternating accusations and justifications can be seen to exemplify the symmetrical and complementary forms of interactional patterning suggested by Bateson (1972) and Watzlawick et al. (1974). Both these processes are related to power:

> *Stuart*—accusation: "She doesn't like the walks, deceiving me about it"
>
> *Diane*—accusation: "Don't consult me, you were furious"
>
> *Stuart*—denial and counter-accusation: "No I wasn't furious with you, I thought you were . . ."
>
> *Diane*—denial: "No I wasn't" . . .

At this point the therapist intervenes, perhaps sensing that this cycle is about to escalate or simply follow a well-beaten path leading to unhelpful negative feelings. The points of denial here may also, by implication, serve a further accusative function, i.e. you don't understand me or you are wrongly accusing me. Also, this can be seen as negating one of the fundamental positive aspects of relationships, i.e. a sense of being understood, accepted, and validated.

Positive vs. negative framing— validation and invalidation

Weber (1992) suggests that, when people form narratives or accounts of their lives, these can be seen in terms of stories and master stories, or narratives and meta-narratives. For Stuart and Diane, the meta-narrative may be that they are in trouble, that their relationship is unsatisfactory. This is probably why they have come for therapy. Within this meta-narrative there are sub-narratives or sub-texts that cover specific situations or events, but most likely these will be invested with the overall negative quality of the meta-narrative. Positive events within this meta-narrative may be framed as exceptions, a one-off, or perhaps an example of what they want more of. More broadly, though, narratives can be seen to contain an overall evaluative component—a positive or negative connotation—with implications for how people should act, think, and feel. Again returning to Stuart and Diane, we can see, for example, that Diane accuses Stuart of acting inappropriately by walking along the cliff but also not showing—by actions to signal attentiveness, e.g. stopping the boys running around—that he was thinking in a responsible way, that he was aware of the dangers and had appropriate feelings, i.e. being worried enough about the dangers. In effect, Diane can be seen as implying that she was having to do too much of the worrying because Stuart was not.

Interestingly, it is possible to see in this conversation the same escalating cycle of narratives that occurred on the actual walk in question. What emerges as they discuss the incident may be a replication or recreation of their relationship—not only the use of the same core narratives, but the same polarizations and escalations as they engage in the struggle to assert their definition of the relationship (Diane and Stuart in fact stated that their quarrels did proceed in this way—Foreman & Dallos, 1996). Systemic therapists have referred to this as uncovering the core processes or enactments in therapy. This process is also a pattern of conversation, and the escalations can be seen as escalations in meanings so that as the conversation proceeds, Diane and Stuart's dominant narratives become increasingly polarized or become pre-emptive (Kelly, 1955)—construing processes whereby our views become increasingly black or white or tunnel-vision like. As in Diane and Stuart's case, this type of construing is accompanied by adjectives such as *always* or *never*—e.g. when Diane accuses Stuart, "You are *never* very attentive".

Acceptability of accounts

Haley (1976b) has argued that sharing insights with family members does not necessarily lead to change and possibly makes the mistaken assumption that they do not know what the problem is. Instead, Haley argues that people have often thought of the possibilities that the therapist has considered and possibly more, but what they want is a diplomatic, face-saving way to move beyond the problems:

> .... husband and wife know perfectly well that the wife's inability to leave the house is related to the husband and the marriage. They do not lack understanding but a way to resolve the problem. To force them to concede that the problem is a marital one is discourteous. Accepting their way of presenting the problem and offering a change within that framework shows respect for them. The crucial difference in point of view centres on whether the therapist thinks that patients need education and self-understanding. If the patient already understands, what she needs is a graceful way out of the problem. [Haley, 1976b, p. 235]

When, as therapists, we offer or suggest accounts to families, we may find that these are rejected—sometimes politely, sometimes not—modified, ignored, and so on. Likewise, in conversations family members scrutinize and evaluate each other's narratives.

What reasons underlie why an account may be accepted or rejected, and to what extent do dominant shared narratives—or perhaps more accurately, shared alternative narratives—come to regulate interactions? Accounts appear to perform a number of important functions: explanation or justification of actions, presentation of self and attempts to maintain a positive self-image, attempts to exert influence on or manipulate others, and, more broadly, to give an overall meaning to one's life (Harvey et al., 1992; Weber, 1992). Some of the key elements in how we evaluate others' accounts appear to be:

1. How well does the account or narrative appear to embrace the events/facts under consideration? For example, Diane and Stuart's accounts encompass the fact that they prematurely terminated the walk, that they were walking along a cliff, and so on. Some features are clearly more open to such verification than others, e.g. whether Stuart was angry or attentive is not contested.

2. Perceived honesty of the account—inferences are made about the motives of the teller, e.g. do they appear to be trying to put themselves in a "good light", to gain power, or to manipulate?

3. Vantage point of the teller—this can be based upon physical aspects such as what facts were available to the person, but it also covers the issue of neutrality or independence. If a therapist, for example, is seen to be neutral, then his accounts may be more likely to be accepted or considered since he has less to gain and also can see, physically and metaphorically, all sides.

4. Presentation of the account—this includes the non-verbal aspects, emotionality, and conventions of presentation. This can include showing appropriate emotions and seriousness and perhaps also being willing to put aspects of oneself in a negative light, suggesting, therefore, that the account is genuinely honest.

As Diane and Stuart's process of interaction indicates, negotiating accounts combines with escalating emotional process. In their account, it appears that anger is a key feature: Diane and Stuart both appear to see each other as becoming angry. Both at the time of the interaction and in their recounting, it is apparent that the process of accusations, justifications, and counter-accusations was also generating emotions of anxiety, frustration, anger, and sadness. These, in turn, fed into the process so that the accounts—and, more specifically, their rejection of each other's accounts—becomes increasingly extreme and polarized. This, in turn, appears to fan the emotional flames, leading to more constrained or pre-emptive views, frequently ending with silence, tears, or angry withdrawal.

Historical context—
the construction of memories

The explanations ascribed to events are embedded in the broader narratives capturing the history of the relationship. Interpretations of current actions are frequently framed within stories or memories of past incidents. These memories can be seen in terms of reconstruction rather than of recall of faithful images from the past. What is remembered and how this is done occur within the broader context of the history of the relationship. Stuart and Diane had been in conflict for some time and saw their current relationship as problematic, which is why they had come for therapy. Consequently, this current definition is the frame or the dominant narrative within which memories are defined. But this is a recursive process, so that the memory (e.g. the reality that they had a row and came back home early) also serves to define the current state of the relationship—"We can't be getting on very well or be very happy, because things like this happen to us."

Narratives and the development of dominant narratives can be seen as an evolving process. Initially, a variety of accounts may be offered for an event, the state of the relationships, and so on. These can be seen as gradually becoming filtered down into a limited set of dominant narratives. Family members may well be aware of alternative narratives, but these may have fallen into disuse and become subjugated as the events and the potential narratives covering them are scrutinized over time (Haley, 1976b; White, 1995). The process whereby this occurs may be complex. It may involve not only, for example, a couple but their children, parents, friends, colleagues, all of whom support or prefer some narratives over others. As we will see in chapter six, the selection may also be influenced by societal and culturally acceptable or dominant narratives in terms of both what alternatives are initially made available for contemplation and which are gradually or quickly rejected. In conversations with others outside the family, accounts may be offered at three or more levels:

- *self*—personal accounts of one's own actions
- *other*—accounts of actions of others in the family
- *relationship*—accounts of the nature of the relationship, e.g. stable, stormy, volatile, on the rocks, etc.

Disclosures—exchanging life-stories

A central narrative underlying Diane and Stuart's case was one of Stuart as cold and attempting to withdraw and escape, and of Diane as needy and wanting to be close. These positions appear to be importantly influenced by the initial conversations at the start of a personal relationship where couples disclose information, i.e. exchange their stories. This usually includes accounts of the families they came from and their childhood experiences—how they came to be the person they are from the melting pot of their families. They described that at the start of their relationship Diane had been very "insecure" and had found great support from Stuart and admired his calmness and strength. Their family backgrounds were very different: Diane came from a lively, gregarious family with lots of displays of emotion, and she apparently had a reputation for having a "bad temper". In contrast, Stuart's family came from the North, and their life had been marred by coldness, arguments, or tense silences. He described how he longed for tranquillity, and his childhood left him with a fear or conflict and a strong wish for a quiet life.

> Stuart: My mum and dad used to have rows . . . I used to hate it . . . better not to say anything. I've grown up with that, found it difficult until I started to realize how you work through these problems by talking about it. . . . I've got this manner of cutting off, and I can distract myself and veer off and go cycling, do something else, enjoy that activity. It puts up a screen, and I feel things are OK now, I'm happy again . . . So in our relationship I have a fear of making people fly off the handle or upsetting them, making them mad . . . real problem for me, between us . . . a fear of upsetting the apple-cart.

Stuart and Diane described how their relationship had originally been close, and they enjoyed physical intimacy early on. Diane had felt very dependent on Stuart but had now come to resent that and felt she wanted to be more independent and not so anxious about things:

Diane: I was anorexic and bulimic when I was younger,
and I also had this agoraphobia. I realize I have not really
dealt with it . . . still going on for me now. Quite a mixed
bag of stuff to deal with. . . .

The stories contained in these initial disclosures can be seen
as a start in the constructing of a set of shared narratives about
each other. These may later be brought out as parts of accounts
to explain each other's actions and justify one's own and, importantly, as predictors of the future.

Construction of memories

Narratives contain a story that strings together sequences of
memories, but these themselves are not simply reproductions
of events that have occurred but are also selected and constructed in an interactional way. Remembering in families can
be seen as a joint, collaborative activity in which partners may
remind each other of the facts—what happened, when it occurred, who was there, what was said—but also of the meaning
of these events, in particular what people's intentions were and
how they felt at the time. There may also be a reflexive view
about what has been learned from the event, how perceptions
of the event differ now, and how in the same circumstances
they might now act differently:

> Relationships are a determinant of remembering, providing crite-
> ria of significance (defining what is worth remembering, and
> how memories are linked together to tell the story of people's
> lives). . . . In the other direction, remembering is a determinant of
> relationships. Relationships can be defined, negotiated, redefined,
> consolidated, disputed, through conversations about the past. Ar-
> guments and agreement occur about what really happened, who
> said what and when, and with what intent; glosses are put upon
> the past, with the aim of defining the present and future paths that
> a relationship might take. [Edwards & Middleton, 1988, pp. 4–5]

It seems likely that even when people are alone, engaged
in private reflection, their thinking derives largely from forms

of communication: phrases and sequences of dialogue formed from conversations between people, with and between family members and other close associates, and even from favourite film scripts (Bahktin, 1981; Vygotsky, 1978b). When discussing significant events in therapy, people not only try actively to recollect the content—what happened, who said what—but have already made the decision that this was an important event worth remembering. In fact, over time the event can take on a significance way beyond its original importance, as symbolizing something essential about the relationship, e.g. an example of what is wrong with it, or of the other partner's unreasonableness, and so on (La Rossa, 1995): "... memories ... are not simply recordings (saved files on the "hard disk" we call our brain); rather, they are stories that, like courtship and divorce narratives, are patched together to distinguish and privilege ourselves" (La Rossa, 1995, p. 556).

The following example is taken from part of the session with Stuart and Diane described earlier (Foreman, 1995). The two therapists were Rudi Dallos (R) and Sally Foreman (S).

Th(S): Both of you keep apologizing—which of you blames themselves more?

Stuart: We suddenly come across these clashes. You take on a destructive urge ... D is very violent sometimes in her responses, an anger ...

Th(S): Since the counselling ... that started a lot of ... ?

Diane: Don't know what you mean (*to Stuart*) ... I can carry on being nasty, but I don't know if I'm so nasty?

Th(R): Can you give an example, Stuart?

Stuart: When you threw rocks.

Diane: Come on, that doesn't really count (*laughter*).

Stuart: You did sort of physically want to hit me.

Diane: Oh, come on, Stuart.

Th(R): Could you describe what led up to it, what happened, what was said, when?

Diane: Only happened the once ... went off to see someone else, had been building up, and I was very annoyed and I did throw him out of the house and throw rocks at him. I was really incredibly furious. I can't remember before or since having that kind of anger.

Th(R): Can I badger you a bit, could you describe it a bit? When did this happen—day of the week, time, what happened?

Stuart: Just after Christmas. I went out to see a friend, a bike ride away. Pretended I hadn't seen anybody. Silly thing to do, she was very annoyed, justifiably, and it just built up, you ...

Diane: I just went out with the kids, took the kids back, dumped them at a friend's house, and I was going to ... I really did lose my rag. I'm not very jealous. Stuart tends to get on better with women than with men. He's got plenty of women friends, he goes out with them. It doesn't really bother me, but this was the kind of friendship he'd built up and not talked to me about, and it had been in the air and several things leading up to it. So stupid ... silly little lies that led up to it, and you could have just told me ... seemed so ridiculous that he would behave in that way, over this going to see someone else really.

Th(S): That's the only time you got angry? Sounds perfectly reasonable to me to get angry then.

Diane: I don't get very angry. I don't lose my rag very readily, very rarely.

Th(R): Was that the only thing you meant when you said she gets aggressive?

Stuart: At the time it did seem incredibly extreme, and in fact we did talk about it afterwards and I said I was surprised how much aggression and anger seemed to come out, and you agreed, sort of, it seemed to surprise you as well. Maybe a one-off, not only that but the whole reason I behaved like that ... kind of fear, that you had a reputation in your family of being bad-tempered, and I had built a fear ... of trying to avoid it. My parents ... really awful.

If quiet and not arguing that was really good, never mind communicating. So in our relationship I have a fear of making people fly off the handle or upsetting them, making them mad ... real problem for me, between us ... fear of upsetting the apple-cart. Counselling helping. You mentioned the apologizing, all part of it, afraid of saying this is what I stand for.

Diane: You make it difficult by being very indirect ... until very last minute ... won't tell me anything a week ahead.

Edwards and Middleton (1988) suggest that remembering consists of three types of utterances: *deixis*—pointing to some event or feature of it, e.g. the statements pointing out the event of Diane throwing rocks at Stuart; *depiction*—statements drawing a picture of what the event was, giving it a context, e.g. that Stuart had gone off to see another woman; *elaborated significance*—the essential meanings and importance of the activity, e.g. that Diane felt that Stuart had told lies and was possibly starting an affair, whereas Stuart felt it symbolized his fear of Diane's emotions. The initial pointing to the event by Stuart was disputed, e.g. Diane says it doesn't really count, i.e. that it is an illegitimate example to draw on to support the idea that she is angry. The focus on particular memories appears to flow from the ongoing narrative being generated in the conversation, i.e. items from the past are pointed to in order to justify or add support to the unfolding story of Diane as angry and emotional, a view that she contests, and therefore she disputes that this item means what Stuart is arguing it means. Stuart and Diane appear to have assigned this memory different meanings and compartmentalized it differently as an example either of Diane's temper or of Stuart's deceptiveness. The initial pointing to the event therefore is itself imbued with meanings since the event is employed to serve different purposes or strategies in their current conversation and the ongoing narratives of their relationship.

Part of the intentions in a therapeutic encounter may be to gain the therapist's support and sympathy in assessing who is wrong or right, the therapist in one sense representing a symbol of some wider consensual reality or social norms of appropriate behaviour. Not infrequently, people in such sequences will attempt various tactics to change the dominant meaning of the memory, e.g. that it was not serious because the rocks thrown were quite small. As we will see in chapter seven, the activity in itself of recalling such events and re-examining them in a relatively calm atmosphere may lead to some changes with very little directive input from the therapist.

Emotions

Remembering is imbued with emotional tones, and what makes the events worth remembering or significant is typically connected to how people felt and their identity—whether they felt good or bad about themselves, happy or sad. Photographs are a powerful example of this, e.g. in triggering memories of the children's childhood, of happy times, reliving the hopes and expectations. In Stuart and Diane's account above, it is possible to see that the memory is very much centred on feelings of betrayal, anger, emotional attack, confinement, and so on. In turn, as the joint process of remembering takes place, these feelings are reactivated and may produce emotional outbursts, tears, and so on in therapy:

> The major grounds for remembering that kept cropping up in our transcripts were to do with the affective reactions to things, including reactions to things that were unusual or novel, things in which the personal identity of the self was at stake, and events that signified something about social relationships between family and friends. [Edwards & Middleton, 1988, p. 12]

George Kelly (1955) and others have also noted the important linkages between understanding, explanations, and emotions. Invalidation—a response that our explanation or story is wrong, incomplete, false, inadequate—or an inability to predict or anticipate leads to emotional responses such as anxiety, threat, anger. In particular, emotions occur when our constructs are in some way inadequate to help us to predict or control the situations we were confronted with. For example, *anxiety* may be driven by the awareness of, or a sense of not knowing, what is expected or what will happen. Aspects of a relationship may provoke anxiety because a person does not know what will happen—whether the other person is committed, how the other person feels, whether our feelings will be reciprocated. Emotional intimacy or expression of criticisms may involve such anxieties, and these may be alleviated by experience or by sharing experiences with others in order to be able to form some coping strategies. Similarly, *hostility* is seen to be a continued effort to extort validational evidence. In a sense, a person is admitting that she or he does not understand the other and does not know how to deal with that person. The response is to resort to hostility because nothing else seems to work. In other words, I may not like someone, but as long as I can find some way of effectively dealing with that person I might not be hostile. Kelly's definitions emphasize that emotions are fluid and changing; each partner is seen as attempting to deal with the demands and fluctuations of their world. He saw problems as associated with an inability to formulate constructs to help understanding and anticipation of natural and inevitable processes of change in relationships.

In families, there is a three-way interconnection between narrative, emotions, and actions. For example, in one family the son believes that his parents think he has been involved in "trouble" and that he is trying to deceive them about it. He expects that they will not believe him, whatever he says. The parents, for their part, believe that their son has lied to them in the past and therefore that they have to force the truth out of him. This frequently repeated interaction may start relatively calmly, though with an undercurrent of anxiety on both parts that it will escalate. As the accusations and counter-accusations start, they experience an escalation of their emotionality: tightness in the stomach, dryness of the mouth, perhaps even a general shaking (Gottman, 1982). Associated with these emotional changes, there will almost certainly be an increasing rigidity in their beliefs and their actions. In Kelly's terms, each will attempt increasingly to try to extort evidence that they are right, and as they do so the escalation increases—most likely, in this case, to be halted by the mother bursting into tears, whereupon the youngster will be accused: "Now see what you have done."

Narratives, empathy, and meta-perspectives

The narratives that evolve in family interactions contain attempts to understand, predict, and influence each other based upon assumptions about the other's intentions, views, and strategies. In chapters two and four, in the examples from Eron and Lund (1993), this is discussed as the assumptions that family members make about each other's "preferred views". What this indicates is that stories and accounts have both a stable and a shifting quality. The accounts that are offered involve both assumptions about others' beliefs and attempts to change, influence, or support these. Kelly differentiated between two types of such awareness: on the one hand, there is commonality—the extent to which people appear from the "outside" and also feel themselves to see things similarly. On the other hand, there is sociality—mutual understanding or empathy—the extent to which each person has an understanding or empathy regarding how the other person sees the world: "To the extent that one person construes the construction process of another, they may play a role in a social process involving the other person" (Kelly, 1955).

Sociality involves an ability to predict how the other person uses the constructs, and this may happen irrespective of the level of commonality. We might understand how someone sees events but totally disagree with them. Likewise, Kelly argues that it is possible to have a high level of commonality with someone but not recognize it, e.g. if we have had little communication or discussion with them. The level of sociality—the recognition of similarities and differences—may fluctuate as a relationship develops: as an example, a couple may both be vegetarians but come to realize that one of them is predominantly a vegetarian for health reasons, whereas the other is a vegetarian on moral grounds. The growth of sociality involves the ability to make increasingly sophisticated predictions about the other's construct system (Dallos, 1991; Duck, 1994).

Shared narratives

Relationships involve the creation of joint action, and central to this is some sharing of beliefs, understandings, and narratives. By analogy, we might say that family life is a little bit like a game in which the participants need to know and agree to some rules, and know that the others know about and are willing to agree to these rules. They also have some ideas about how the others will play, what their intentions are, how much they want to win, whether they are playing for fun, and so on, as well as about how the others see each other and themselves. In addition, as we have seen in the section on memory, members develop a shared history of experiences that they have taken part in together and how these are seen. Also, family members develop a shared history of memories and experiences that they tell each other about but have not experienced together, e.g. when husband and wife talk about what kind of a day they have had at work, or what their childhoods were like. These become shared experiences in the sense of sharing each other's accounts of these events. The responses from family members can alter, reinforce, or contradict the original meanings attached to the events so that a shared set of meanings may be constructed. Stuart and Diane had told each other about their family backgrounds, and these can achieve the status of joint, shared memories. In fact, over time family members may forget who the original teller of a particular story was, and the memory achieves the status of a family or joint memory.

From the conversation in families, some shared ways of viewing events will emerge—a shared belief system. This does not simply mean agreement but may mean the coexistence of alternative or even competing narratives. Nevertheless, some shared dominant themes are likely, e.g. Stuart and Diane were both artists who viewed self-expression, creativity, and opportunity for growth and self-expression as important. They differed in how this could be achieved, not in whether this was central or not. They appeared to agree about their domain of discourse— what things were seen to be worth talking about, arguing over, investing with emotional commitment, and so on. In these terms, divorce and separation, for example, may be less to do with disagreement than with growing apart in terms of ceasing to care, or of refusing to see the other's dominant concerns as central or relevant.

A shared belief or narrative system can be viewed in terms of a metaphor of a deck of cards containing an array of options or choices that are seen by the family members to be possible, e.g. a couple may not agree about the choices they *should* make, but there is likely to be more agreement about what choices *are* possible. Their shared belief system sets out the domain of perceived choices or the "cards in the game". Evolution and changes are possible and are prompted by the influences of peers, friends, and local community and by the wider cultural changes in attitudes and expectations regarding relationships (e.g. gender roles).

An important area of negotiation and potential conflict for any relationship can be the development of a set of understandings and agreements about the relationship itself. It is necessary that a set of constructs or narratives is developed about the various relationships in a family. Secondly, it is necessary for there to be some agreement or shared way of seeing these relationships: the roles people will play, tasks, how to divide up their time, obligations, rights, intimacy, and dominance (Procter, 1981, 1985). Who occupies each role may change: for example, if the father becomes ill, one of the sons may temporarily step in to take over some aspects of his role, either doing it or parts of it like him or in distinct contrast to how the father would have done it. Obviously, if there is total disagreement about these, then the relationship is likely to dissolve into endless arguments and inaction and will probably fall apart. The agreement is about the domain of choices seen to be possible—about the roles seen to be necessary and about who should fill them. However, both of these may be more or less negotiable—they represent choices seen to be available at any one time in the relationship.

SUMMARY

This chapter has outlined some approaches to examining family life and experience from a story of family members as attempting continually to generate narratives about themselves, each other, and their relationships. These narratives are developed to offer a sense of continuity, stability, and identity to themselves and to their relationships. However, family life makes a variety of demands for change, and consequently the narratives need to be adapted, to evolve or be modified, or even to be rejected in favour of new ones in order to make sense of and deal with changes. In turn, the narratives that are held shape the nature of the changes—how events are interpreted colours what changes are perceived to be necessary. At times, the narratives may appear to be inadequate or "not to fit" with the changed circumstances, events, feelings in a family. Also, family members may have wildly different stories of what is happening. At these points, we, as therapists or observers, might consider that the family's narratives may have become distortions, denials, and myths. This theme is developed in the following chapters, and we can consider the following as some points of focus generated by the discussions in this chapter:

1. The family members' stories are attempts to fit shifting events, sometimes dramatic changes such as at life-cycle transitions.

2. Narratives differ in their content and their structure, such that some stories appear to be tight, rigid, and inflexible, whereas others may be flexible, loose, or even vague. These differences influence how much and in what ways the shifting events and experiences can be incorporated into the narrative.

3. The emotions, conflicts, and anxieties that are associated with periods of change are likely in some cases to lead to rigid or pre-emptive construing, which may recursively feed back to increase the crisis, the tension, and the rigidity of thinking.

CHAPTER FOUR

Choosing narratives
and interacting

In the previous chapters, it has been suggested that strategic
and structural therapies contain many ideas that are consistent with the recent movement towards a narrative
approach to therapy (Anderson et al., 1986; Hoffman, 1993). For
example, strategic approaches may look more different to
these newer forms of therapy than they really are and, in fact,
may share many of the same constructivist premises. However,
strategic approaches—with their emphasis on finding pragmatic ways of disrupting the vicious cycles of failing attempted
solutions to problems—have been criticized for being manipulative, and even dishonest. One of the key techniques—reframing, which attempts to suggest a new way of viewing the
relationship which does not involve the problem—has likewise
been criticized on the grounds of playing "fast and loose" with
reality. It is argued that some reframing will suggest anything
that appears to work, no matter whether the therapist in
any way genuinely believes the reframe. In contrast, Efran,
Lukens, and Lukens (1988) point out that "There is a subtle but
critical difference between taking liberties with established definitions and proposing fresh problem-solving frameworks" (p.

107

34). Trainee family therapists often appear to have difficulty learning to employ reframing because it sometimes feels false or disingenuous, e.g. when a reframe is one that they are not totally convinced about themselves. This leads to feeling unsure about whether the family will accept a reframe, or to fears that they might offend the family.

Strategic and structural therapists have responded to such criticisms by suggesting that constructivist therapies can be vague and loose and offer little idea of what works or about therapeutic direction: "In general, the narrative/constructivist approaches have come under scrutiny for being 'soft' on thera-peutic direction and therapist responsibility, and vague about the question of what actually works in therapy to bring about change" (Eron & Lund, 1993, p. 292).

If we agree that people's understandings, accounts, and nar-ratives in families are active and serve various purposes in shaping their lives with each other, then this allows us to also entertain the possibility that family members act strategically. They can be seen to have beliefs about each other, about them-selves and about their relationships, have ideas or plans about what they want and need from their relationships, and try in various ways to achieve these. This is not to suggest that people are inevitably underhand and manipulative, but instead that they do plan and anticipate what effects their actions might have. If a husband buys his wife some flowers, he almost cer-tainly has some anticipations about what may result. In effect, he has a plan that may include wanting her to feel good, to forgive him, to enhance the chance of sexual intimacy, or even to make him feel good about himself. It is not necessary to subscribe to psychodynamic theory to accept further that people may hold some of these intentions more or less uncon-sciously.

It is even possible that some of the unease felt about strate-gic therapy approaches is because they confront us with the un-comfortable possibility that we are all, to some extent, man-ipulative, especially in seeking to gain power, advantage, and control over others. Furthermore, because of the legacy of psy-chodynamic thinking, there is an assumption that connotes the unconscious as sinister, "dark", and "nasty" and hence presumes that unconscious plans and intentions are predominantly negative. In Haley's story of the alcoholic wife and in Bateson's account of the double bind (in chapter two), it is precisely this assumption of negative destructive unconscious forces that promotes the view that it is necessary to attempt to manipulate people out of their patterns of destructive actions and feelings rather than to encourage change by open discussion of the beliefs underlying these. Alternatively, with a more benevolent and positive story about the unconscious it becomes much easier to envisage the possibility of engaging in co-constructive conversations with families. It is possible, of course, that Haley is also right: sometimes a more indirect or manipulative approach may be the only one that appears to be able to assist a family. Part of the problem may be our tendency to generalize: if strategic approaches work in some cases, then why not apply them to all? In fact, it may not invariably be necessary for therapists to conceal their opinions and feelings from families, and to do so in some cases may even be counterproductive.

An attempt to suggest some integration of strategic and narrative approaches is a focus of this chapter. Eron and Lund (1993) have outlined the basis of such an integration and, most importantly, combine this to suggest a model of how problems in families can be seen to evolve. Their model revolves around the brief therapy idea that family life inevitably poses difficulties. These, however, may be construed in a variety of ways, and each alternative view suggests a different course of action or attempted solution.

ALTERNATIVE NARRATIVES

An example of an ordinary difficulty—teenage misdemeanours—may help to illustrate this:

Jenny (age 13 years) asks if she can invite her classmate Betty round to her house after school. Though Jenny's parents have some reservation about Betty, because she has a history of being "wild", getting drunk, and tinkering with drugs, they agree. Mother is out when Betty visits, and the girls apparently have been "happily" occupied while father was preparing the dinner. The girls delay in coming when called to eat, and, when they do eventually appear, Betty starts being violently sick and father thinks he can smell alcohol. At this point, Betty's mother arrives to collect her and immediately asks if the girls have been drinking. Since Jenny has previously taken a strong moral stance against alcohol and drugs, her father is confused. The following day, Jenny admits that they had drunk two bottles of wine, that it had been her idea, and that she actually drank more than Betty. She does not appear to have a hang-over, and there is some apparent pride and amusement, especially on the part of her brothers, that she appears to have been able to hold her drink so well.

Later that evening, Jenny's concerned parents discuss what has happened and what course of action to take. Their discussion revolves around and includes a contemplation of some of the following narratives:

1. *Contagion*—Betty is a "bad influence, and she has led Jenny astray. This fits with the fact that she has a history of "problems": she has been known to get drunk and has experimented with drugs.

2. *Lack of attention*—Jenny's mother has been working (training) and has not been with Jenny as much as previously and is distracted and tired when she is with her.

3. *Conflict with friends*—Jenny says she has fallen out with her best friend, and it may be that she feels she needs Betty and engaged in the deviant behaviour in order to cement their friendship.

4. *Sibling modelling*—Jenny's older sister's (age 17 years) has just recently found a boyfriend, is becoming sexually active, and has started to drink alcohol occasionally. Until recently, she had been very close to Jenny and, though older, had acted at a similar age.

5. *Conflict with father*—there has been some conflict between Jenny and her father, and, since he was at home at the time,

Jenny's actions might have indicated rebellion and contempt towards him.

6. *Normal adolescent pranks and misdemeanours*—many adolescents act in deviant ways, try out adult activities, and test their parents' rules.

7. *Family/marital problems*—the family is a complex step-family, and the parents feel responsible since there has been a history of marital conflicts, and they fear that Jenny may be responding to these.

8. *Over-protectiveness*—the mother thinks that she may be a "little" over-protective (father is sure she is very much so), so children cannot admit to embarking on adult activities, do so secretly, and overact when they do.

9. *Precociousness*—Jenny's half-brothers on her father's side were brought up as more independent than her half-siblings on her mother's side. Jenny is showing a temporary copying of her father's side of the family and their ways of acting

10. *Copying father drinking*—the father drinks somewhat and has previously encouraged Jenny to have a "drop" since he believes controlled drinking is a reasonable way to learn how to "handle it". Jenny's mother strongly disagrees with this view and believes in total abstinence for children.

11. *Caring friend*—Jenny is seen as caring, sticking up for the "underdog"; possibly she felt sorry for her Betty, who had been in trouble, and the drinking may have been her a way of affirming her loyalty to friend.

These alternative narratives or explanations were evaluated within the broader perspective of Jenny's history and her previous behaviour. She had been seen as a "good" girl and had expressed very little interest in use of drink or drugs—on the contrary, she was morally opposed to their use. In discussing the girls' action, the parents showed preferences for some narratives over others, and directly and indirectly implied varying amounts of blame and responsibility to each other. In so doing, they also communicated some feelings about their own relationship.

This story may be repeated in innumerable families in different ways, such as staying out late, getting into fights, or stealing. It also serves to start to illustrate a number of aspects of the role of narratives in family life:

1. Families actively construct narratives that attempt to explain events.
2. Alternative narratives are generated in a similar way to Palazzoli's account of progressive hypothesizing.
3. The narratives are scrutinized to see how effectively they cover or connect all the "facts" or events.
4. Many of the narratives contemplated are held in common by all families and connect the family to their local and wider culture. These alternative narratives are therefore not infinite but constrained by the wider societal discourses that the family is located in.

Such an ordinary example of family life is revealed to be astonishingly complex. Moreover, the complex web of interpretations and construction of narratives has an "unfinished" or open quality. The meaning of many actions can never be fully determined since there is often insufficient information to decide. For example, the two sets of parents did not discuss this incident together in great detail, nor with the girls present, so even many of the basic "facts" cannot be verified. A narrative is assembled about events often from fragments of information and woven together into a story that makes apparent sense. In doing this, people often fit in the missing pieces by reference to their store of knowledge about similar events. One point of reference or a source of potential meanings may be their own past, e.g. the parents may form inferences about the girls' actions based upon how they acted at that age. In turn, the recall and meanings given to such memories may in part be interpersonally determined. Each parent may strategically decide to express or conceal some memories from the other, e.g. the mother may decide not to reveal too much about how "wild" she was at that age, since her husband might take this as a threat or a sign that his wife is allied with the daughter

against him. Also, their evaluations of their past actions may
have various glosses put on them for the "children's sake". For
example, parents may "pretend" that they regret their own
adolescent misdemeanours, whereas in fact they are secretly
proud and savour the memories of the fun they had. Needles to
say, children are immensely skilled at detecting such ploys, the
"glint in a parent's eye", and at "rekindling" their parents by
now reliving for them some of the fun their parents had in the
past, and now miss.

HYPOTHESIZING

Arguably, Palazzoli et al.'s (1980) idea of progressive hypothesizing (see chapter two) captures the essence of a constructivist approach:

> By hypothesising we refer to the formulation by the therapist of an
> hypothesis based upon the information he possesses regarding
> the family he is interviewing. The hypothesis establishes a start-
> ing point for investigation as well as verification of the validity of
> this hypothesis based upon specific methods and skills. If the
> hypothesis is proven false, the therapist must form a second
> hypothesis based upon the information gathered during the test-
> ing of the first. [p. 4]

Kelly (1955) argued that all of us, not just therapists, are
continually generating explanations, hypotheses, and stories in
a similar manner. He distinguished between enduring hypotheses or narratives that are essentially a person's world views or
core beliefs of the world, and the more fleeting explanations
that occur from moment to moment. The former may be part of
our conscious belief system, whereas the latter are more trans-
ient but may accumulate to lead to a reappraisal of our more
enduring views. Kelly argues that the fundamental views are
relatively resistant to change, and great anxiety may be experienced if a person feels compelled to alter these radically. Other
beliefs that are linked to these are less central: how a particular
person or episode is seen may be more amenable to change
than broader, core beliefs about the values of family life, such as
fidelity, honesty, and fairness.

FIT OR VALIDITY?

Palazzoli and Kelly both agree that it is reasonable to argue that our stories have to fit or represent reality or events sufficiently adequately to be able to predict others' actions and anticipate the future—in short, to manage our lives "reasonably" well. Chapter six explores further how realities can be seen to be distorted both by families and, more broadly, by the inculcation of societally shared schemes of distorting ideologies or "false consciousness". Returning to Jenny's case, it could be argued that some of the potential narratives fit better than others. When parents or other family members engage in discussions of such incidents, some evaluations are made of these alternative narratives, some are consigned to the background, whereas others are supported and become dominant. But how is this done? Research on how people form explanations suggests that two types of processes are employed more or less simultaneously. On the one hand, people work upwards from the "facts"—what actually happened, how the events connect together—and a narrative is inferred from these facts. But, at the same time, people also appear to work from general ideas that start from a broad proposition about what sort of a situation or context is being considered, and attempts are then made to see if the actions fit this (Antaki, 1989). In Jenny's case, it is possible to start *deductively* with a general view of a context about adolescence, and this may lead to viewing, or deducing the meaning of, her specific actions as an example of normal delinquency. Alternatively, it is possible to start *inductively* from her specific actions—that she had become drunk, had never previously done this, had drunk to considerable excess and in an obvious way. In this way, the facts point towards a general narrative of her actions as an example of a spontaneous bit of "silliness" rather than the signs of a more serious or chronic problem. Both processes of hypothesizing may occur, and the agreement between them is assessed, possibly leading to a revision of the explanations if they appear to offer contradictory conclusions. In addition, interpersonal checking of the interpretations with other members of the family, with friends, and with others may occur (a form of inter-rater reliability testing). More "objective" sources may also be solicited, e.g. testing the credibility of tentative explanations with relative strangers.

It can be argued, therefore, that some narratives endure or come to dominate because they are more valid—they fit the facts better. But why do some fit better than others, and what does "fit" mean? It could mean that some narratives keep the peace more successfully, i.e. they satisfy unconscious needs and thereby perhaps distort the truth. In contrast, adopting a radically constructivist view, there is seen to be no objective reality, or facts, or truth to account for; consequently, all narratives are therefore equally valid—some just appear to fit better:

> We are talking only of views, not of reality or truth, because we believe that views are all we have, or ever will have. It is not even a question of views that are more or less real or true, or progressively approaching the truth. Some views may be more useful or effective than others in accomplishing one's chosen end but this is a pragmatic criterion, not one of "reality". [Fisch, Weakland, & Segal, 1982, p. 11]

Speed (1984), however, argues that one possible reason for the apparently extreme position suggested above is a polarization effect resulting from theorists of a cybernetics persuasion attempting to distance themselves from the deterministic and linear individualistic approaches that had previously been predominant. There are some interesting parallels with the rather cavalier handling of reality in some versions of psychoanalysis, e.g. it is not made explicitly clear, by Freud or some later post-Freudians, whether actual sexual abuse is fundamentally different from imagined or fantasized sexual abuse. This debate has been particularly pertinent recently with the discussions of "false memory syndrome". Confusions may arise because visions of the material world of events and those of the social world of perceptions, feelings, and actions are being treated as equivalent. It can be argued instead that there may be a variety of ways that an act—e.g. of sexual "abuse" (the term itself conveying a meaning, one previously called more neutrally incest)—can be interpreted. But is it much less defensible to suggest, therefore, that it is pointless to ask whether or not it "really" occurred? There are many areas of experience in families where the debate about "truth" is at such a basic level—who is the father of a child? ... who hit whom? ... who stole some money? ... which of the parents has been unfaithful? ... and so on. The truths about such events can readily be distinguished, what they mean is arguably more contentious and relative.

Perhaps one of the core issues for family therapists is that often we are working in the area that lies between these two extremes of material and semantic truths. The example concerning hypothesizing from the work of the Milan team, which was quoted in chaper two, illustrates this point. The activity of the team in that situation was similar to that of the everyday processes in an "ordinary" family. As Kelly (1955) suggests, people are involved continually in formulating hypotheses, explanations, and stories. Families spend considerable time engaged in generating such hypotheses or alternative stories. More broadly, Cecchin (1987) has suggested that hypothesizing is connected to curiosity: "Curiosity is a stance, whereas hypothesizing is what we do to try to maintain this stance" (p. 411). He suggests further that:

> Families are wonderful story tellers because they have such interesting scripts to describe. They come to therapy with these scripts tightly written. Their problem is that their scripts do not help them to function in a way that *they* find useful. As clinicians we offer the family new scripts (based upon our hypotheses) to which the family responds by adjusting its scripts that, in turn, helps us alter our scripts, and so on. When we feel unable to develop hypotheses, we know we have accepted the family's script and, thus, have lost our sense of curiosity. [p. 411]

But does the process of therapy in fact offer families "new" scripts? Instead, for families like Jenny and her parents it may be the case that:

1. a range of alternative stories is generated and considered to encompass events as they arise;
2. therapy allows some of the submerged narratives to resurface;
3. there is a societal domain of "acceptable" or legitimate narratives driven by the dominant discourses or ideologies of mental health, family life, gender, and so on;

4. the social or cultural context constrains what stories are allowed to be entertained as legitimate possibilities.

Viewing families and their stories in these ways might place less pressure on therapists to try to be creative "for families". Instead of being over-concerned about an inability by the therapist or the family to generate new scripts, we can see that both are faced with a difficult problem: how to generate—or, more correctly, support—an alternative narrative when the choices of narratives available do not seem to fit the "facts", recognizing also that some alternatives may be dismissed because they are culturally unacceptable—too "odd" or "weird". Cecchin (1987) goes on to add perceptively:

> We notice that it is often difficult for students [of family therapy] to grasp the idea of hypothesizing or to hypothesize about a system. This is probably because we have been raised in cultural contexts in which the common belief is that teachers know more than students. [p. 411]

Perhaps students do not have difficulty hypothesizing per se, but Cecchin is right concerning the dominant discourses about teachers and students. But maybe there is more to it than this: students often reject the hypotheses that spring to mind because they are not seen as properly systemic, or because they regard them as obvious. It might be more appropriate and useful to try to imagine what the family's hypotheses are, what they have considered in the past, what they have rejected and why, what they think now, and how they might think about events in the future. Perhaps not surprisingly, the therapists' hypotheses— the stories that they have contemplated—and those contemplated by the family appear to be a constrained set. Part of the reason for this may be that due to living in the same societal reality people share the same stock of available narratives. What may be seen to be new narratives may more accurately be what Goffman (1975) calls transformations or variations on dominant stories. In contrast, when a therapist works with a family from another culture, then the potential stories contemplated may differ radically between them (Carter & McGoldrick, 1988; Lau, 1984).

SURVIVAL POTENTIAL
OF NEW NARRATIVES

There is a need to consider the viability or survival potential of narratives that have been generated within the context of the therapy room. How removed are these from the dominant stories in society outside the therapy room? Stories that are too far removed from the consensual realities may quickly atrophy in the melee of the external world. Some indications can be gained of the likelihood that stories may persist from the family's reactions to the therapist's suggestions of alternative narratives. Cecchin (1987) points to this when he suggests that there is a recursive process whereby a new script may be offered to a family and they respond by adjusting their script. Therapy starts to resemble a process of mutual discovery, with the family and the therapist coming to understand each other's points of view and progressing to co-construct a version of events that is mutually acceptable.

Case example—competing stories

The Bales family consisted of three adult children, Pat (age 23), Kathy (age 20), and David (age 19), and Mr and Mrs Bales. The two daughters had left home. David, though still living at home with his parents, refused throughout to attend therapy. The problem was presented as continual quarrels and tension in the family, supposedly caused largely by Mr Bales' difficult behaviour. He had a long psychiatric history, with a previous diagnosis of manic depression for which he had been hospitalized. The "illness" was said to have been triggered by shell shock during the war. Mrs Bales was the breadwinner in the family. Mr Bales had been employed in various temporary or part-time jobs but was now retired and receiving a small pension from the Army. It appeared that he was virtually ostracized by the rest of the family at home, the two daughters and, to a lesser extent, his son continually siding with Mrs Bales against him. Mr Bales complained that no one listened to him, that he was excluded, e.g. they shunned him and would not even eat with him. Some of this painful pattern was also apparent in the sessions, where the daughters would occasionally giggle in concert and exchange knowing looks and expressions of exasperation with each other and with Mrs Bales while he spoke. However, Kathy, the younger daughter, admitted that she was similar in some ways to her father, especially in that she "shared his volatile temper". The daughters, though no longer at home, visited almost daily, apparently to "check if their mother was all right", but they tended to ignore Mr Bales completely on these visits.

The edited extract is from the first interview with the family, following some discussion of the conflicts and family difficulties:

Therapist: Who's the family peacemaker?

Mr B: There isn't one and that's why we are here (*all laughing*); in my estimation, if there was a peacemaker we would be drawn to peace. We're like a boat with a hole in it and nobody's blocking it up and we are letting it sink and sink. And its been like this for the last fifteen years.

Therapist: Sounds like someone must have put their finger in the hole occasionally, otherwise the boat must have sunk?

Mr B: Point is, I've been to the doctor's time, time, and again. "Look here, Sir, something's got to be done about it as it's going on and on", and this is why we are here, it's gone on too long.

Therapist: So maybe you are the peacemaker, and maybe the way you've done it . . .

Pat: Dad? (*looking very puzzled*)

Therapist: Maybe it sounds crazy, maybe you've done it by having your symptoms, and your illness is a way of getting something done . . .

Mrs B: In your own way . . .

Therapist: . . . about what's going on in the family. I don't know, maybe . . .

Mr B: Because I had my breakdown. I've seen men shot and I've learned to pray and said I wouldn't like my son to go into the same position . . .

Mrs B: You amazed me when you said that, because you said having the symptoms kept us together, when I thought personally that's how we got into this mess, because of all the illness and symptoms. That's the way I've kind of viewed it really.

Therapist: Well, it's early days yet, I don't know, who can tell, but sometimes things work in peculiar ways, but I'm not saying that is the case.

Pat: I'm more puzzled than I ever was now (*laughing*).

Kathy: When we were very young, we have always been brought up on that, thought that's what normal family life was, dad shouting, we used to get hit quite a bit, we thought that was normal. It was not until he got put into hospital that we realized . . .

Mrs B: I used to think, what can it be? I wondered if it was me (*laughing*) because I was not very domesticated and that used to worry him and everything.

Therapist: Something happened a moment ago, you got very upset, Mr B?

Mr B: Yes, I was shell-shocked [in the Second World War], I caught the blast of a mortar bomb . . . you can't explain to people because you haven't lost an arm or a leg . . . you can't put over a picture. . . . I don't want people to feel sorry for me because I've got an incurable disease . . .

Pat: He used to get ill, he used to start watching war films and why bring it back when it wasn't very nice memories, but he was always watching those films . . . we couldn't understand that, seeing as how it upset him so much, why watch them, relive those memories again?

Mr B: If you shut something away in your mind, you cannot . . . it's like warfare, if you cut the enemy off you cannot capture them, if you cut the war films off and I'm not going to see them, cut off . . .

Therapist: What it sounds like to me is that you are saying that watching war films . . . is a form of treatment . . . you keep facing it . . . and eventually you are desensitized to it, you stop reacting?

Kathy: But it's been quite a long time (*the women scrutinize each other and do not looking convinced*) . . . you used to get agitated, we were thinking that you might hit us . . .

Therapist: The other side of how that makes you feel is how it affects your family. Sounds like they get a bit worried because they don't like to see you upset . . .

Mr B: If I thought it made a great big difference for me mentally or physically I wouldn't blasted well watch them. If I thought they were very upset in their flats that dad was at home, upset about me watching them [war films], I'd be very upset (*all laughing*) . . .

From this extract it is possible to see the interplay of a number of dominant narratives in the family:

1. Mr Bales as "ill"—he was seen to have some serious form of mental illness. The fact that he has been hospitalized supports this view for all of them, but not so much for Mr Bales.

2. Family conflict: they all seem to agree that there is conflict and that it upsets them, but they differ as to the cause. Mr Bales thinks the conflict is the cause of the problems and the fact that they don't have a peacemaker, whereas the others appear to view Mr Bales as largely the cause of the conflict and the problems.

3. Mr Bales is an awkward, difficult personality. Even if he is not ill, he is seen as awkward, bullying, and emotional.

4. Mrs B wonders if she was not an appropriate wife, not domesticated enough, which used to worry him.

5. Mr Bales is the source of the problem, but it was due to external circumstances—shell shock. A variation of this narrative is that Mr Bales makes it worse by watching war films, which upset him.

6. Lack of help from the professionals: Mr Bales says he has been to the doctor repeatedly, but nothing has been done to help.

7. More implicitly in this extract but clearer elsewhere, Mr Bales suggests that there is a lack of love in the family and,

by implication, a lack of love for him, i.e. he is upset by how badly they treat him.

Finally, the therapist offers another version of events, a different story, which is that Mr Bales' symptoms are an indirect way of trying to obtain some help. This clearly contrasts with the dominant or preferred stories in this family, which seem to be that Mr Bales is the source of the problems, and, were it not for his problems, things would be much better. However, Mrs Bales appeared to be offering the idea that she may not have been an appropriate wife, "not very domesticated", a subjugated narrative that alludes to the story of Mr Bales as not simply the cause of the problems but as himself being troubled by them.

Conflicting stories

In the B family, it is possible to see a number of contrasting or conflicting stories in operation. A question that arises is whether these are individually held, i.e. does each member of a family have her or his own personal stories? One version of constructivism is that stories, constructs, and beliefs are inevitably personal and unique, and hence each person is an "island" of personal beliefs. In contrast, it is possible that family members share stories, beliefs, and explanations. It appeared that the women in the family, and to a slightly lesser extent David, were in agreement that Mr Bales was the cause of the problems due to his illness. However, it was also clear that Mr Bales was aware that this is how they saw him and that he did not completely agree with this. In turn, the others knew that Mr Bales saw the situation differently, that he saw it as more of a family problem and as due to lack of respect for him.

Kelly (1955) referred to this awareness of others' beliefs and stories as sociality. It has also been termed meta-perspectives (Laing, 1966), i.e. how I think you see X and even how I think you think I see X. In effect, family members hold their preferred stories but at the same time are aware of each other's beliefs and preferred views. From this, they are able to anticipate not only each other's actions, but also each other's thoughts, feelings, and beliefs. Furthermore, these anticipations may operate so that deviations from expected actions or stories may be met with surprise and even a variety of means of reinstating positions. As an example, if any member of the B family articulated a completely new story of the problems, they might be reminded that this was inconsistent with their previous views: "Oh, you've changed your tune." By analogy, the ideas in a family can appear to show a homeostatic process such that ideas that are "too deviant" from the accepted norm may have various operations performed on them, such as censure, ridicule, or criticism, so that the dominant shared view, or "party line", is re-established. Like actions, some remarks—and the thoughts presumed to behind them—can become defined as "too way out", leading to various forms of censure: "How could you say that, you must think . . . !"

Inability to anticipate what will be said (e.g. when someone articulates a radically different story from the "usual") can cause confusion and anxiety. In fact, there may be an experience of no longer knowing someone, of losing contact or rapport with them, if they appear to alter their views radically. A sense of being cheated or betrayed may accompany a recognition of having been "taken in", believing something that another did not really mean. Associated with such uncertainty about another's narratives may be an emotional sense of insecurity or anxiety about what they may say or do next. In Kelly's terms, there may be less anxiety associated with relating to someone whose views, even though distasteful, are consistent than when another's views are apparently chaotic and unpredictable.

SHARED NARRATIVES

Harry Procter (1981, 1985) suggests that the stories that family members develop consist of opposing points of view. In effect, family stories or accounts can be seen in terms of Kelly's idea of a construct—a bipolar classification:

> Consider the example [from Watzlawick et al., 1974] of the nagging wife and withdrawing husband. Her perception of him may be: "He is lazy and inactive and he needs prodding into action".

He may see her as: "She is always nagging me, why doesn't she wait and let me make my own mind up and stop rushing around?" Each has a perception of the other that governs their actions, each anticipates the other and acts in accordance with these anticipations. The message that each gets from the other validates and confirms the perception that each holds. What develops over time is a shared construct system. In this particular example, the basis of the couple's interaction seems to be a shared family construct, which may be "lazy, withdrawing" versus "busy, nagging". [Dallos & Procter, 1984, p. 80]

In turn, each partner has an awareness, a meta-perception, that this is how the other sees them. They do not necessarily agree on each other's perceptions or stories, but they know them. In fact, their disagreement about each other's stories is what drives the relationship or, arguably, maintains the homeostasis.

Some of the key aspects of this idea of shared stories and beliefs in families can be summarized as follows:

1. Family members develop a set of stories about their relationships with each other.

2. They also agree, at least to some extent, to hold some common ways of seeing events and their relationships.

3. The understandings in families are patterned and shared in an analogous way to their patterns of behaviour.

4. The understandings can be seen to consist of a limited number of shared constructs or dimensions of understanding.

5. The members of a family may use a variety of terms, and these carry subjective meanings for them, sometimes not immediately accessible to outside observers.

6. They may employ a variety of different terms all of which effectively cover the same range of events. In other words, the basis of their understandings or belief system may "boil down to" a few major, or "core", constructs or dimensions.

Family members appear to share beliefs not simply in terms of agreements, but in terms of holding shared dimensions along which they are positioned in relation to each other (Procter, 1981). In effect, they agree on what is worth arguing or disagreeing about. For example, the couple above appear to share the view that the issue of whether a person is active—busy, as opposed to lazy and inactive—is important. Eron and Lund (1993) share such a dialectical view in stressing the interplay between beliefs and actions. They suggest that the basis of many problems in families is a cycle of behaviours and beliefs resulting from two conflicting but interlocking narratives. It is, of course, possible that a family may appear to contain more than two stories, but it may be that these inevitably distil down to two contrasting constellations of views.

EVOLUTION OF PROBLEMS

Systemic theory approaches, including constructivist views, have tended to fight shy of attempts to explore the evolution of problems. An exception to this has been the concept of the family life cycle and the relationship between key transitional changes, crises, and the emergence of problems (Carter & McGoldrick, 1988; Haley, 1981). Typically, the concept of the family life cycle and transitional crises has been employed in order to help the therapist understand or formulate a hypothesis about how the problems may have been precipitated by critical configurations of demands at transitional stages. This helps the therapist to generate a story about how the problems have arisen. However, it is quite likely that family members also have their own developmental stories. In fact, this is essentially what a narrative is—an account or story about how the current situation has arisen, what events/experiences in the past have moulded individual personalities, ways of relating, and so on. Families when asked about their problems often spontaneously provide a life-cycle story, e.g. how their relationship was fine until the first baby came along, and then, with the pressures of work, they drifted apart:

> As we tracked the development of problems in families, we began with the premise of many strategic therapists . . . that problems evolve from the mishandling of ordinary life difficulties

which usually occur at key transitional points in the life cycle (for example, marriage, divorce, birth of a child, separation, illness, children leaving home, death). We found that at these times people began to act differently, but their views of self and other may also become more fluid and unsettled. [Eron & Lund, 1993, p. 29]

The complexity and potential stresses involved with transitional stages has also been described in a variety of studies outside the family therapy literature (La Rossa, 1986). These include shifts in roles, identity, intimacy, power, and patterns of relationships. In the change to parenthood each partner is likely to start to see themselves in some radically new and different ways, e.g. as parents not just adults. They may start to view each other differently and form new expectations of each other, such as responsibilities for childcare and financial provision. The conflicts and mutual criticisms that may emerge can lead each of them to conclude that these in part imply that their partner now sees them as less attractive and competent. Since one of the central aspects of relationships may be a sense of validation, being accepted and valued for what we are, these shifts may have very powerful effects. Illnesses, especially unforeseen ones, can have effects that demonstrate many of these components:

. . . in the stroke victim case, the event of major illness may challenge the prevailing views of self and other at all three levels. It is likely that the man begins to see himself differently: as less capable, less independent, and less able to help others. He may begin to see his family differently: as more solicitous and more critical of his capabilities. Finally, he may begin to see his family seeing him differently: to imagine that they see him as helpless and incapable of caring for himself. [Eron & Lund, 1993, p. 297]

These changes, Eron and Lund argue, frequently lead to "dysjunctions" when people feel that others are seeing them in ways they do not like and find distasteful or objectionable. In short, a narrative starts to emerge in which one or more members of the family contradicts the preferred family view of that person. With the Bales family earlier, Mr Bales's preferred view of himself appeared to be that he should be the respected father in the family. He expected the children to acknowledge him, to listen to him, and perhaps to put up with his occasional moods because he had a right to express his feelings about the terrible things he had gone through for his country and for his children. Instead, the family tended to see him as moody, a bully, at times ridiculous or rather sad and hopeless. Kelly (1955) suggests that when people are confronted with such a schism between how they want to see themselves, attempts are made to force things to be the way they want to see them: people attempt to distort the evidence to support their views. This frequently involves hostility, anger, frustration, and attempts to coerce people into accepting one specific version of events. Unfortunately, this is typically seen simply as aggression and bullying and, in response, generates negative reactions leading to the very opposite of what the person wishes to achieve.

Eron and Lund (1993) try to identify the points in the family's history where such dysjunctions have occurred and then to chart the pathways in terms of the attempted solutions:

1. A critical transitional event takes place leading to shifts in self-perceptions.

2. In this emotionally charged situation, members may become more vigilant and sensitive and start to see others seeing them in ways they do not like.

3. Attempts are made to rectify these perceptions, e.g. if I think I am not respected by others I may try to command respect or become depressed and withdrawn. Either reaction may set a problem-maintaining cycle into motion.

4. As the problem cycle proceeds, it becomes increasingly more fixed, and the disjunctive narratives are reinforced, leading to more of the same behaviour.

5. Ways of seeing the situation and each other's behaviours become rigid, so that eventually people become convinced that a problem really exists, usually in one person. Since people tend to believe that they have acted for valid and good reasons, it is hard for them to see how their own beliefs and actions may contribute to shaping the problem.

This analysis bears many resemblances to studies of the natural processes of account-making discussed in chapter three. The critical transitional stage may involve an emotionally charged climate in which perceptions, attention, understandings, and memories may become distorted in various ways. As Harvey et al. (1992) have shown, the first stages of the process of a traumatic event tend to be denial, numbness, intrusive thoughts, distractedness, over-vivid memories, and preoccupation with the event. In short, our cognitive processes, including problem-solving abilities and attempted solutions, are not at their best. For example, following the birth of a child a young couple may find themselves tired, insecure about their parenting skills, overwhelmed by the new responsibilities, but also feeling that they "should" be happy and overjoyed at the arrival of their child. Consequently, there may be considerable ruptures between preferred views of self and each other, which, fuelled by the emotionally charged climate, lead to a variety of cognitive distortions, such as selective focusing on negative aspects of one's own and others' actions, over-generalizing that the situation is hopeless, and so on (Beck, 1967).

Eron and Lund (1993) emphasize that in order to understand why a particular attempted solution is selected and why it has the effect of promoting a problem, it is necessary to explore the family history and gain an understanding of the dominant narratives and how these make up the family members' views of themselves and of each other. As an example, they offer the case of a young man who has left home to start college. Having being successful and popular at school, he finds college difficult, not getting the grades or the social life that he expected. He starts to call home more often, sounding worried, which is a disconcerting new experience for his parents, who had been used to their son being confident and successful. They respond with concern, which unsettles their son, who is used to being seen—and prefers to see himself—as confident, competent, and independent. This undermines his confidence, and the situation spirals, so that he becomes increasingly less confident. In turn, his parents lose confidence in themselves as parents and blame themselves for not having prepared him for independence. The worried telephone-calls continue, and one attempted solution that the parents suggest is that he moves to a college nearby. However, this further convinces the son that his parents see him as incompetent:

> At the point when the family enters treatment, the young man has dropped out of two more colleges closer to his parents' home town, is unemployed, and is literally petrified to leave his parents' house: his symptoms are a metaphor for his failed transition. [Eron & Lund, 1993, p. 300]

The dominant story that starts to emerge is that both the son and his parents have "failed" (see Figure 4.1). As the situation becomes more desperate, this story starts to dominate and becomes increasingly constraining. The accompanying emotions of anxiety, guilt, and frustration appear to constrain thinking further, i.e. the perceptions and narratives become increasingly tunnel-vision-like.

These difficulties—the trials and tribulations of children first leaving the nest—are extremely common, but we may speculate about why in this family things went along this particular path. An alternative scenario might have been that the parents recognized the son's distress but held onto the idea that they were competent parents who could offer him enough support to get through. Parents in this situation sometimes make the

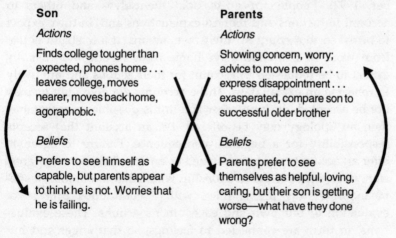

Son	Parents
Actions	*Actions*
Finds college tougher than expected, phones home... leaves college, moves nearer, moves back home, agoraphobic.	Showing concern, worry; advice to move nearer... express disappointment... exasperated, compare son to successful older brother
Beliefs	*Beliefs*
Prefers to see himself as capable, but parents appear to think he is not. Worries that he is failing.	Parents prefer to see themselves as helpful, loving, caring, but their son is getting worse—what have they done wrong?

Figure 4.1. Development of a dominant story of failure (after Eron & Lund, 1993).

suggestion that the youngster persevere for some time, perhaps until the end of the college year, and then make a decision. However, there may be a variety of reasons why events proceed along one path, why one story emerges rather than another. For example, the parents may feel distressed themselves, and this comes across to their son; or they may hold an unspoken belief that this particular child is more vulnerable, perhaps because they feel he was not given enough love as a child. Such feelings of guilt may then surface to promote the development of one dominant story, and its accompanying attempted solutions, rather than another. A conversation with the family that explores these various narratives, underlying beliefs, and the events and feelings surrounding past occurrences may be more effective and potentially long-lasting than, for example, a directive task that aims to block the parents' actions of overconcern, or a reframe that just focuses on this cycle.

NARRATIVES AND CHARACTERS— HEROES AND VILLAINS

In creating a narrative, which involves describing their own and others' actions, people are inevitably formulating questions about why they, or others, have acted the way they have (Weber, 1992). People appear to hold themselves and others to account for actions and request explanations and, in turn, expect to be asked to account for their own actions. If a husband is late from work or if a child stays home from school, they usually expect to be requested to account for their actions and are likely to rehearse an explanation. These accounts we give may or may not be accepted, or, if no other account is possible or acceptable, then an apology may be offered, i.e. an account that accepts responsibility for a negative consequence. Failure to agree to offer an account may be construed as an act of insolence, aggression, or rejection of the relationship worse than the initial misdemeanour. Family life is filled with a continuous process of evaluation of our own and each other's actions. These evaluations, in turn, are connected to feelings, so that anger and humiliation may be experienced if an account is rejected, or it is implied that it is a lie or a fabrication. An experience of loss of face or damage to one's character may accompany being compelled to accept an account that puts the person in a "bad light".

When a family attends for therapy, the accounts they offer of the problems, their lives together, and their relationships appear as stories that contain a plot and members of the family as the characters. Each character is depicted as playing a part in the story, making a contribution to the plot which is more or less positive, i.e. there are villains, victims, heroes, and heroines. On one level, the story is about their actions, but more significantly it is likely to contain assumptions about their intentions. Attribution/accounts (see chapter three) theorists have suggested that events are framed in terms of explanations that are predominantly either dispositional or situational. The former assigns cause and usually responsibility for the action to the person, whereas situational explanations focus more on external circumstances. For example, the young man at college might be seen as vulnerable, having a weak disposition or, in situational terms, as caught in a web of family transaction or unlucky in having a stressful time at college. Family therapy in its various forms can be seen as essentially offering situational explanations or narratives for problems in that causes are seen to be external to individuals. However, there is a consequent danger that the family itself becomes "personalized", in becoming seen as the cause of its own problems. In effect, systemic therapy represents a fundamental shift to a situational explanation in regarding problems as caused by the family situation, not as due to inherent individual factors.

POSITIVE CONNOTATION

Understanding that people in families inevitably engage in explanations—creating narratives that contain positive or negative evaluations—helps to elucidate more clearly the power of positive connotation developed by the Milan team. In positive connotation the therapist suggests to the family that the problem(s) can be seen in a more positive light in contrast to the negative perceptions that have tended to prevail. An attempt is made to propose a convincing explanation in terms of how each member of the family is acting for "good", positive reasons. These reasons are predominantly framed as for the mutual beneficial interest of the family as a whole, and frequently these are stated as being unconscious. This, in effect, creates an alternative story in which the symptom is put in a different light:

> Understanding the use of positive connotation as a strategy, we believe, requires that the therapist should accept that people come to therapy with fixed ideas about the way things are. These ideas usually include the belief that problem behaviour is bad. In order for the therapist to carry out his primary aim, which is to introduce differences into the belief system, he may want to convey the idea that a problem is not necessarily bad. [Campbell, Draper, & Huffington, 1989, p. 56]

The narratives that families construct place each of them in different roles, with differing amounts of responsibility and blame for what is happening. The struggles over which narratives are adopted as the dominant ones may relate precisely to the fact that they cast people in varyingly positive or negative lights. If the struggle to find a mutually acceptable story cannot be resolved, a form of stalemate may develop, often accompanied by members of the family taking sides. This, in effect, means taking sides with one story as opposed to another. In the Bales family, there were a number of possible stories that had currency and were more, or less, acceptable to each of them: that he was a bit of a bully, awkward, or crazy was not acceptable to Mr Bales but was to the children and to Mrs Bales; that the children were disrespectful was acceptable to Mr Bales but less so to Mrs Bales, since she felt that he was at fault because had been too hard on them.

The acceptability of the stories also relates to strategic positions, e.g. the children appeared to gain power in the family by being in a coalition with their mother and having the run of the house. Since they had left home, this was less central, and they may have been more willing to accept a story that features the relationship between the parents as a source of the problems.

Positive connotation can be seen, therefore, as a form of arbitration in families: there is something in it for everybody—everyone wins. This is not intended to be a pejorative view of families. From the inside, it can at times be impossible to be cool, detached, and rational and try to take on board everyone's feelings and points of view. There will almost certainly be times when people are blamed or are in the dog-house for a while. It may be, as Eron and Lund suggest, that it is a matter of "bad luck", deprivation, or circumstance that in some cases one person comes to occupy permanently this "sick" role.

SUMMARY

This chapter has attempted to employ ideas from a variety of constructivist approaches discussed in the previous chapters to offer a model of family dynamics and the evolution of problems. Some connections between strategic and narrative approaches have been outlined. In particular, it has been suggested that narratives, beliefs, and constructs invariably have a strategic quality in the extent to which they are employed to predict others' actions and construct interpersonal plans. Narratives evolve in order both to explain events and to shape desired courses of actions and "preferred views of self" in the family. Family dynamics are fuelled by the tensions between these competing stories among family members. These competing meanings can be seen to display dynamic properties of escalation and polarization and elicit attempts to maintain the symbolic status quo—e.g. by a variety of operations, such as censure, ridicule, and criticism, that may be performed to bring deviant meanings into line with the dominant family narrative.

It is suggested that all events in a family have a more or less enigmatic quality in that alternative explanations are invariably possible. Family members can be seen, like family therapists, as engaged in a process of progressive hypothesizing: any new circumstance calls forth a range of possible explanations, and from the flux of the family interactions some dominant explanations emerge. These, however, have a more or less temporary and propositional nature and are open to renegotiation or revision. The dominant views that emerge can play a significant part in shaping the evolution of problems in families. The view of any particular difficulty is embedded in family members' beliefs, and these shape the particular attempted solutions that thereby follow. It has also been suggested that the narratives that evolve, especially in relation to problems, are not neutral but position people in varyingly positive or negative ways— they assign blame and responsibility for which people are called to account. From this point of view, one of the active ingredients of attempts at "restorying" and "positive connotation" can be seen to be the extent to which they allow each person in the family to be her or his "preferred self", i.e. to hold a more positive part or character in the family story.

CHAPTER FIVE

Dominant narratives—social constructionist perspectives

Constructivist approaches to family therapy have made a significant contribution in revealing how the patterns of family actions can be seen in terms of the interweaving of family members' actions and beliefs. Yet this still locates the source of the patterns and the associated problems predominantly within the sphere of the family itself. However, it is possible that the patterning is produced not just by the idiosyncratic dynamics of each family but is necessitated by the demands of the wider society within which a family is located. Frequently observed patterns, such as that of the "over-involved" mother and "disengaged" father, need to be understood more broadly as being determined by the wider societal structures and ideologies that shape family life, especially the relations between men and women:

> The pattern of family behaviour so frequently encountered by family therapists, that of the "over-involved" wife/mother and disengaged and absent husband/father, suddenly appears in a new light: as a necessary form. That necessity derives from its ability to reproduce the personality characteristics, relationship

patterns and behavioural orientations that are functional for continual operation of the contemporary social formation. [James & McIntyre, 1983, p. 126]

This is not to suggest that all aspects of family life and experience are totally determined by structural and ideological factors, but equally it should be no surprise that given such preconditions certain forms of family arrangements are commonly found. Furthermore, it is important to recognize that though families may show variations on this pattern (e.g. differences in degrees of "over-involvement" or "disengagement"), nevertheless the underlying core structure of gender relations may be fundamentally similar across many families.

Central to this idea is that "mothering" is presented as "naturally" fundamental to a woman's identity, and this importantly shapes family life, including the mother's important contribution to re-producing the contrasting male role:

> Women's mothering in the isolated nuclear family of contemporary capitalist society creates specific personality characteristics in men that reproduce both an ideology and psychodynamic of male superiority and submission to the requirements of production. It prepares men for participation in male-dominated family and society, for their lesser emotional participation in family life, and for their participation in the capitalist world of work. [Chodorow, 1978, p. 124]

Despite social changes, women are still more likely than men to carry the burden of care for children and to be more centred around the home than men. This is not simply a personal choice but one shaped by a variety of economic and practical necessities dictated by the society they live within. However, associated with any given society is a web of discourses or ideologies, such as that women are "naturally maternal" since they are seen to be more emotionally responsive, nurturant, non-competitive, and so on. In this way, a set of roles and beliefs about family life is reproduced across the generations.

Systems theory's inability to take account of such wider societal factors that shape the patterns of interactions that family therapists observe has been seen by some as a major indictment and testimony of its failure (James & McIntyre, 1983; Williams & Watson, 1988). However, it has been suggested, in contrast, that in fact second-order cybernetics is quite capable of being utilized to take such factors into account:

> The second-order cybernetic view argues, in a manner similar to that of the feminist critics, that it is the observer (or therapist) who draws distinctions that "create the reality". . . . By including the observer as part of the system observed, second-order cybernetics acknowledges that the system considered relevant is a construction of the observer drawing the distinctions. . . . Drawing distinctions is, thus, not only an epistemological act, it is a political act. [McKinnon & Miller, 1987, p. 148]

They argue that acknowledging that the therapist is involved and becomes part of a family–therapist system can potentially be a useful step towards recognizing not only her personal influence, but also wider cultural factors. The therapist's beliefs are in turn shaped by wider ideologies: those of the institution or profession she represents and, in sum, society at large. Hence these wider factors inevitably play a significant role in the therapeutic encounter. McKinnon and Miller (1987) add, however, that systemic therapists, including the Milan team, have significantly ignored the issue of how their own position is inevitably a political one. At an obvious level, it is easy to ignore the imbalances of power that may result from the different social positions occupied by the therapist and a family:

> By defining the therapeutic situation as one of mutuality or "co-evolution", Milan therapists, all too easily, presume that the therapist and client are equal contributors in constructing the therapeutic reality. . . . most obvious, is the situation of the white therapist with the black family, or the male therapist with the single-parent mother. [McKinnon & Miller, 1987, p. 151]

Such a critical perspective, a focus on the "politics of therapy", had been forcefully advocated previously as part of the anti-psychiatry movement (Cooper, 1970; Foucault, 1967, 1975; Laing, 1966). Therapy, it was argued, inevitably involves a process of social control, namely in assisting, if not coercing, people to conform to the norms and expectations of the society they live in. Especially when the presenting problems contain elements that are anti-social (e.g. violence, abuse, or theft), then therapy can easily come to be seen as corrective—fixing people so that they do not engage in these anti-social activities. Of course many, if not most, therapists resist attempts to turn their work into such corrective procedures but this may nevertheless be partly how we are seen, not least by the families with whom we work. However, the political aspects of therapy may be seen to be much wider. White and Epston (1990) suggest that therapists may also, at times unwittingly, engage in a political activity by upholding or failing to challenge dominant definitions of problems. Foucault (1975) has argued that these dominant views are largely based on a "scientific" approach that proposes that problems have an objective reality and that the "truth", scientifically established can be discovered about these. An influential case in point is the view that psychotic disorders are due to an organic, biological cause; the precise nature of this has yet to be identified, but the assumption is that, given time, a scientific approach will be able to arrive at a definite and objective causal explanation of, for example, schizophrenia.

White and Epston (1990) argue that it is this fundamental view that a scientific approach can establish the objective "truth" of disorders that is a central political issue in therapy. More specifically, this view also regards societal, or even relational, factors as secondary, if not irrelevant. Many families can be regarded as having been immersed or indoctrinated into such a view and therefore see their problems in such a "problem-saturated" way. However, this scientific view of problems is related to power, e.g. the power invested in the medical profession or the power of dominant sections of society to define problems as signs of personal weakness rather than as indications of social inequalities. In effect, to challenge these definitions is also to challenge the existing structures of power:

> . . . in joining with persons to challenge these practices, we also accept that we are inevitably engaged in a political activity. (We would also acknowledge that, if we do not join with persons to challenge these techniques of power, then we are also engaged in

political activity.) This is not a political activity that involves the proposal of an alternate ideology, but one that challenges the techniques that subjugate persons to a dominant ideology. [White & Epston, 1990, p. 29]

THERAPY AND POLITICS

An interesting and important question is why therapy is generally seen as needing to exclude "political" discussion? Answers to this question include the idea that therapists must be neutral and that it is not their job to engage in political discussion, especially since it might be an abuse of their power to "indoctrinate" clients. Another is that problems are private, to do with emotional experiences, personal relationships, childhood experiences, i.e. not predominantly to do with wider political issues. Not least, the issue may be that if therapists become overtly political, they may lose their jobs. Arguably, though, a discussion of some political issues—e.g. the impact of a variety of the structural factors that may oppress a family, such as unemployment, poor housing, or racial discrimination—may be relevant. Furthermore, a discussion of how they have experienced various ideological oppressions—such as racism, gender inequality, or class prejudices—may help them to view their problems as less personal and more external and social. Feminist-inspired therapies have, perhaps, recently done most to advocate such a critical, political approach (Goldner, 1991; Harre-Mustin, 1991). However, White and Epston's point is that, in challenging the dominant narratives or ideologies, therapists need not be intending to propose or impose their own alternative ideologies. Instead, to engage in some critical reflection on what oppressive ideologies and practices might be influencing a family can be seen as a valid component of therapy. Furthermore, reflection by therapists on how they may at times unwittingly be perpetuating these ideologies can also be appropriate.

Any given society can be regarded as containing a range of norms or ideas about what are deemed to be acceptable and legitimate ways of behaving, feeling, and thinking (Becker, 1974; Mead, 1949). Attached to these are ideas of roles or appropriate parts that people are expected to play in society—father, mother, employee, child, brother, lover, and so on. More recently, a number of writers have argued that it is more appropriate to consider the "self" and concepts such as roles and norms as fluid and changing—*distributed* across different contexts—rather than as fixed or invariable (Bruner, 1990; Gergen, 1985). At the same time, it can be argued that there are sets of common ideas running through these different contexts in any given society which map out the possibilities of people's identities. For example, the roles of father and mother regulate family life both informally and formally, as in laws relating to obligations, rights, and safety in the family. Foucault (1975) has emphasized that these norms operate through our internalization of regimes of knowledge. These may function so that we monitor ourselves and carry out surveillance of our own and each other's actions: "In these circumstances, persons will perpetually evaluate their own behaviour or engage in operations on themselves to forge themselves as 'docile bodies'" (White & Epston, 1990, p. 24). This is also referred to as the "normalizing judgement": internalized ideas about what counts as truth, which in turn dictate definitions of what it is to be normal, are applied by people to themselves and to those intimately involved with them. Rather than social control through more obvious direct forms of coercion, control is seen to be enforced by the people themselves. These internalizations may be in the form of people's internal dialogues or conversations, e.g. the condition of anorexia may involve frequent berating of the self to be slimmer in order to conform to some desired notion of beauty. Psychotic disorder may involve internal conversations that view the "voices", including the internal, as deviant, strange, bizarre, or a sign of organic illness. In effect, this can be a self-sealing narrative which, by disqualifying these internal dialogues, short-circuits any possible useful awareness, insight, meta-narratives about the "voices". This scrutinization of the self according to norms has also been discussed in terms of "secondary labelling", i.e. taking on board others' definitions of self as deviant and odd and incorporating these into an internal image or definition of self.

CONSTRUCTIVISM
AND SOCIAL CONSTRUCTIONISM

Constructivist approaches have been invaluable in highlighting how the beliefs that family members hold serve to shape their actions, choices, and attempted solutions to what are perceived to be the problems. In addition, they add an important dynamic component in stressing how it is disagreements between members of families that are often at the root of relationship struggles and failed patterns of attempted solutions to problems. Also (as discussed in chapter four), the idea of preferred views is helpful in revealing how the struggles over meanings can be seen in terms of attempts to remain true to a positive, desired narrative about one's life, or a narrative in which the self is located in a positive, valuable role. However, these preferred views can be seen as not simply personal preferences but as shaped by shared societal values, norms—ideologies.

Constructivist approaches to family therapy, however, have tended to stress individuality and uniqueness, though there has been some recognition that the beliefs that shape people's actions are related to wider social norms or beliefs (Jackson, 1965). Systemic thinking has made possible a major extension in showing that the processes of constructing meanings occur between people and not merely at the individual level as, for example, in cognitive therapy or personal construct theory.

However, though it can be argued that the fundamental individualism remains, nevertheless pioneers such as Watzlawick have obviously been aware of the importance of the wider societal context: "Culturally, we share many conventions of punctuation which, while no more accurate than other views of the same events, serve to organize common and important interactional sequences" (Watzlawick et al., 1967, p. 56).

An important difference between constructivism and social constructionism is that the latter takes as its central point that there are social realities. It is not simply suggested that there is a "real" objective world "out there", but that there are dominant beliefs, explanations, ways of thinking about the world, and in particular a shared language that constructs how we see the world. The fact that these socially constructed views continually change does not mean that, at any given moment or point of history, they do not have a real existence as influential shared ideas. This sensitivity to how families are immersed in the reality of their culture highlights how constructivism, in contrast, tends to isolate families from society. Instead of simply exploring new narratives, a social constructionist approach to therapy tries to consider how a family's creativity is shaped by dominant narratives, and what is co-constructed in therapy must engage with this wider societal systems of beliefs. Such therapy often includes an explicit discussion of these societal beliefs, as in Goldner, Penn, Sheinberg, and Walker's (1990) approach, in which couples are encouraged to discuss critically how their ideas are shaped by the commonly held expectations of gender roles and male–female relationships.

SOCIAL CONSTRUCTIONISM

A variety of societal influences may shape people's experiences in families, including institutionalized structures and practices. Adequacy of housing, income, type of locality, and educational opportunities are determined by the family's position in the socioeconomic pecking order. Dominant shared beliefs or ideologies define expectations, ideas of identity, gender, and other family roles, and a system of perceived rights and obligations. These beliefs may shape not only the practical, more obvious aspects of life, but even the most intimate, supposedly "private" moments, such as expressions of sexual intimacy and moments of family sorrow and joy. Even in our moments of solitude, our private internal reflections consist of verbal dialogues and images imported from our cultures. For example, the words and phrases that we use in speaking with ourselves connect us to our immediate and historical cultural legacy of ideas and meanings. Feminist analyses have been particularly helpful in drawing attention to how language itself contains and perpetuates a variety of assumptions, directs our attention, and may perpetuate ways of thinking that support inequalities, e.g. in terms like housewife, "good" mother, and single parent.

Social constructionism shares with systemic theory an emphasis on the centrality of relationships: becoming a "person" is to be involved in a social world of meanings through our interactions with others. It also shares with constructivism a view of people as actively engaged in formulating meanings, attempting to understand, predict, plan, and reflect on their own and each other's actions (Gergen, 1985; Goldner, 1991; Hoffman, 1993). In addition, it emphasizes that all aspects of our existence are fundamentally social: from the moment of birth we can be regarded as immersed in a social world that offers us not only a view of the world, but epistemological orientations, ways of knowing or thinking about this world. Rather than predominantly starting with a perspective on how the individual is actively making sense of his or her world, this process of making sense is itself seen as a socially constructed and mediated activity.

Some key family therapy concepts, such as the idea of "family life cycles", strikes chords with social constructionist ideas. For example, the family life cycle embraces the idea that each of us is simultaneously involved in a variety of social groups, e.g. a woman in a family may simultaneously be a mother, a worker, a daughter, a lover, middle-class, white, and most generally a woman. Our sense of self is therefore seen as fragmented, complex, and multiple. At any given moment, and in different contexts, one aspect of our identity may dominate over another. There may also be strains and conflicts between these different identities which are defined by the various social systems to which we belong, e.g. the identity of a mother and career woman. These societally constructed identities may themselves shift and leave us with ambivalent or contradictory images of ourselves, e.g. the shifting ideas of masculinity and fathering may lead to many men being confused about who and what sort of identity, what sort of person, they should be. Social constructionism suggests that our social world is actively created by the interactions between and within groups of people in society. What is created is a set of ideas, or shared beliefs/ideologies, which lead to various practices, including ideas about what the structure and behaviours comprising families *should* be like. More widely, the practices or regimes that follow define our access to money and housing, work opportunities, educational structures, and a variety of intrusive measures, such as surveillance of care of the children and acceptable behaviour inside and outside the home.

CONSTRUCTION OF EXPERIENCE

The dominant narratives can be seen to shape both our futures —what we expect, aspire to, images of existence—and, at the same time, the past—how we make sense of what has happened. Like buying clothes off the shelf, we attempt to fit our experiences into the narratives that are available:

> There exist a stock of culturally available discourses that are considered appropriate and relevant to the expression or representation of particular aspects of experience ... persons experience problems which they frequently present for therapy when the narratives in which they are storying their experience, and/or in which they are having their experience storied by others, do not significantly represent their lived experience, and that, in these circumstances, there will be significant aspects of their lived experience that contradict this dominant narrative. [White & Epston, 1990, pp. 27–28]

These narratives may in turn shape our aspirations and dreams; they map out what we believe to be possible and desirable— e.g. spontaneous romance and mutual compatibility, harmonious family life—and we may experience distress when our experiences do not appear to fit or match up to these ideal narratives. As another example, childbirth is surrounded in narratives of joy, self-fulfilment, closeness of the parents, and so on, but the reality for many may involves elements that do not fit—tiredness, irritability, self-doubt, distance, and lack of intimacy between the parents. The more strongly this ideal version or narrative is accepted as the "truth" of how things should be, as normal, the more distress and guilt people may feel if their experience appears not to fit this (Carter & McGoldrick, 1988; La Rossa, 1986). Such ruptures between our preferred nar-

ratives, or societally sanctioned dominant narratives, and what
we are actually experiencing can, as we saw in the last chapter,
set in motion patterns of failed attempted solutions which are
driven by attempts to reconcile our preferred views with a view
of ourselves as incompetent, abnormal, or deviant.

The production of dominant systems of ideas and meanings
—ideologies—is regarded in social constructionism as shaped
and maintained according to distributions of power. As a telling
example, people of the lowest socioeconomic groups and ethnic
minorities generally have poorer physical and mental health:
put simply, they die younger and appear to have generally
more tormented lives. However, until recently it has not been
acknowledged that these differences are due to basic inequalities in our society but, rather, were attributed to "poor health
habits", "fecklessness", and so on. The crushing effects of pov-
erty and stress have frequently been minimized in terms that
extol the virtues of personal autonomy and choice. Such
conceptualizations can be regarded as systems of knowledge or
ideologies that serve to disguise or justify the privileges of
the most powerful groups. In short, the dominant classes have
privileged access to a variety of means—education, the media,
commerce, and industry—to promote systems of thought that
maintain their superior opportunities and position:

> The ideas of the ruling class are, in every age, the ruling ideas . . .
> the class which has the means of material production has the
> means of mental production, so that in consequence the ideas of
> those who lack the means of mental production are, in general,
> subject to it. [Marx & Engels, 1846, p. 35]

The foundations of social constructionism and feminist approaches to family therapy have derived the basis of their position from Marxist theory, in particular the proposition that
dominant groups in society have the power to produce and
sustain dominant beliefs or ideologies. The dominant sections
of society—the ruling classes—are seen as able to disseminate
and enforce by a variety of practices those beliefs that suit and
maintain their positions of dominance. These ideologies may
also serve to distort, as in the popular and pernicious view that

society is structured according to fundamental abilities and that the poor are in that position because they have less ability, are less intelligent, or don't want to work.

POWER AND DISCOURSES

The terms "discourse" and "ideology" are at times used interchangeably in much of the literature. It is useful, however, to point to some important shades of difference:

> Inequitable relationships are most effectively maintained by the ideologies that obscure the existence of inequality and mask the continuous and pervasive conflict of interest between the groups concerned. By ideology we mean a socially produced construction of ideas and explanations, a set of procedures and practices which both account for and organise the social system. [Penfold & Walker, 1984, p. vi]

On the other hand:

> A discourse is a group of statements which provide a language for talking about—i.e. a way of representing—a particular kind of knowledge about a topic. When statements about a topic are made within a particular discourse, the discourse makes it possible to construct the topic in a certain way. It also limits the other ways in which the topic can be constructed. [Hall, 1992, p. 291]

Ideology has typically been used in the sense of a set of beliefs that produce knowledge that serves the interests of a particular group or class. Foucault (1975) points out that ideology has been employed to suggest that there are some true statements about the world, versus false statements, and that by coming to know what is true, real, or *fact* we can more clearly distinguish between truth and fabrications. Politically, this has been exemplified in early Marxist and feminist positions that emphasize that *real* inequalities exist, and ideologies are constructed to deny these because they serve to maintain the interests of the ruling classes of men. In contrast, Foucault in his conception of discourse argues that statements about the world are rarely ever simply true or false—"facts" can always be construed in different ways:

Foucault's use of "discourse", then, is an attempt to side-step what seems an unresolvable dilemma—deciding which social discourses are true or scientific, and which are false and ideological ... values enter into all our descriptions of the social world, and therefore most of our statements, however factual, have an ideological dimension. [Hall, 1992, p. 293]

One interpretation of Foucault's use of the term "discourse" is that it plays down "real" structural inequalities—oppression and abuses of power. The combination of discourse with the term ideology, with its emphasis on a more or less deliberate misleading or denial of "real" inequality, may be a more realistic picture of the strategies for gaining or maintaining power between sections of our society and in turn within families.

Structural power and "ideological" power are interrelated: each reflects and maintains the other. Those who are dominant (e.g. in terms of holding particular resources) are also likely to be able to ensure that their beliefs, ideas, and opinions are more influential than those who are subordinate; this in turn may justify inequality. According to Williams and Watson (1988), ideology "covers up" inequality between the genders by justifying it in terms of it being natural, God-given, functional, or complementary. Ideology also disguises inequality by labelling reactions against oppression as "madness" or "mental disorder" or "abnormal", and by encouraging those who are in a subordinate position to explain their experience as not to do with social inequalities, but to do with there being "something wrong with them".

Similarly, Lukes (1974) states that a more subtle and insidious facet of power is:

... the power to prevent people from having grievances by shaping their perceptions, cognitions and preferences in such a way that they accept their role in the existing order of things, either because they can see or imagine no alternative to it, or because they see it as natural and unchangeable, or because they value it as divinely ordained and beneficial. [Lukes, 1974]

Ideologies and structure can be seen to shape experience in various profound ways, e.g. by virtue of men and women belonging, of being located within the wider groups comprising society. A husband is a member of the family, but he also belongs to wider classes or groups—men, workers, bosses, sons, relatives, competitors, and so on. Likewise, if a member of a family is defined as mentally ill, that person becomes identified as belonging to a wider group of mentally ill people. Membership of these various groups is not a neutral act but has important consequences. Various privileges and sanctions may be associated with these, e.g. access to work, finance, and freedom and also an imposition of identities. Forms of classification, segregation, and confinement may result, as for those designated as mentally ill. They could also lose a variety of privileges and have their rights violated in various ways by examinations, physical treatments, and confinements. Also, their work was not (and still typically is not) paid at normal rates; instead, in occupational therapy departments, for example, they were paid a token sum for the work produced, even though this was of an equivalent standard to that produced commercially. More subtly, the membership to these various groups confers identities that set out personal expectations, aspirations, and ideas of self and how we should relate to others. For women, this has typically involved an identity of mothering, of beauty, and of lower expectations of achievement and independence than men.

Foucault (1975) has been highly influential in pointing out that in any given culture there can be seen to be dominant narratives or discourses. In the early days of psychotherapy, for example, the dominant narratives had been that problems were due to individual factors or disorder. With the advent of interactional approaches, the dominant narratives have moved, to some extent, to a view that problems are due to a variety of transactional processes within the family. Though family therapies have argued for a "neutral" approach, a systemic approach has been seen more critically from the outside, e.g. parents' rights groups as accusative, blaming, and implying that family dysfunctions cause the pathology.

POWER
AND THE CONSTRUCTION OF REALITY

Knowledge and power are seen to be inextricably intertwined, and a prime aspect of this is the rise in influence of scientific thought, medicine, technology, economic analyses, and so on. These forms of knowledge make claims to "objectivity", i.e. to be fundamentally true; a good example here is the idea of the organic, "scientifically verified" nature of psychotic disorders. Access to these bases of knowledge is regulated, e.g. the selection processes for training for medicine or to gain entry into the higher levels of the political domain where confidential knowledge is guarded. In turn such knowledge has important implications for practices—what is done. Medicine is a good example, with its wide range of institutions, hospitals, equipment, assessment procedures, legal rights, and so on, all of which can be employed to control what is done to people. However, Foucault clarifies that knowledge or discourses do not operate simply in this fairly straightforward way. Instead, he argues that discourses operate in both positive and negative ways. By positive he does not mean "good", but that they operate to construct ways of thinking about the world: "Positive . . . in the sense that power is constitutive or shaping of people's lives . . . in 'making up' persons' lives . . . negative . . . contributes a theory of repression" (White & Epston, 1990, p. 20).

In this way, the positive effects of power and knowledge are to promote dominant ideas or "truths" that people accept and that thereby come to shape their lives. The negative aspects are the processes whereby ideas are suppressed, abandoned, ignored. The acceptance of these "truths" makes people into "docile bodies", i.e. apparently willingly accepting these truths unquestioningly and thereby being shaped and controlled by them. In this way, the person supposedly experiencing mental health problems is as likely to accept the dominant medical/ organic discourse as the cause of their problems as are the relatives and medical staff. These dominant narratives are carried both through the vehicle of language and by practices of various sorts. Colloquial terms—such as crazy, mad, insane, nervous breakdown, and bizarre—direct our gaze so that experiences of mental distress come to be seen in ways that suggest that there is some inevitable, fundamental nature to the differences between people who are mentally ill and those who are normal. Interestingly, studies of the mental health of the general population, of the "ordinary person in the street", suggest that in fact the incidence of emotional distress indicative of mental health problems is extremely wide. But many people who have suffered extreme distress do not attend for therapy and appear to resolve their problems in a variety of alternative ways.

The "practices" resulting from and maintaining discourses can be seen, for example, in the welfare structures associated with rights to benefits for families or the structures that encourage financial dependence in women, such as maternity leave, loss of employment opportunities, and so on. These not only have practical consequences but implicitly, and at times explicitly, convey the message that it is "natural" and expected for women to be dependent and nurturing. Similarly, these practices may be played out in the details of family life in terms of how domestic arrangements are organized within the family. The discourses are also imported to regulate the shaping of gender differences within families, e.g. parents impose surveillance on themselves and their children to ensure appropriate socialization, including the inculcation of "normal" gender roles. Even more intimately, families enact practices whereby internal experiences and the extent to which they are made public are regulated, e.g. that there are some thoughts that children might have that should not be talked about, that must remain private and are even shameful.

CULTURALLY AVAILABLE STORIES

Foucault proposed, then, that society contains a repertoire of dominant narratives that shape our thinking and experience: how we think about ourselves, our inner conversations, and how we interact with each other. Not all stories have equal status, and in fact he argues that some are made peripheral or subjugated. Examples of these are narratives that are relegated to being historical, e.g. attempts to frame Marxist ideas as "out of date" and no longer relevant to modern society. Also, local or sub-cultural narratives may be dismissed as naive, simplistic, or superficial within the dominant scientific/logical framework. This can apply, for example, to racial differences, so that until recently many third-world cultures were referred to as "primitive" societies. Another example may be the common references to young people's views and enthusiasm for change being labelled as idealistic or unrealistic fantasies, and women's arguments regarded as "hysterical" or over-emotional.

Foucault's ideas, as we saw above, point to a view of society as containing a hierarchy of narratives, with some relegated to the periphery. In contrast to constructivist views, this suggests that narratives and their formation are not simply or predominantly personal. Families do not have an infinite number of ways of viewing events; instead, there is a limited array of narratives, which have been made available to us through our socialization or immersion in our culture. This sets limits to our thinking and serves to constrain our perceived domain of options or avenues of action. Significantly, this analysis also suggests that people attempt to employ these dominant narratives to fit their experiences. Family members can be seen to have unique patterns of experiences/histories, but they will attempt to select a dominant narrative to embrace these.

A young couple, Julie and Damian, discussing their sexual problems, offers an illustration:

Julie: Is it that you get frustrated because you think you should be doing it once a week? . . . I don't . . . we don't sit down with other couples and ask them how often they have intercourse . . . it's only what society says . . . I think he's governed by what things should be, or driven by desire.

Damian: Both . . . not just because I feel we should . . . I've got to feel right . . . I'm not just a machine.

Julie: I think he would do it every day if I wanted to.

Damian: I don't think so ... I know deep down that if she
wanted sex I would, but it's never been tested that there is a
limit for me.

[Foreman, 1995]

This brief extract reveals several dominant discourses that
have been identified as common themes in heterosexual relationships. One of the most common is a biological—male sexual
drive—discourse which suggests that men have a greater phys-
iological need for sexual "release". In contrast, this suggests
that women have less of a need for sex and are more interested
in relationships and emotional intimacy. A more "modern" or
permissive discourse suggests that sex is fun and a good physical activity (like aerobics or jogging) which is essential for good
health, and regular sex also helps to cement the relationship.
These can be seen to operate in this extract overtly and covertly.
Julie suggests that Damian is like other men in needing it, and
he implies that he at least partly agrees with this: "I don't think
so" but "it's never been tested". Julie says she does not feel a
need to do it so often, which fits with the discourse that women
need it less. She also implies that the permissive discourse,
"what society says", sets norms or expectations that drive
Damian but not her. In effect, Damian and Julie can be seen as
contemplating alternative explanations or stories of their relationship and sexuality, but this contemplation is constrained by
the wider domain of available discourses—the dominant narratives. They can attempt to wander outside the perimeters of this
domain, but then they risk a variety of subjugating processes,
such as being seen and seeing themselves as eccentric, weird,
odd, deviant, or perverted.

An awareness of these discourses does not necessarily inevitably mean that people can easily transcend them. White and
Epston (1990), as we saw above, suggest that developing "resistance" or a subversive position in relation to such discourses
is an essential part of therapy. An influential example of the
application of a social constructionist perspective has been the
analysis of power and gender relations in families (Goldner,
1991; Harre-Mustin, 1991). This reveals all aspects of family life,
from the daily routines to the most profound experiences, to be

shaped by culturally shared discourses of gender. Work with families where there has been violence between couples reveals that, rather than being deviant, these relationships may more accurately be seen as embodying *in extremis* the dominant assumptions in society about relations between the genders. The men seem to be caught in attempts to establish a culturally sanctioned view of themselves as dominant, in control, and invulnerable and the women as nurturant, sensitive, and responsive to, and needing others. Though not excusing or encouraging a denial of responsibility for the violent partners, the feminist systemic perspectives emphasize the processes of unconscious internalization by men and women of these dominant discourses of gender which shape their "personal" beliefs and narratives. These filter our perceptions of self and others and shape what kind of relationships we expect and attempt to create. When there is a rift between these expectations, frustrated attempts to coerce others to fit into the prescribed roles may then lead to threats and ultimately to violence (mainly by men). Women, too, may in some cases stay in such relationships predominantly because of their socialization and induction into ideas, such as that men are naturally more aggressive, women more nurturant, and, most importantly, that the violence is an indication of their failure to manage the relationship. The previously dominant view of the family as being women's domain carries with it the responsibility for managing everyone's feelings, including their anger.

EXTERNALIZING THE PROBLEMS

White and Epston (1990) discuss the idea of externalizing problems to free people from oppressive "problem-saturated" ways of seeing themselves. Part of the process of problem formation and maintenance is an internalizing of the problem so that it is seen as an individual or even family "fault", something residing in their individual personalities or even in their relationships:

> "Externalising" is an approach to therapy that encourages persons to objectify and, at times, to personify the problems that they

experience as oppressive. In this process the problem becomes a separate entity and thus external to the person or relationship that was ascribed as the problem. [White & Epston, 1990, p. 38]

The techniques for doing this include treating or speaking about the problem as an object or entity outside the person or the family. As an example, White and Epston cite how a woman supposedly suffering from schizophrenia had been encouraged to resist the all-embracing, "totalizing" nature of such a definition of her identity by discussing how she could combat or resist the "voices" that were harassing her. Discussions focused on some successful instances of how she had been able to "defy the voices' influence". White and Epston's approach appears to have the effect of reducing the all-pervasive nature of the labelling associated with problems. Instead of discussing problems with a totalizing narrative in which the problems completely encapsulate the person, so that the symptoms become the defining part of that person's identity or relationships, they can be identified as just one part of his or her identity. This approach also fits with the increasing attempts to define problems more specifically in terms of profiles of competencies and deficiencies (Boyle, 1990). Therapeutic discussion invites people to look at the ways that they may have been "conscripted" into pathological identities. One part of this can be to explore how they have come to enforce the oppression inherent in such labels on themselves by engaging in self-criticism, self-blame, and self-accusations. A related aspect is to explore with family members how they may be imposing these on each other and also conscripting the whole family into a pathological identity—that they are a pathogenic family or a "problem family".

Constructivist approaches have repeatedly drawn attention to the fact that family members may disagree, sometimes violently, about their explanations and narratives. These have been seen as essentially interpersonal disagreements or struggles over the punctuation of events. More recently, this has been discussed in terms of the competing stories that family members hold and that define previous and future events. The analysis of questions about the meaning of a problem, or symptoms, is similar to the processes of deconstruction employed in the analysis of literature and the social sciences. Deconstructing involves taking constructs apart, analysing and tracing their historical origins, examining their inner logic, exploring their contradictions and inconsistencies, exploring the situations that concepts are employed in, and considering what implications there are for action. When we engage in this process with families, it is not unusual to find that the conflicts are not so much about disagreements, but about different uses of a concept. Deconstruction can be employed as an activity that invites alternative meanings to be considered, which, by opening up the definition of a concept, can encourage or at least lay the groundwork for some mutually acceptable definitions to emerge.

The social constructionist perspective brings into focus a number of questions:

1. Are these disagreements fundamentally interpersonal, or are they related to wider conflicts and contradictions within and between competing societally shared beliefs or discourses?

2. Is it possible that some narratives, by virtue of being different from the dominant societally shared ones, are seen as deviant and are marginalized, excluded, or punished?

3. To what extent do family members create their own narratives or predominantly draw from and adapt narratives from a societally shared pool?

4. Do some of the distortions/fabrications occur because of attempts to contort personal experiences into common socially acceptable ones?

From studies of families, couples, and individuals with "severe" disorders, it has frequently been argued that they show features of being deluded, out of touch with reality. One of the key symptoms of schizophrenia, for example, is taken to be a combination of bizarre thoughts, rambling disconnected speech, delusions, and distortions of reality. Something in the story-production process appears to have gone wrong. Another way of putting this is that such people offer stories about them-selves and their circumstances, but these are stories that we feel we cannot make sense of. Even more clearly, distortions, fabri-cations, concealments, and lies are evident in the stories of family members where gross abuses—such as incestuous rela-tions, physical violence, or emotional attacks—have occurred. But what is it about some narratives or stories articulated by families that leads us to label them as bizarre? Since there are significant differences in what is seen as deviant between and even within societies, this suggests that such definitions are to some extent relative. One argument is that it is not merely the content of the narratives, but the internal flaws in the fabric of these over and above any disconnections with what is societally acceptable. However, even this is contentious since there are many examples in literature where odd ways of constructing narratives is acceptable, even highly applauded. It is also inter-esting that we have a shared knowledge of what counts as acceptable and as unusual: e.g. in role-plays people can be very convincing in mimicking psychotic symptoms, including biz-arre speech. This was powerfully illustrated by Rosenhan's (1973) studies in which students feigned psychiatric symptoms to gain admission into a psychiatric unit. When they then re-verted to "normal" behaviour, however, they had great diffi-culty convincing the staff, since a powerful, self-fulfilling expectation or labelling had quickly become established, and their protestations of sanity were regarded as further signs of acute disorder.

UNIQUENESS, COMMONALITIES, AND DOMINANT NARRATIVES

Family life can be seen as consisting of unique sequences of events, feelings, and actions. How these events are interpreted may not be unique but should be seen in terms of the dominant narratives available. However, these may frequently fail to cap-ture or adequately explain people's lived experiences:

> . . . those aspects of the person's life, and those qualities that he or she experiences in relationships with others, that he/she can

appreciate, but that do not fit with that which is specified by these unitary knowledges, that is do not conform to the norms and expectations proposed by these knowledges. [White & Epston, 1990, p. 32]

In other words, there will be times when people experience a gap or schism between their experience of relationships and the available discourses. Various attempts can be made to resolve this schism: for example, denial of the events, attempts to contort the dominant narratives to fit the experiences, alternation between different narratives so that events are at one moment seen one way and later another, or denial of one's experiences (i.e. as not real, not valid, or crazy). The latter appears to apply particularly to serious problems of "mental health", i.e. where the persons' experiences are ascribed a narrative of not making sense, a meta–non-narrative. Given that people are regarded as makers of narratives, to assign someone's narrative as nonsense, crazy, or meaningless is to stop listening to them and to make them, therefore, into non-persons.

Families in therapy demonstrate both uniqueness and commonalities, a sense of their experiences being individual and different but also as referenced to dominant narratives. It is also apparent that family members are in a dynamic flux precisely because they differ in their narratives. These differences can take a variety of forms:

1. subscribing to different narratives as most fitting events;
2. disagreeing over the details of an agreed choice of narrative, i.e. disagreeing about what the narrative is about;
3. employing a narrative in a pre-emptive, rigid way, i.e. shaping a narrative to be more rigid than it is commonly perceived to be;
4. narratives become polarized as a result of frustrations, failed attempted solutions;
5. misunderstanding about each other's narratives and consequent conflicts;
6. strategic use of narratives by members to achieve their own purposes of gaining power.

This list could be extended considerably, but two points arise: the first is the need to consider how the narratives constructed relate to family dynamics. The second is that there is a translation process between the narratives "out there" and how they are understood in families. It is possible that, since there is always a translation process, it may be pointless to talk about the influence of narratives and better to focus on personal meanings. However, this misses the point that people do attempt to contort their experiences into the dominant narratives. Therapeutically, it can be helpful to use these dominant narratives as points of reference with families and to consider how they may be interpreted differently and to consider what different implications such alternatives may have for their lives. In some cases, narratives that have been unhelpful may progressively become less central or even disappear. But some caution is needed since attempts to reject or dismiss well-entrenched narratives too rapidly may be anxiety-provoking, since these are the foundations of the family's belief system. The new ground has to be established before a migration of identities and beliefs can be embarked upon.

It is also important to be aware of the fact that the dominant narratives may also be contradictory and conflicting. As an example, the narratives of masculinity contain ideas of strength, emotional control, and competition but also of sensitivity and need for love and attachment. Some men experience these as incompatible—that, if they show love and dependency in a relationship, they may be seen as weak and will be rejected. These discourses may present us with inherent paradoxes or dilemmas (Goldner, 1991) that promote troubles between the sexes. What people often experience as personal dilemmas or failures may in fact be a widely promoted false idea and fuels the associated illusion of private solutions (see chapter six). This is the widespread view that individuals or families can solve these dilemmas, and if they cannot it implies that they are inadequate in some way.

Case study: the Masters family

The following is an extract from a session with a family where the conversation includes both an explicit discussion of political issues and an exploration of how some of these relate to the dynamics, conflicts, aspirations, and preferred views of self and each other in a family. Some members of the therapy team regarded this particular family as over-intellectual, denying of their emotions and feelings for each other, and unable to express anger and love for each other clearly. However, in the session, through engaging with and pursuing their shared interests in politics and the arts, a discussion results in which universal themes of political resistance, integrity, and moral positions in life are brought to the fore. Most importantly, some of the constraining and subjugating assumptions within dominant discourses, especially regarding mental health, were revealed. This allowed the discussion to move away from "problem-saturated" and essentially medical narratives of their "son's" problems, to a less oppressive view that connects his struggles and confusions to widely shared experiences (Anderson & Goolishian, 1988).

The family consisted of the parents, their son Tony (age 26), and his older sister Monica (she was married, lived some distance away, did not attend the sessions, and was said to be relatively "problem-free"). Tony was seen to be the source of the problems.

The current problems were said to have started when Tony became withdrawn while studying to gain entry to university. His parents were both teachers and held strong socialist views. Tony had attended various political demonstrations with his father. The parents also had strong cultural interests, especially in literature, theatre, and the arts. Tony was apparently unsettled at university, showed no interest in his literature course, did not attend lectures, dressed "eccentrically", consumed illegal drugs, and generally ceased to look after his health. His speech and manner were said to have become "bizarre", and he eventually dropped out of college. This was repeated several times on different college courses. He eventually abandoned university study and took various part-time jobs, usually ending up with no money, facing eviction, and hungry. He became increasingly angry with his parents and demanded money when he visited, leading them to dread his visits and to feeling "terrorized".

The situation escalated, with Tony displaying bouts of highly excited and "bizarre" behaviour accompanied by withdrawal and apathy. His parents felt that they no longer understood or could communicate with him and eventually had him placed temporarily in a psychiatric unit, where he was diagnosed as having schizophrenic-type symptoms. However, following this confinement, the "urban terrorism" increased, and, after Tony had repeatedly "burgled" his parents, they contacted the police. This led to a term in prison on remand for Tony over the Christmas period.

The family were eventually informally referred to therapy by a family friend who was a social worker. A dominant theme in the sessions was that Tony felt his parents had "sold out" on their political values, whereas he had continued to be an angry anarchist. The following is an extract from a session following his release from prison (he had received a three-month suspended sentence):

Therapist: How do you feel about the sentence?

Tony: Quite reasonable; when I was first remanded inside I was very angry. Looking back on it now, it's quite amusing, kept me away from the scene of the crime. Gave me a chance to reflect on what I wanted to do with the future . . . looking back on it, it was quite a useful time. I also found that I didn't want to go back to prison . . .

Mr M: We felt *we* were up against it. When we had a chance to recover, I felt *you* were up against it . . . I did feel I owed you and I was free and you weren't.

Mrs M: It gave us a pause . . . pre-prison time was one of the worst we can remember for the last ten years . . . we had a chance to recover. I hadn't slept in weeks . . .

Therapist: Can I ask you, Tony, what your parents think you want from them?

Tony: I think they think I want money, desperately short of food, and that I want rescuing by them—that happened in the past. I think if they hadn't rescued me so many times in the past I might have got through this more easily, but because they rescued me each time it became a lifeline which was tying me down. I took less care of what I was doing because I knew I would get help, but when help was not available . . . everything blew up . . .

Therapist: Are you saying that you wanted to be rescued— were they right?

Tony: At that time, yes.

Therapist: You seem to be saying you wanted to be rescued, but deep down it was not what you needed . . . you needed to be left to become a man, and it seems like now you have done?

Tony: I see more clearly what happened now . . .

Therapist: You told me last time about some of the interests you shared. Could you tell me a bit more about that? . . .

Mrs M: We are all readers.

Mr M: Sport.

Mrs M: You two share sport, I'm not interested . . .

Tony: We do have a lot of interests in common . . .

Mrs M: Artistically, but musically we are very different.

Tony: Mine is wider!

Mr M: Worse!

Therapist: What is the musical interest that you share?

Mrs M: We both like jazz.

Tony: I sometimes find classical music makes me very restless.

Mrs M: You like punk rock.

Tony: As I'm getting older, my musical interests are widening . . . core of it is punk, the politics of the music . . .

Mrs M: Sound of it, noisy.

Tony: That's the point of it, to annoy as many people as possible, the political philosophy. It grew up in 1976, a direct result of the National Front marching in the street and getting stronger . . . when I first bought the Sex Pistols, they said why does anyone want to be anarchy [title of one of the tracks], it doesn't make any sense?

Mr M: That discussion has been going on ever since.

Tony: Yeah.

Therapist: Jazz was also revolutionary and subversive ...

Mrs M: In its time.

Mr M: I'd forgotten it was subversive.

Mrs M: All innovative work.

Tony: I'm sure Beethoven was.

Mr M: People were outraged by his music in its time ...

Tony: The Clash [punk band] started out hard-core punk, but gradually absorbed jazz and reggae sounds. As I get older ... absorb different types of music ... blues ... can't be angry all your life ... it's too tiring.

Therapist: Do you think its a question of being angry or directing anger? It's sometimes said that people are radical when they are young but stop in middle age—do you think that?

Tony: True, in a lot of cases, time of anger in 50s, freedom and human rights movement ...

Therapist: You don't have to lose your ideals.

Mr M: True, in our case we've hung on to ours.

Tony: True of some people, hang on to their ideals very much ... Graham Greene is still radical, but some people sell out when they become successful ... the system becomes useful to them ...

Therapist: Can you think of people who are right-wing and then become radical?

Tony: I think something radical has to happen to their lives.

Mrs M: Become unemployed ...

Therapist: Jonathan Swift perhaps stayed very critical and political throughout his life, critical of the monarchy, went to prison?

Mr M: He was an awkward cuss, liked to offend archdeacons ... I find that quite sympathetic ... (laughs)

Tony: I read his book recently. He set out to offend just about everyone in authority.

Mr M: I think he worked quite hard at it.

Tony: I think he saw it as life's achievement to offend as many people as possible . . .

Therapist: What about Geoffrey Chaucer, he was fairly critical but wealthy as well . . . ?

Mr M: Yes and rude as well . . .

Mrs M: And he had a good go at the friars as well . . .

Tony: He was on the fringes of the court, so it was not a question of him attacking something because he didn't have it . . .

Mrs M: He didn't like the church too much . . .

Tony: Yes, certainly the Roman Catholic church and their selling absolutions . . .

Mr and Mrs M: Yes . . .

Therapist: Not just having a literary digression here . . . it raises the idea, doesn't it, of whether we have to sell out . . . it sounds like you have made life quite difficult for yourself though . . .

Tony: Yes, life has been quite difficult, not just the last few months but for quite a long time now.

Mr M: But you have partly chosen that.

Tony: Oh, yes, but some of those crises were seen as crises from the outside. I was reasonably contented . . . from my position of views of the world everything seemed to be very hard . . .

Mrs M: You did seem to be throwing things away, opportunities . . .

Tony: But they were opportunities I didn't want, doing what was expected of me, jobs I didn't want to do, didn't enjoy . . .

Mrs M: But L_____ University, you chose that . . .

Tony: I'm not saying it happens all the time.

Mr M: Did seem to us to be a self-destructive element, bad things going on for you ...

Tony: I was never sure of what I wanted to be, kept trying different things, never found my position, spot in life, never had a sense of direction. So I had no real incentive to succeed in what I wanted to do ...

Mr M: You just retreated. Pity, because we were supporting you with what we thought you wanted to do, both financially and psychologically, but you didn't actually want the support any more. It left us up the creek.

In this extract, one dominant theme seems to be the sense of powerlessness felt both by Tony and by his parents: Tony's sense of impotence to change the world and find a direction for himself, and his parents' frustration at not being able to "help him". The "problem", in a sense, appeared to be winning over them all. One of the intentions of the session was to pursue some alternative narratives that stressed the connections between the family and could assimilate Tony's anger within the narrative of the family's shared commitment to a politically radical, but constructive, stance. An attempt was also made to consider how these related to, or connected with, their beliefs about Tony' state of mind. The parents' beliefs (also shared by Tony) reflected the contradictions and ambiguities of cultural discourses of mental health. On the one hand, they contemplated "traditional", predominantly medical views of mental health, and, alternatively, they agonized over the possibility that they had failed as parents and caused Tony's problems. The conflicts for the parents seemed to centre around a negation of their preferred views of themselves as "caring" and "helpful" by Tony's response to their efforts, including his accusations that they were "weak", hypocritical, and uncaring and had "sold out". One way that some consistency could be achieved and the dysjunction between their preferred views of self and actual selves was for Tony to be fully conscripted into a pathological, "ill" identity. The parents would therefore not be to blame for his condition, since he was ill and they could take care of their son. However, this did not fit Tony's experience of himself fully, and he alternated between being "ill" and being "angry" and deeply resenting and resisting attempts to conscript him into a pathological identity. In fact, he clearly stated that one of the things that had made him most angry and resentful was that his parents had previously had him placed in a psychiatric unit. He was much less resentful about the spell in prison, which gave him an identity of being a bit "hard", and he felt some pride that he had coped with prison fairly easily.

The session moved from a discussion of anger in the family—from the resentment at Tony's attacks on the parents, his resentment at his imprisonment—and on to a discussion of his ambivalence towards his parents—both needing to be rescued by them and resenting their help which stops him becoming an adult. However, running through this discussion, a narrative of rebellion, radical politics, and resisting inequality in society started to emerge. This seemed to embrace and unite the parents' radical politics and Tony's criticisms of people who sell out. It is revealed that Tony and his father went on political demonstrations together, but somehow Tony's radical, critical position had become turned inwards on his family. Through a discussion of their joint interests, literature, and music, the narratives around "selling out" versus maintaining a radical critical position were considered—a narrative of directed and constructive anger, in contrast to the one of betrayal of values and "selling out". This added a different turn to the radical/anarchistic narrative, which hitherto had ended in the bitter inevitability of "selling out". The family enthusiastically considered various historical cultural figures who continued to be both radical and lived constructive rather than self-destructive lives. The discussion in this literary format also seemed to fit with the parents' preferred views of themselves as interested in culture and showed Tony, as he enthusiastically contributed and in fact lead the discussion, to have been positively influenced by their interests.

However, the literary references also revealed how this family, and all families, are immersed in the history of ideas of their culture. Perhaps not all families will be quite so "cultured", but their images, ideals, and aspirations will nevertheless be shaped by the society they are immersed in. For example, Tony actively participated in a discussion of the influence of punk music on his view of the world. He had made connections with this and identified with the growth and maturation of the musicians. But, in their conversation, the themes underlying this music—rebellion and resistance to inequality and dishonesty—are seen as transcending historical eras, with similarities identified with themes in the fifteenth century such as the exploitative practices of the church. Perhaps most importantly what emerges is some recognition that the family is caught up in universal dilemmas: the conflicts between the generations, search for identity, conformity versus rebellion, and being crushed versus standing up against the system. What is more, there is a recognition that these are dilemmas for which there is no absolute or true solution. All families struggle with these issues, and possibly the more perceptive they are, the more they are painful and uncomfortable. At best, there are only compromises of one sort or another. But, as Foucault (1975) suggests, we can become subjugated into the view that these are solvable problems and that it is an indication of personal inadequacy or weakness if we fail to do so.

It seemed likely that, for this family, their wider political perspective became confused and lost in the face of their son's struggles, in part because they also appeared to have absorbed the dominant views of mental health, i.e. that there was something wrong with Tony, that he was ill. Unfortunately, the radical politics of mental health tended to be seen as blaming parents (Bateson, 1972; Cooper, 1970; Laing, 1966) and offered little solace. Tony's narrative, on the other hand, was that he felt aimless, anarchistic, did not like much of what he saw in the world, and wanted to change it but could not. Perhaps even more, he held these views in a political context (Thatcherite Britain) in which his socialist views were under great attack. As the discussion of such issues continued within the family, the problem of Tony's anger started to be externalized as something he could usefully direct, rather than as indicating some pathology that consumed him and threatened to destroy him and his family. His parents were also more able to move towards their preferred views of themselves as caring, radical, cultured, and active rather than as weak and having sold out. Tony was also able to clarify that he had felt oppressed into trying to fit in and do things he did not want to do.

SUMMARY

The patterns of family dynamics that therapists frequently observe may be shaped not just by the interplay of the actions and personal beliefs of family members, but by their internalization of wider societal discourses. These can be seen not only to shape their personal beliefs, but to confront a family with a range of practices, including sanctions of various sorts, if they deviate from acceptable forms of actions and beliefs in any given society. In particular, a significant discourse for therapy is the idea that problems are caused by individual inadequacy of various sorts. Though systemic therapy has done much to challenge this scientific and individualistic ideology, it has run the danger of simply moving this "up" one level to seeing problems as caused by family dynamics. In contrast, it is possible to see many problems as resulting from inevitable dilemmas and difficulties posed by the culture in which the family is located. What is more, these problems may become acute because family members themselves are deeply steeped in, and oppressed by, this dominant ideology, which locates problems as predominantly the responsibility of them as individuals or as due to their interpersonal dynamics. The choices family members make, including their attempted solutions to their difficulties, can be seen to flow from a reservoir of societal discourses which, having been internalized by them, may constrain them, with the support of various agencies, to a limited set of beliefs and choices of action. In effect, to regard families as "unique", though in some sense respectful of people's individuality and power to transcend their circumstances, is also to ignore the wider forces that constrain them and ultimately to lay blame for problems squarely at their feet.

CHAPTER SIX

Narratives, distortions, and myths

There may be many moments in therapy when therapists feel that the narratives that are being articulated by a family, couple, or individual are very different to how they see what is going on. This may be based on an apparent contradiction between how a family or couple appears to be in the session and what they say things are like at home and elsewhere. Two parents, for example may say that they are in agreement about how to handle the problems that their child is demonstrating and are united in their approach at home but, in the session, show non-verbally quite different reactions to the child's actions, fail to be able to agree on any consistent plan of action with the child, or tell quite different stories about how the current state of events arose. More dramatically, when there have been incidents such as physical or sexual abuse in a family but this has been denied by some members, then it is very compelling to view members of such a family as engaging in distortions, denials, and fabrications. An apparently straight-forward explanation is that the perpetrator does not wish to admit to the acts, since these are not only morally deviant, but have criminal sanctions against them. Other members may be seen to collude partly out of fear and perhaps out of "shame" at admitting to being part of "such a family".

People's actions and their narratives, including the attempts they make to explain their actions, are coloured by feelings of fear, guilt, sadness, anger, and shame. However, these emotional reactions are not simply due to some innate biological states but can, in themselves, also be seen as socially constructed. The words available to describe emotions vary between cultures, and there are complex rules about what emotions are appropriate in different contexts and how people "should" feel in various situations, e.g. sorrow not laughter at a funeral, enthusiasm not apathy during sexual intimacy: "feelings are not substances to be discovered in our blood but social practices organized by stories that we both enact and tell. [Feelings] are structured by our forms of understanding" (Rosaldo, 1984, p. 143). Feelings are bound up with the dominant narratives and conventions of a culture that prescribes how people *should* act and feel. Various acts also have prescribed sets of emotions attached to them, e.g. failure of a relationship or being rejected in amorous advances are associated with a set of images about what feelings are typically experienced and how people should act. Even in their private moments, people may find themselves experiencing and reacting to these events in terms of socially prescribed ways, e.g. getting drunk, talking to a friend, or even speaking to oneself using commonly voiced phrases learned from parents and others.

Perhaps one of the most vivid examples can be seen in the concept of "romantic love" enshrined in language. In Western cultures, this concept has dominated literature, art, and music for several hundred years. It sets out an image of a set of feelings that most people expect to experience and offers a yardstick by which people are likely to appraise their feelings in a relationship, e.g. whether what is being experienced is "true love", infatuation, or merely lust (Averill, 1985; Hendrick & Hendrick, 1988). Yet it is a relatively recent concept. Historically, it is not a set of feelings that people invariably expected to have or even sought. The expectations that a culture embodies about such an experience have considerable implication for relationships. An obvious example is that sexual activity was, and arguably still is, made more acceptable if the partners profess to be "in love". For women, until recently, too readily engaging in sexual activity could lead to negative stigmatization as "easy" or a "slut". Hence, a structure is established that encourages people to attempt to shape their ambiguous feelings to "fit" this particular discourse. This may encourage people at times if not to lie, then at least to distort their feelings even to themselves in order to be able to declare that they are "in love" when they may not feel anything but mild passion.

There may be many other examples of people attempting to feel what they think they "should" rather than what they do. In families and other intimate relationships, this can become all the more central since people know that expression of certain feelings, or even acknowledgement of having them, may be sanctioned or punished in various ways. Possibly one of the most problematic areas currently are sexual feelings between parents and children. Such strong sanctions prevail regarding sexual abuse that, for many families, it is extremely difficult to admit to any such feelings at any level. However, some sexual feelings between members of families (other than just the spouses) are arguably inevitable and universal: ". . . often coinciding with the girl's entering adolescence; at such a time, the blossoming out of her biological and psychological personality will quite normally foster a father's infatuation" (Palazzoli, Cirillo, Selvini, & Sorrentino, 1989, p. 69). One solution for many families is to pretend and to create a myth that these feelings do not exist, and to deny manifestations or counter-indications of such feelings in their behaviour.

Not only are emotions socially constructed, but so too are the pathways or temptations into falsification, fabrications, and lies. The stronger the societally constructed sanctions regarding certain areas of emotional experience, the more it might be expected that distorting and fabricating activities will abound. This has, of course, been suggested by Freud (1905), but it might be a mistake to assume that processes of repression have ceased in the twentieth century. It may therefore be the case that family therapy has been involved in a twofold error: (1) giving relatively inadequate emphasis to the emotional aspects of family life, (2) assuming that the emotional aspects of family life are largely a "private, family affair". But a feeling of rupture between what we think is going on and what the family thinks is a two-way street. It is not restricted to our experience as therapists, and families may, likewise, feel that the therapists see things in a way that makes little sense to them. Recent interest in family perceptions of therapy has highlighted that unvoiced differences between their perceptions and expectations of therapy, and those of the therapists, may significantly inhibit the progress of therapy (Reimers & Treacher, 1995). As an example, in the first session with the Gregg family below, the family voiced various concerns and criticisms about the course of family therapy that they had experienced previously. They saw their problems as predominantly resulting from their son's psychotic illness, a view that was in stark contrast to the therapy team's predominant view of the problems as largely due to a highly enmeshed and confused family system.

Case study: the Gregg family

Henry was 28 years old and had been diagnosed as suffering from a psychotic–schizophrenic disorder for over eight years. He had returned from a psychiatric hostel both to live with his parents over Christmas and because his parents felt that the hostel was not meeting his needs and he was making little progress. The family had previously attended for family therapy, but with a different therapy team.

> Therapist: You were saying that you were unhappy with the previous therapy sessions. Why weren't they of benefit, how could they have been a benefit? What kind of meetings would be helpful now?

> Mr G: There was far too much emphasis as far as I could see on historical psychiatry, why he [Henry] was like he was, reiteration of questions we were asked about personality differences between the three of us. Whereas Pat [Mrs Gregg] and I felt that certainly in the later months at the

P____ unit, since Henry came off the drugs, I would have liked an emphasis on the occupational side of things. We both used to say that he's not doing anything, lying in bed, and all the staff would say is "if he's not self-motivated there is nothing we can do about that" . . . We thought that when he had come off drugs, in fact that was an ideal time as there would obviously be a change inside him. Something could have been done on a more practical side, and we continued for some months after that on what we considered to be rather irrelevant questions and answers, on which most of the time was spent, with Henry doing very little talking, Pat doing a little, and me doing 90%, and it seemed to me that it wasn't really productive.

Therapist: So, one of the things you would like to see is Pat and Henry talking more, and the second, to focus on these practical issues?

Mrs G: Yes, I don't want too much of that, because . . .

Mr G: (interrupting) No, he means you talking and Henry talking and me sitting, because you feel you don't like talking in this situation and Henry closes up like a clam because he's not happy about it..

Mrs G: You're easy about it because of your training for your job . . .

Mr G: (interrupting) . . . but it becomes a one-on-one situation because I do all the talking.

Mrs G: . . . because you are that sort of person.

Mr Gregg: I even said to him today [Henry], you say what you think about things if you are asked, or even if you are not asked . . . (looking at Henry) . . . he's just about asleep . . .

Therapist: Henry, what about you? Your mother and father have said what would be helpful. Do you want to tell me what would be useful to you?

Henry: (silent . . . looking towards parents, especially father . . . continues silent)

Mrs G: Henry, come on . . .

Mr G: (*overlapping*) . . . come on Henry (*both appeared to be very agitated at Henry not replying*)

Therapist: They've said two things, practical and occupational. Is that what you think it would be useful to talk about?

Mr and Mrs G: Come on Henry, come on . . . (*again appearing agitated*).

Henry: Like what . . . ?

Therapist: Well, where you are going to live.

Henry: I know where I'm going to live.

Mr and Mrs G: You do?

Henry: Yeah, where you are (*pointing to Mr Gregg*).

Mr Gregg: Not on a long-term basis, you know you can't for several reasons . . .

Henry: (*looking at therapist*) I don't know where I'm going to live . . .

Therapist: So it would be useful to talk about that?

Henry: It would be, yes (*looking at Mr Gregg*).

It was extremely difficult to avoid seeing the Gregg family in terms of a narrative that featured a dominant intrusive father and a very high level of enmeshment between the parents and Henry. A compelling hypothesis was that, being caught up in this process of enmeshment, Henry had found it extremely difficult to develop any sense of his own identity and had remained dependent and childlike. Mr Gregg, despite initially saying that he wanted to give the others a chance to speak, repeatedly interrupted and dominated the conversation. The parents seemed to become extremely agitated as Henry did not reply to questions and instead looked towards them, apparently waiting for them to prompt him with an answer. Their relationships also appeared to have a "game-playing" quality, e.g. Henry seemed to be playing a game with his parents, laughing and giggling at their agitation at his lack of replies or his "silly" comments. The parents, and Henry to some extent, appeared to engage in a continual process of "mind-reading"; in particular, the parents repeatedly appeared to be thinking and answering for Henry and completing his sentences for him. Mr Gregg, likewise, had the habit of interrupting his wife, finishing off her attempts to speak, and prompting her:

Therapist: (*to Henry*) So you do some conservation work . . . tell me a little bit more.
Henry: What do I do? Well, . . . part clearing (*laughter*) and err, working, err, well I've done some pond work (*laughing*).
Mrs G: (*beaming smile*).
Mr G: (*looking serious, apparently not amused*).
Therapist: What do you mean pond work?
Henry: I've been in a pond.
Mrs G: (*laughing*) You've been in a pond . . .
Mr G: (*not smiling, looking serious*).
Therapist: Whose pond, what pond was that?

The parents' narrative appeared to be imbued with a medical discourse that their son was suffering from a form of mental illness (schizophrenia). They felt that he needed to be occupied in order to avoid him acting in a "stupid" manner or becoming frustrated and generally seemed to see themselves as caring parents who were trying to do their best. In contrast, they felt that the therapists they had been involved with previously had blamed them for causing Henry's problems and that discussions around this had been a waste of time. What was needed, they felt, were some practical measures to help Henry. In fact, they had not wanted to attend this initial session and appeared to be alienated from therapy, not, they said, because they did not want to "discuss their feelings", but because they felt that such a discussion in the past "had not got them anywhere", had been of "no benefit to Henry, or them".

Such a schism between the family's and the therapists' perceptions may be quite common, especially at the start of therapy. The view that a family holds, their dominant narratives, may appear vastly different to what strikes the therapists. In fact, in this case the communicational patterns were so compelling that most members of the team found it virtually impossible not to think about this family in terms of classical enmeshed and double-bind features.

FAMILY SECRETS

Traditionally, systemic approaches have included the view that some families, especially where psychotic symptoms are evident, are engaged in pathological processes of denial, fabrication, and mystification. Such "suspicion" was a current that directed some of the explorations of the therapy team with this family. As the sessions proceeded, the focus moved on to a discussion of the stresses and strains that the parents had experienced over the years, and they were invited to a session on their own to discuss their own feelings and needs following some hints that they had a few issues that they had never had a chance to discuss. They proceeded to reveal that they had both had several affairs over the years, had been very unhappy in their marriage, and had frequently thought of divorce. However, they felt unable to do this because of financial considerations and because they had "rubbed along" for so long now. This was perceived by the team as the expression of an important family secret and what was underlying the continual over-involvement of Henry in their dynamics. The revelation of this secret seemed to allow the couple to release Henry from his position of worrying about his parents. When he was away from home, Henry admitted that he was continually preoccupied with thinking about and being concerned for his parents. In a subsequent session, the possibility of the parents separating was discussed with him, and he reacted calmly, saying it was "up to them", but he would continue to have contact with both of them and that it was a pity if they could not work it out since they had been together for so long. The revelation of the secret was seen to be important, perhaps not because of its significance as such but because it enabled the secret use of Henry in a power struggle to change.

Such secrets contain elements of deceit, distortion, and fabrication since they usually involve a false reality being presented behind which the secret can be concealed. The cause or the reason for the development of family secrets has been considered to be anxiety-laden and unresolved unconscious interpersonal conflicts (Palazzoli et al., 1989; Selvini, 1992; Wynne, Ryckoff, Day, & Hirsch, 1958). Such ideas are consistent with the early theorizing in systemic family therapy, which started with assumptions about defensive unconscious processes, e.g. that the "function" of homeostasis was to protect a family from disintegration, which might occur if the unconscious conflicts surfaced. The concept of the "family myth" captures this notion of families as engaged in unconscious processes of distortions. One common example of such a "myth" has been seen to be the common belief held by two parents that their child *has* a problem that is largely unrelated to their relationship: "Whenever there are disturbed children there is a disturbed marriage, although all disturbed marriages do not create disturbed children" (Framo, 1965, p. 154)

This idea is embedded in the concept of triangulation and, more specifically, "conflict detouring", in which it is proposed that the conflict between the parents is expressed in some way through a child who displays symptoms. Consistent with this, family members are likely to see the problem as residing in the child rather than as a response to other relationship conflicts, especially theirs. In effect, this represents a conflict between the family's narrative and the therapist's. Sometimes these competing narratives may be quite rigidly held by both parties. However, it is another step to suggest that one of these is a myth, though there may be occasions where the family's narrative (and sometimes the therapist's) may seem to be not just an alternative narrative, but a downright distortion or fabrication—a construction of unreality.

However, the possibility that families—or even therapists—engage in such distortions raises some central questions:

1. Are such distortions predominantly attempts to fit in with what is seen to be socially acceptable?

2. Are these distortions fuelled and coloured by emotional processes, such as shame and guilt associated with this need to be socially acceptable?

2. Do family members hold distortions/perceptions and create myths, or is it that alternative narratives are present but subjugated or dormant?

4. What are some of the links between processes of distortion and power?

These questions revolve around the issue of the processes whereby people learn to distort experience in a variety of ways. There are a number of interconnected strands to what such distortions may entail. At the most basic level, there may be a denial or distortion of the facts, e.g. that sexual abuse has occurred. At another level, there may be differences in how things are seen. It may be that members of a family really do see things differently to the therapy team or to some consensual reality—how most people might see an act, e.g. as an example of sexual abuse or violence. This often entails disputes about meanings of actions, such as whether an act was sexual abuse or merely a fatherly caress. At a different level still, it might be that family members recognize and perceive an event in a similar way, or know how it is commonly perceived, but wish to cover up their recognition since this would involve having to accept responsibility and possibly blame. In one session with a family where the teenage daughter had alleged that her father had sexually abused her, he continued to deny this throughout. However, at the end of the session, he turned to the therapist and asked, "Do you think it is possible that I did it but that I cannot remember it?" This question suggested that he was aware that the act had taken place and what it meant to others, but he wanted a "way out" by framing his memory as out of his control, that he could not remember.

The driving force underlying the creation of myths and distortions may be the fear of punishment and reprisals of various sorts. In the case of abuse, this is clear in that criminal sanctions are involved. In other areas of family life, this may be more convoluted. Bateson (1972) in his theory of the double bind implied that underlying the distortions was a fear of showing one's true feelings. Likewise, others have suggested that families may become caught in such spirals of distortions out of a fear of catastrophe if true feelings of conflict, anger, and power struggles are revealed, and hence a facade of "niceness" may be constructed (Palazzoli et al., 1989; Wynne et al., 1958). Similarly, in the context of marital violence Goldner (1991) has argued that many violent husbands, in fact, experience themselves as particularly powerless, dependent, and vulnerable immediately prior to a violent act. Subsequently, they may attempt to deny the facts of the violence or the extent because of the anticipation of punishment, humiliation, ridicule, or loss of status. Until recently, use of violence in marriage was to some extent condoned, or at least excused by notions such as the wife being provocative, hysterical, or denying the man in various ways, especially sexually. Men's use of such justifications is therefore both a personal ploy, but also one that is a distortion or myth that may be shaped by a wider culturally constructed distortion that conceals that such violence is legitimatized in order to control women.

FAMILY MYTHS

Ferreira (1963) suggested that unconscious fantasies and conflicts not only operated at the level of the individual, but could also work as a collective unconscious fantasy or "family myth". Aspects of a family's past, especially traumatic or distressing events experienced by the parents, grandparents, or even more distant relatives, are seen to have become shrouded in defensive myths that serve to cover up memories that are too painful for them to accept. This can involve not only denial but the fabrication of stories or myths, a sort of Orwellian rewriting of history. Such myths, it is argued, become debilitating when they serve continually to falsify and mystify experience in the family, leading to spirals of denial and fabrication:

> . . . the term "family myth" refers to a series of fairly well-integrated beliefs shared by all the family members, concerning each other and their mutual positions in the family life, beliefs that go unchallenged by everyone involved in spite of the reality distortions which they may conspicuously imply. . . . The family myth describes the roles and attributions of family members in their transactions with each other which although false and mirage-like, are accepted by everyone as something sacred and taboo that no one would dare to investigate, much less challenge. [Ferreira, 1963, p. 457]

The function of family myths is seen to be to preserve the family stability, or homeostasis, and to avoid the possibilities of disruption or disintegration of the family or relationships within it, by providing a response to real or perceived threats to the viability of the family. A family myth can be seen to represent to the family what a defence mechanism is to the individual. Families were seen as calling upon the "family myth" whenever tensions and stresses in the family reached such a critical point that a real or fantasized threat to disrupt or even break up the family was perceived. In effect, the myth was seen to operate rather like a safety valve:

> the family myth functions like the thermostat that is kicked into action by the "temperature" in the family. Like other homeostatic mechanisms, the myth prevents the family system from damaging, perhaps destroying itself. It has therefore the quality of a "safety valve", that is, a survival value. [Ferreira, 1963, p. 462]

One of the most pervasive family myths that family therapists encounter is, of course, the belief held by the family that the only real problem is that one of them is ill. Were it not for this member, things would be pretty well all right, and they would be quite happy. (A common myth perpetuated by us as family therapists can be that if only the family's internal dynamics were functional, then they would not have the problems).

CONFORMITY TO DOMINANT NARRATIVES AND EXPECTATIONS

An example of the complex mechanisms by which a family myth is produced and maintained in a family has been described by Pollner and Wikler (1985). They cite a case of a family who were initially encountered at a large psychiatric institute to which they had turned in their search for a remedy for their daughter Mary's unusual behaviour. The members of the family agreed that Mary (age 5½ years) was a verbal and intelligent child but that she was "malingering" and refused to speak in public in order to embarrass them. Following extensive clinical examination, Mary was diagnosed as severely retarded and unable to perform at anywhere near the level of ability claimed by her parents and Mary's two older siblings. Videotapes of the sessions with the family were examined in detail and suggested that their transactions were permeated by "subtle, almost artful, practices that could function to create the image of Mary as an intelligent child".

The narratives in the family in effect ascribe "agency" and purpose to her actions, which to outside observers was blatantly missing. The authors describe six strategies whereby the family operate in a concerted way to attribute intelligence to Mary's actions and which served to distort the reality of their situation. These are summarized (from Pollner & Wikler, 1985) in some detail here because they offer some insightful descriptions of the ways that fabrications can occur:

- *Framing*—this involved the construction of a frame, such as a game of "catch", wherein virtually any activity that Mary displayed could be attributed with intelligent meaning. If she stood passively and let the ball drop out of her hands, it could be framed as deliberately dropping the ball or not wanting to play.

- *Postscripting*—this was the reverse, in the sense of giving meaning to Mary's actions after the event. The family tracked any action that she might emit and weaved a meaningful story onto it, such as if she were acting in a goal-directed way. For example, at one point Mary's sister dropped a block on the floor while Mary was banging a block on the table. As Mary sat down her sister said, " O.K., let's find that block".

- *Semantic crediting*—here, a range of reflexive behaviour responses, such as a startled reaction to a noise, were integrated by the family with simultaneous verbal requests to Mary. Though she was in fact responding to the non-verbal stimuli, the family interpreted her response as showing a comprehension of verbal instructions.

- *Puppeteering*—in some instances, rather than waiting for Mary to do something as a basis for the implementation of an attributional strategy, the family might subtly manipulate her physically towards an object. This would be accompanied by a verbal instruction and touch or by positioning themselves so that she was forced to move in a particular direction. The result could appear and would be credited as Mary making deliberate, planned actions.

- *Putting words into Mary's mouth*—this involved the construction of a dialogue or episode wherein each utterance, such as a gurgle emitted by Mary, was interpreted by one member of the family at a time. As an example, in one sequence she was encouraged to talk by asking her to say her name and age for a reward of money. Her following gurgles were interpreted for her as, "She's bargaining for more money".

- *Explaining in the "bright" direction*—despite the previous strategies there were times when Mary's behaviour was obviously inadequate. Such inadequacies were explained away by an overriding incorrigible belief that she was "intelligent", and so therefore these were lapses explained as being due to her "not wanting to play", "teasing, "pretending", or "malingering".

The concept of family myth has tended to imply that the motivation for the distortion is internal to the family. An alternative explanation, which incorporates a family life-cycle perspective, suggests an inability in this family to come to terms with the fact that Mary would not develop as *expected*. The recognition that a child is seriously handicapped has been likened to a process of bereavement for a family (Black, 1987). There is a need to face up to the pain that the child will not develop as they had hoped and that this will involve some possible difficulties for the family. Most basically, it destroys the hope that they can develop as a "normal", relatively happy, trouble-free family. Some of the tasks at this stage for the family would be to foster Mary's development; encourage education skills; encourage some independence for Mary; for Mary's parents to readjust their lives to having more time for themselves throughout the day, possibly a return to work for Mary's mother; for Mary's siblings to adjust to treating Mary as an equal, as another child, not as a baby; and so on. However, in this family, due to Mary's difficulties many of these expected tasks could not be fulfilled. Instead, a more complex and demanding set of tasks is presented, such as adjusting their lives to caring for a child whose abilities will delay these expected developments and require all the family to make sacrifices and invest considerable amounts of their time in caring for her.

By constructing a "myth" of normality, the family members may have tried to avoid confronting these painful narratives. Possible each of them was personally aware of the "reality" of the situation but continued the pretence in order to protect the others. As such a system of distortion grows, the practices that served to maintain this myth that Mary was "intelligent" and that there was nothing wrong with her become established. Consequently, the emotional cost of exposing the myth increases since to do so would reveal all of them to have been deceiving themselves, and each other. Perhaps it may also contain the underlying fear that surely someone in the family must be extremely vulnerable to the truth being revealed for this distortion to have arisen. Over time, the safest course of action for all may be perceived to be to adhere to the myth. More generally, a frequent component of the experience of a tragic loss is an initial period of disbelief, sometimes followed by a denial of the event.

However, the family's sense of loss here can be seen as not simply a private affair but as socially constructed in terms of an image of how they "should" be. In fact, the family's behaviour was in some ways appropriate for the treatment of a child of below 2 years of age, which was roughly the level of Mary's actual functioning. Rather than constructing a false belief system anew, they can be seen to be attempting to hold on to a previously appropriate frame but which no longer tallied with the external reality. Perhaps until a little while after this age they had been able to view themselves as a "normal" family, i.e. in terms of their life cycle. As they drifted away from this possibility, their mourning can be seen as both for the loss of their hopes about Mary, and also the desire inculcated in them by society to be a "normal" family.

Families exist in relation to a local community and are also required to adjust and integrate with other systems. A family myth, such as that "we are a happy family", or that a stepparent loves his son even more than his own, may be driven by an attempt to conform to socially acceptable values. Of course, not only the family but society can create a model of family life which is based on "myths" supported only by a shaky foundation of unrealizable expectations. One of the periods when families are confronted with the needs for change, and consequently some reappraisals of what they are and should be as a family, is at the time of major transitional stages in the life cycle. Faced with what they may perceive to be expected of them as a family, but which they may not be able to face, or with contradictory expectations, one solution may be to turn away from reality or, more likely, to attempt to maintain a version of reality that had been reasonably appropriate in a previous stage of the family's existence. Both the motivation for, and the content of, family myths can be seen as social constructions that serve to avoid the family having to view themselves in terms of negative or painful narratives. Seeing themselves in terms of these may raise the fear of tensions and conflicts, which are perceived as potentially threatening to the viability of the family. Furthermore, it is possible that there are "meta-narratives" that imply that if such negative narratives apply, then the family is in "danger", is not viable, and should split up. The threat of such disintegration in turn raises fears and tensions, which may confirm and aggravate the negative perceptions.

OUTSIDE THE REALITY
OF THE THERAPY ROOM

The greater the extent of a family's acceptance of cultural norms, the greater is likely to be their experience of frustration, guilt, embarrassment, and loss when their experience does not match these. It is likely that this family had high expectations of their child, which were embedded in ideologies of "normal" or even "excellent" development and progress. These may, in turn, have been fuelled by expectations of school, friends, and other relatives. A family myth can, in this way, be seen to evolve from a melting-pot of a mix of sources. It is also usually

presented, perhaps in an embryonic form, for external validation to various professionals, who may be taken in or experience
pressure not to challenge a myth for fear of the negative emotional consequences for the family. Even mild acceptance of the
myth, however, can serve to maintain or strengthen it. Alternatively, challenges may result in a family experiencing further
crises or, alternatively, adopting a resolute stand against outsiders who "do not understand". "Bombshell" interventions,
which starkly confront or challenge such myths, may be extremely hit-or-miss, perhaps producing positive change but,
alternatively, resulting in further withdrawal, spirals of denial,
and isolation. This is possibly the case with paradoxical interventions, which may leave no straw for families to hold on to
and may therefore result in relapse, perhaps with a return to the
patterns of distortions or myths:

> Work with paradoxes aroused a great deal of enthusiasm in those
> early years. However, the sensational therapeutic results achieved
> at first became fewer and less substantial as time went by, and in
> some cases the initial success proved short-lived. [Palazzoli et al.,
> 1989, p. 9]

One possible reason for this failure and that associated with
brief and paradoxical approaches is that a puncturing of a family myth is inadequate in itself, since a family has to continue to
live in the culture context in which the emergence of the myths
was necessary. With the Gregg family, the medical narrative of
their son's "illness" would very quickly come into play again as
soon as they had left the therapy room. Families have to leave
the artificial reality constructed in conversations in the therapy
room and go out to live in the "real" world outside. Many of us
perhaps remember our first experience of experiential group
sessions—a sense of euphoria and oneness with the world. It
can be disconcerting to realize subsequently that not everybody
wants to be hugged or to talk intimately about their feelings.
Perhaps the use of a prescribed relapse, or at least a warning of
it, helps precisely because it offsets such potential disappoint-
ments that are likely when re-encountering in the future the
dominant narratives that were part of the context out of which
the problems initially evolved.

DISTORTIONS AND POWER

Haley (1976b) has continually emphasized the centrality of power in families, especially in terms of who has the power to define the nature of relationships. Similarly, Palazzoli et al. (1989) have come to the view that struggles over power—in particular, a position of rigid stalemate between the parents—is the active ingredient of psychotic disorders in the children. Unfortunately, to ascribe such processes of fabrication and distortion to families is also to adopt a negative, even blaming, stance. This has been a criticism of the double-bind hypothesis and, more recently, of Palazzoli's approaches, which equate problems with dysfunctional family dynamics or pathological "family games". This critical stance regarding family processes is fairly evident:

> A father openly lavishes praise and esteem on his firstborn daughter, endlessly extolling her wisdom and diligence. This behaviour is implicitly aimed at his wife: He feels she is neglecting him and he uses this ploy to signal his lack of regard for her. For a tactic of this kind to work itself into an intricate game, there will have to be collusion, which, in turn, sparks reactive behaviour in all the other family members, each busily working to his or her own ends. [Palazzoli et al., 1989, p. 68]

This appears to offer a starkly pointed criticism of the parents' games and not a "pretty picture" of family life. At the same time, it is hard to avoid the perception that sometimes one or more members of a family appear to be being "kept in the dark".

Unfortunately, though revealing, such analyses tend to obscure the wider cultural issues of power, such as those relating to gender and the oppressive aspects of pathological identities (Foucault, 1975; White, 1995). As an example, such issues of power within the family and their roots in wider gender-related inequalities started to emerge in the conversations with the Gregg family where previously the main direction of the discussion had centred on Henry's disorder:

> Mr G: You get black moods on occasion, don't you, Henry?
>
> Mrs G: He [Henry] has certainly hit me a few times, hasn't

he (*looking towards Mr Gregg*) . . . not recently but he has been abusive to me . . .

Mrs G: I don't know why he does it. I feel like these two men are very close and have a great deal in common and I feel out of it, I'm the odd one out, female, and my daughter is a long way away . . . I've got to be much more aggressive, and I've got to hang on to my identity somehow because my husband is a pretty strong personality . . . I have a personality of my own, but it's different obviously. But this business, if we [Henry and I] are by ourselves there is nearly always trouble. When Jill, a friend of mine, came over he was just berserk, shouting, and of course I got upset. I'm female and I burst into tears and all that sort of thing and I feel very much on my own . . . I feel very left out at times because they get on so well . . . I feel I am almost fighting for my life. It sounds rather stupid, that, because Jim [Mr Gregg] is a very strong character. I can be quite strong in a different sort of way to Jim, but . . . no, life for me is not very pleasant . . .

Therapist: Who would you say is suffering the most in this situation?

Mrs G: I think I am.

Therapist: So you are the person who would most like something to change and be sorted?

Mr G: I would, yes.

Mrs Gregg explained that she felt extremely powerless, that at times her experience was of "fighting for her life" in relation to two strong men (her son and husband) who had a lot in common and often appeared to be against her. In the sessions, however, she usually adopted a warm, supportive attitude towards Henry, smiled at his antics, joked with him, and so on. This was in stark contrast to Mr Gregg, who presented a rather stern, no-nonsense face towards Henry. However, at home Mr Gregg spent considerable time with Henry, frequently visited him when he was staying away, and offered extensive advice to staff about what Henry needed.

THERAPISTS' DISTORTIONS

The focus on issues of power also presented another twist to the interpretation of the issues in this family. Rather than simply seeing the problems in terms of a "secret" about their affairs, a set of narratives about power, inequality, and women's role in families emerges. This new narrative, however, was much less comfortable for the team since it raised deeper issues about gender in their own relationships and the possibility that family problems could not simply be solved by a confession of some private misdemeanours. In fact, it could even be suggested that the team were in some way colluding with a distorted view of this family's problem as mainly due to the parent's deceit-fulness, rather than as, at least partly, arising from the inevit-able, and often unequal, power struggles between the sexes. Certainly, in this family Mrs Gregg appeared to be in an unequal and powerless position.

Consideration of the impact of such wider societal processes raises many questions, especially in the face of such pathologi-cal dynamics as in this family. One obvious question is: "If such gender-based inequalities are so central, why don't all families have a psychotic son?" Some of the team, on the other hand, saw Henry as less crazy, and certainly far more sensitive than many young men of his age who had never received psychiatric treatment! More contentiously, it might also be suggested that, in families where such feelings of oppression in the mother are not resolved, problems are almost certain to emerge. Mrs Gregg had, in fact, also received treatment herself for depression and anxiety, and Henry, despite his apparent "silliness", was very tuned in and sensitive to his other feelings of desperation.

FALSE CONSCIOUSNESS:
DISTORTIONS, DENIALS, AND FABRICATIONS

It has been suggested that families internalize the processes of mystification and distortion inherent in the society in which they are located (Cooper, 1970; Laing, 1966). An alternative view is that families not only absorb dominant societal narra-tives, but that forms of distortions and fabrications are inherent in some of these narratives. Following from this is the question of the ways in which society may promote distorted or fabricated ways of viewing issues of power and inequality. Arguably, power is one of the last taboos in our society—it may be acceptable to possess it, but less so to be seen to be obviously striving for it. Perhaps this is part of the issue in families: since it is socially unacceptable to appear to be too hungry for power over others but yet legitimate to possess power, people may, then, attempt to exert influence by a variety of covert means and manoeuvres. In addition, covert moves may be the only effective or possible course of action for the less powerful members of families—women, children, and the elderly (Foreman & Dallos, 1996; Williams & Watson, 1988). To admit to a covert tactic is to lose the power that it might provide—to "give the game away"—and hence it "pays to conceal". Even a cursory examination of the practices of power in various cultures, especially Western ones, suggests that it is riddled with just these denials, distortions, and fabrications. One of the key falsifications and distortions is not that the powerful have gained power because they have striven, coerced, manipulated, and strategically manoeuvred for it, but that it fell into their hands because of their natural ability or even superiority.

Postmodernist perspectives emphasize narratives and discourses in society as a shifting web of meanings created at a local level between people in groups, such as families. Similarly, Foucault's account and related developments in the study of discourses and their operation tend to underestimate the extent to which some narratives appear to represent fabrications, denials, or lies. In contrast, the idea of "false consciousness" originally proposed by Marx and Engels (1846) suggested that ideologies are derived from structural inequalities. They serve a purpose, and some are clearly more beneficial to some groups at the expense of others. It serves the interests of a dominant group, therefore, to promote and maintain certain versions of the world. This can but need not necessarily imply that some groups are "deliberately" creating falsifications, not that they recognize their ideologies as false. Quite the opposite, in fact: ideology may be most powerful when a statement or perception appears to be naturally and self-evidently true, so obvious that it hardly needs to be spoken. False consciousness is not seen as something that is simply imposed on people, but as a set of beliefs that is personally internalized and held to be true: that is, people actively participate—by holding to such beliefs—in their own oppression and control:

> false consciousness ... the holding of beliefs that are contrary to one's personal or group interest and which thereby contribute to the maintenance of the disadvantaged position of the self or the group. ... Examples might include accommodation to material insecurity or deprivation, developing needs which perpetuate toil, aggressiveness, misery or injustice ... deriving a kind of comfort from believing that one's sufferings are unavoidable or deserved, ... and thinking that whatever rank is held by individuals in the social order represents their intrinsic worth. [Jost & Banaji, 1994, p. 3]

Jost and Banaji (1994) have suggested that the processes of false consciousness can be seen to operate at the level of groups of people like families or work groups. These display a tendency for the members to justify whatever existing state of affairs has become established—what Jost and Banaji term "system justification". False consciousness in groups can be seen to be evident when a set of beliefs is held that serves to justify an existing state of affairs that clearly operates at the expense of the individual's or family's self-interests. However, in order to accept this view, it is also necessary to accept the proposition that the world is not simply a creation, but that some events are "real". Prime candidates for this suggestion are actions within families such as physical violence, rape, material deprivation, and actions done to families such as removal or arrest of members, verbal and other forms of abuse, confinement, or removal to impoverished, deprived, or dangerous areas, material deprivations, and so on. It can, of course, be argued that these events can be seen as having a variety of meanings; however, it is hard to see how many of these actions do not represent negative consequences, irrespective of the subtleties or nuances of meanings that might be attached to them.

Research studies in a variety of situations (Jost & Banaji, 1994) suggest that people frequently hold beliefs about themselves that are clearly counter to their best interests. For example:

1. Women tend to be described by terms such as passive, irrational, and incompetent, and these terms may be employed not only by men, but also by women themselves. Men, in contrast, are more likely to be seen as aggressive, competitive, selfish, and hostile.

2. Working-class people and the poor have been found to be subject to stereotypes as lacking in abilities, unintelligent, incompetent, and lazy and tend to accept and apply these terms to describe themselves.

3. Victims of violence in many cases blame themselves for in some way having caused or provoked the attack. This has also been seen to a considerable extent in studies of domestic violence, where not only the attackers (usually men) but also extended family, friends, and professionals may support this distorted view.

It appears that:

> Once a set of events produces certain social arrangements, whether by historical or human intention, the resulting arrangements tend to be explained and justified simply because they exist . . . the disadvantaged come to believe that the system is part of the order of nature and that things will always be like this. [Jost & Banaji, 1994, p. 11]

Beliefs that support the interests of dominant groups—e.g. the white race, men, the powerful and wealthy—are absorbed by the less powerful and taken to be justified, inevitable, or true because they are encapsulated in the systems in which they find themselves:

> . . . people are apt to underestimate the extent to which seemingly positive attributes of the powerful simply reflect the advantages of social control. Indeed, this distortion in social judgement could provide a particularly insidious brake upon social mobility, whereby the disadvantaged and powerless over-estimate the capabilities of the powerful who, in turn, inappropriately deem

members of their own caste well-suited to their particular leadership tasks. [Ross, Amabile, & Steimetz, 1977]

Our belief system and the narratives that we employ may be constructed by our more or less passive but continual immersion in and exposure to ideas, e.g. from our family and friends and through the media. The absorption of beliefs and ideologies may occur unconsciously, and, hence, people may not be aware of having been exposed to information that leads them to hold beliefs that are to their own disadvantage. A study by Devine (1989), for example, found that subliminal presentations (very brief presentations that preclude conscious perception and awareness) of racial stereotypes of black Americans later influenced whites' judgements of an ambiguously described person. Developmentally, as a result of being exposed to a particular system in which, for example, blacks, the poor, and women typically occupy inferior positions, children may accept intuitively that they occupy these inferior positions because they are less able. If they happen to be a member of one or more of those groups, then this self-labelling may function in a self-fulfilling way to locate them in those positions and further support the false beliefs about their own lack of abilities.

JUSTIFYING
THE FAMILY STATUS QUO

Becoming a member of a particular group (e.g. the unemployed, single parents, "mentally ill") has attached to it a set of beliefs and identities. Moreover, there may be general changes in beliefs that encompass inequalities and are ascribed, or come into play, as a person becomes a member of a less powerful group. For example:

> . . . an instinctual or sensual gratification, an emotional nature both primitive and childlike, an imagined prowess in or affinity for sexuality, a contentment with their own lot which is in accord with proof of its appropriateness, a wily habit of deceit, and concealment of feeling. [Millet, 1970, p. 18]

Components of this stereotype or set of beliefs have been applied to designate the differences between blacks and whites, men and women, adults and children, the mentally ill and mentally healthy. The beliefs that emerge to differentiate different groups may be quite restricted and, to a large extent, predictable from the power positions of groups in relation to one another. In relation to violence and abuse in families, this stereotype has frequently been voiced to describe women and employed to justify physical restraint or even violence, e.g. the "violence-prone personality" (Foreman & Dallos, 1996).

The assignment of one person to an ill position in the family can be seen as an example of the kind of justification processes that Jost and Banaji (1994) discuss. Rather than asking why a family chooses to keep one member in that role, it can be seen as an example of a much wider process whereby once some process of assigning has taken place, the members of a system will inevitably attempt to justify its existence. As an example, Henry is seen to be mentally ill because he is occupying the role of a mentally ill person. What is more, family members may employ just such a process of justification to explain away various forms of social inequality and oppression, even their own, because they are immersed in a variety of narratives that lead them to do just that. This leads to a circular process: since the family view him in this way, this in turn may shape his actions, which validates the social label of him as "ill". Significantly, as people lose aspects of power, such as job and money or an attractive partner, they become all the more vulnerable to such a view of being inadequate because they appear to occupy a low status position.

KEEPING POWER STRUGGLES SECRET

Realizing that the sort of processes that had been ascribed to family pathology exist in the wider culture does not completely explain how and why dysfunctions emerge, but it can certainly help us to adopt a genuinely more neutral or understanding position. Palazzoli et al. (1989) argued powerfully that some of the key ingredients promoting the development of psychosis in a family are:

1. a rigid power struggle, usually between the parents, which has become stuck or is in a stalemate;

2. a child being induced to take sides in this game without end and in which no one can win;

3. an eventual awareness by the child that his or her loyalty and sacrifices for one or other parent has been to no avail and only resulted in being betrayed ultimately by the favoured parent;

4. the game or struggle between the parents and involvement of the child is kept a secret.

The ingredients of this dynamic are universal to all families—namely, struggles over power, mutual blaming and accusations, and attempts to solicit the support of others. Yet, as we have seen, the prevalence of false consciousness in society should expect us to see just these sorts of denials and distortions around issues of power. In contrast to Palazzoli's blaming tone regarding families, we can expect such struggles over power in all families. One question is how we can engage in a discussion of power in a way that will allow these issues to emerge. It could even be argued that to employ indirect means of attempting to alter the family dynamics without openly discussing issues of power may run the risk of colluding with a denial of its centrality to family life. An important question is, how much choice do families actually have to construct their dynamics? It has been a premise of systemic thinking that all families are unique, and possibly this has drawn attention away from the commonalities—what is not unique, what is not really open for negotiation in family life. This starts to reveal that perhaps much less is unique than was originally thought. For example, with the Gregg family the parents' decision to keep their affairs a secret from Henry can be seen as not just a personal choice to conceal this, but as one that is driven by societally shared discourses that define morality. Also, there is a widely shared discourse that such revelations may damage the children emotionally, and that therefore some things should not be said in front of them. Both what families choose to present—their public face—and what they choose to conceal from the world, and even from each other, are in part shaped by dominant narratives that they have internalized from a variety of sources.

SUMMARY

Any given society can be seen to contain a range of narratives that families internalize in various ways and employ to map their experiences. These narratives are ubiquitous, are often presented as obvious truths, and may be absorbed more or less passively and outside conscious awareness. However, they are not neutral but are versions of events that may, in some instances, present distorted views of the world that serve the interests of particular groups in society more than others. This need not necessarily be seen as a conspiracy by those groups to deceive others, though it is a possibility that in some cases the distortions are deliberate. The dominant narratives are internalized by family members and serve to construct and maintain their own disadvantage. Falsifications and distortions may influence family life in a variety of ways. They may distort the nature of the relationships between, for example, men and women in families. They may offer false or unrealistic explanations of events, e.g. problems of mental health being portrayed as either individual or relational problems. These distortions, in turn, are employed to construct a process whereby family members have a tendency to justify the "status quo". In effect, the family dynamics and organization that have evolved come to be seen as inevitable and as resulting from the inherent characteristics, including the abnormalities, of one or other member.

Attempting to steer their lives employing a "distorted map" may mean that family members, in turn, attempt to cope by distorting their own experiences, thereby compounding the falsifications. Specifically, instead of viewing "family myths" as a private phenomenon, such distortions can be seen to appear as a response to an experience of powerlessness and negative framing, resulting from the internalization of dominant discourses that distort a family's experience.

CHAPTER SEVEN

Evolving
and dissolving problems:
a co-constructional approach

"I sometimes think that 99 percent of the suffering that comes in the door has to do with how devalued people feel by the labels that have been applied to them or the derogatory opinions they hold about themselves."

Hoffman, 1988, p. 79

T his chapter will attempt to draw together and illustrate an approach combining ideas from social construction-ism and systemic therapies. Such an approach, instead of starting from an assumption that there is a problem to be treated, asks questions about how various sorts of problems are constructed in any given culture. How is the concept of depression or schizophrenia employed, not just in professional settings but in everyday conversations in families? It indicates, perhaps above all else, that the understandings that families hold are shaped by the dominant beliefs in a given culture. These beliefs, in turn, colour the nature of experiences in families—how people's actions and feelings are ascribed meanings and shape others' reactions. One important implication of this for therapy is that problems can be seen as not confined to some individuals and their families, but as common experiences —a part of all our lives. This touches on concepts from the brief therapy models and the idea that problems arise from attempted solutions to ordinary difficulties that are common experiences. Another way of putting this is that problems can be seen as part of a continuum. The severity of problems may vary at different points in each person's life, and consequently one person's problems may be more severe than another's at a given time. However, we are united by a language and shared images of distress that allow us to know something about what the experiences of various painful conditions may be like. Even though we may not taste them as fully as do others, they frame our lives, perhaps in our intentions to try to avoid such experiences, e.g. attempts to avoid depression, anxiety, stress, and conflicts. Where would the tourist industry be, for example, if many people were not so concerned (and encouraged to be by the media, etc.) to protect themselves from stress and depression?

In therapeutic work, it is likely that problems are encountered some way along their evolutionary pathway. This may tempt us to think, when we see them "fully grown", that they are somehow different in kind from the sorts of problems that might be generated by ordinary, everyday difficulties. The view held by therapists about "life" has far-reaching implications for how clients are treated and what is seen to be success in therapy, a "good outcome" or signs of positive change:

> Giano (previously diagnosed as schizophrenic) is just fine. I have only very positive things to say about him. He hasn't been taking any medicine for three years. . . . He has a girl friend and he's crazy about her. He's lost weight and looks wonderful—you should see how handsome he is now! I saw Gina some time ago and she told me you folks had worked a miracle, . . . [Palazzoli et al., 1989, p. 141]

> Daphne (psychotic and previously frequently erotically provocative to both parents) made no further advances to anyone, including her mother, and thus had more time to devote to her own problems. Gradually she began to solve them all, and in time she

became a ski instructor and became engaged to a nice, suitable boy. [Palazzoli et al., 1989, p. 135]

Sarah (Tekka's mother) . . . reported that Tekka (21 suicidal episodes, resulting in psychiatric hospitalisation) . . . was off the lithium, and was living in her bus on the Cape. "She looks much better now, and the sparkle is back in her eye." Despite this positive picture, Sarah expressed continued anxiety. "I'm trying not to worry, but Tekka still seems so fragile to me. It's fifty-fifty whether she's fine or has another episode. But there's nothing I can do about it. I just have to trust she can take care of herself." [Hoffman, 1993, p. 184]

These extracts offered by Palazzoli and Hoffman appear to embody widely differing ideas and expectation of "change". Palazzoli's accounts have a fairy-tale quality of miracle cures and families living happily ever after. In contrast, Hoffman offers a down-to-earth view of therapy as of some limited assistance through life's complex and inevitably troubled journey. These differences may follow directly from the theoretical bases that are adopted. Hoffman's commitment to a social constructionist position, which regards problems as related—at least in part—to wider societal factors, leads to a view of therapy as necessarily limited. Therapy may offer some benefits, but it cannot simply eliminate the wider societal forces that shape people's experiences and their problems. Palazzoli's approach, on the other hand, which views problems as the result of a variety of devious family games, offers a more optimistic, though perhaps unrealistic, view of the enormous changes that can occur if only a family can be induced to alter its dynamics. A social constructionist view suggests that, since a range of narratives and structures exists in society which promotes inequalities, mystifications, and distortions, then it should be expected that many people experience problems. Families who participate in therapy are therefore not necessarily fundamentally any "different", except that they may possibly be more sensitive, or even have higher expectations, which lead them to wanting their lives to be better.

There is considerable evidence that suggests that psychiatric problems are much more widespread in the general community than is commonly thought (Goldberg & Huxley, 1980, 1992). When "normal" people are interviewed about difficulties they have experienced, it is not uncommon to find that they report incidents that are as severe as some symptoms that bring people in to seek professional assistance (Dallos, Neill, & Strouthos, in press). Consistent with a brief therapy model, such accounts indicate that a variety of factors—such as availability of some form of support, e.g. friends, work colleagues, a teacher, extended family, parents—helped to alleviate the difficulties and prevent an escalation into serious pathology. These accounts also suggest an element of "luck" in that some—seemingly almost chance—input from peoples' support network helped to direct the difficulties along a non-pathological pathway as opposed to one that could have involved becoming labelled as "mentally ill", with a consequent destruction of identity, self-respect, and confidence.

The extract presented below is from an interview conducted as part of a research project exploring people's life paths and their accounts of the emergence of difficulties and ways of coping. Two groups of people took part in the interviews: one group was composed of people who had a psychiatric history; the second group of people were randomly selected, with no psychiatric history known to the interviewer. Participants were asked, as part of a semi-structured interview, to focus on one or more significant positive and negative turning points along their life path. In particular, they were asked to describe the path that negative events had taken, and to contemplate alternative pathways that they might have taken, for better or worse.

The extract is from an interview with Karen (age 34), a nurse and a recent graduate in social sciences. Karen was recruited as part of the random "normal" population, but it turned out that she had had a psychiatric history. In fact, most of this random "normal" sample had experienced severe difficulties at some point in their lives which they felt, "but for fortune", could have led to "psychiatric disorders". Karen revealed in the interview that her childhood had been difficult, her father had suffered from alcohol problems, and she had experienced difficulties at school. Following a referral by the school to social services and

to the child guidance service, family therapy had been suggested, but her father refused to take part in such "pointless
nonsense". She described in some detail a critical low point in
her life, when she had made a suicidal attempt ten years previously after she lost her job as a senior nurse:

Karen: The manager told me they didn't want me to do the
job and basically they were firing me, or sacking me, or
whatever. I couldn't handle that. I thought, I had only
trained as a nurse, I couldn't do anything else. It got me
into all sorts of problems around that, and of course I was
away from home. I didn't have my friends, my support
network, didn't have anything to counteract that with. So,
I took an overdose and ended up in D___ mental hospital
with a reactive depressive thing . . . I felt I was a failure, I
was never ever going to achieve what I wanted to achieve,
and because the managers had been very underhand in
the way that they dealt with things, it felt very subversive
. . . So I remember feeling very cheated, feeling very angry
that I had failed. I suppose I tried to blame myself rather
than the system. But in fact it was partly the fault of the
system, looking back on it now, because they didn't actually give me the right direction for following the system
. . . I kept thinking, what am I going to do?, how am I going
to go back to my parents and tell them that I have failed?
how am I going to tell them that I have lost my job?, all
those sorts of things, and in a sense I thought they would
accept more easily if I had an illness, than if I'd just lost my
job. So in a sense the overdose was a way of me getting
acknowledgement for a reason to be able to go back and
say I had lost my job . . . That is what was actually going
on, that actually gave me a reason for having lost my job,
rather than not being able to cope . . .

Interviewer: Were some of the staff helpful in the hospital?

Karen: They were, I'm not decrying hospitals, it was just a
mistake, staff were fine, . . . often they don't do very much
. . . No, they just let me sound off at them, and just be
around, and I played a lot of Scrabble (laughs) in that time

... I think going into hospital was a big mistake actually, because it automatically put a label on you as someone who had had a problem, a psychiatric problem ... I found that as soon as I got that label my whole world in a sense changed, because I became someone who came under certain prejudices and people responded very differently to me. People wouldn't actually accept my qualifications ... the label was the thing that people looked at and not me ... had I had the insight, or been older when it happened, I would have taken myself off to a retreat somewhere, or something like that, and done it differently ... gone off on a trekking holiday, just away from the situation and actually worked it through ...

Karen saw her problems as developing from a variety of sources: her troubled family background, the negative work environment, loss of her job, and isolation from her friends. At the time, she felt vulnerable and inadequate and blamed herself. Her actions of taking the blame onto herself and taking an overdose fixed the definition of the problem as personal. Consequently, her hospitalization, which made sense at the time, further supported a construction of the problems as personal. This slide into a definition of a problem as due to individual pathology can occur rapidly and, as Karen explains, is something she regrets and which has placed a negative label on her. Retrospectively, she sees the problems as largely related to a destructive work context which placed her in an untenable position. She also sees her own actions at the time as informed by an individualistic view of mental distress, i.e. in such circumstances discourses of personal weakness, failure, and inadequacy may dominate a person's inner thoughts and lead that person into accepting a view of her/himself as "ill".

Her account captures and helps to summarize some of the strands outlined in the previous chapters:

1. People are actively engaged in trying to make sense of their circumstances and act strategically in attempting to influence others and manage their relationships; e.g. Karen was trying to work out how to tell her parents, how they

would react, and what was the best course of action at the time.

2. The beliefs underlying the strategic actions attempted are, in turn, shaped by dominant narratives that constrain what choices are perceived to be possible.

3. The dominant narratives exist not only as ideologies, but are manifest in various structures and practices; e.g. a medical view of mental distress is manifest in the actions of doctors, such as medication and confinement to psychiatric units.

At the point of experiencing distress, people are therefore confronted with constraints on how they see their problems in terms of the dominant ideologies and structures around them. To resist these alone can be a tall order, and, as Karen indicates, she initially succumbed to these powerful influences and started down a path of "mental illness" and became labelled. For her, this not only incurred stigma but, practically, has prevented her from attaining promotions as a nurse, despite now being exceptionally well-qualified. She added that part of her subsequent empowerment came through her university studies and reading of critical and alternative views of mental health.

Other accounts from this piece of research suggest that, like Karen, most of the "normal" participants had experienced serious difficulties in their lives. What appears to discriminate between these and those developing full-blown "pathology" was the availability of support at the time, which avoided individualistic and pathologizing definitions taking hold. We know relatively little about the "natural", ordinary ways that people cope with life's inevitable difficulties. However, the work on the formation of accounts and narratives suggests that engaging in conversations with others—and their positive, affirmative reactions—assists people in dealing with serious problems. The reactions of significant others, such as family members, to these evolving narratives may be extremely important in determining whether troubles deteriorate or diminish.

However, it may be over-optimistic to assume that family members or friends can easily provide this support. In fact, to expect them to do so can, in effect, ascribe blame to them for being uncaring or unsupportive. Instead, White (1995) argues that we are all directed towards such pathologizing because this is the dominant discourse in many societies. For example, the legacy of psychoanalytic theory leads to a view of problems as resulting from personal pathology. Even systemic analyses can run the risk of ascribing blame to faulty patterns of interactions or communications in the family. At a personal level, we may also gain some comfort in an uncertain and stressful world by perceiving symptoms and problems as indications of some personal aberration. To see these as due, instead, to wider social forces, inequalities, and oppressive practices suggests that all of us may be vulnerable, and fear of becoming "mad" is perhaps one of the greatest fears there is:

> Pathologizing discourses have the potential to bring to us a degree of comfort . . . and make it possible for us to ignore the extent to which the problems for which people seek help are so often mired in the structures of inequality of our cultures, including those pertaining to gender, race, ethnicity, class, economics, age, and so on. [White, 1995, p. 115]

As the extract from Karen's interview indicates, the initial events that can lead to problems are common and are shared by many of us, e.g. stress, a sense of failure, and rejection at work. Typically, these lead to self-accusations and a sense of personal inadequacy. In fact, people frequently verbally abuse themselves and talk to themselves either internally or out loud for being "so stupid", "pathetic", "weak", and so on. When, as in Karen's case, others are not available to offer some support to help us to talk back to these internalized accusers, and if this is coupled with an awareness that more of such criticism would likely be forthcoming from a central figure in one's life (her father), then an escape into pathology can seem like a "haven":

> . . . in order for people to break from these self-accusations and attributions of personal inadequacy, from the stress that is informed by the expectations about what it means to be a real person in our culture, and from the experience of guilt . . . they must step into the site of "illness" . . . this is a sad reflection on our culture. [White, 1995, p. 118]

As Karen's account also indicated, the temporary haven and sanctuary that the illness label provided was short-lived. It left her with a spoilt identity, as someone who could never be trusted again to hold a demanding position of responsibility in her profession.

EVOLUTION OF PROBLEMS

Eron and Lund (1993), in agreement with such a view, suggest that problems can be seen to have an evolution that can often be traced to disruptions precipitated by the demand to accomplish significant life-cycle transitional changes. For example, those changes associated with children leaving home or the birth of a first child may throw a relationship off course. They argue that a key aspect of what happens is the extent to which people's preferred views of themselves and their relationship appear to be threatened. Various actions may then follow as attempts to realign themselves with this preferred view; e.g. a young couple after the birth of a child might feel that they are more distant towards each other, that they they are not intimate enough—sexually and emotionally. In effect, they may feel that their relationship is not how they want or prefer it to be. Attempts may then be made to rectify this, such as complaining to each other about the situation, going out more, or recruiting a parent to help with the children to give the couple some time together. If these attempted solutions do not have the desired effect, and instead the couple find themselves becoming ever more distant, then a range of emotional responses—such as frustration, anger, sorrow, and resentment—may accompany this recognition. These may cloud the clarity of their thinking and thereby serve to ensure that the "failing" solutions become locked in. Both what are perceived to be problems and what courses of action these imply can therefore be regarded as shaped by dominant narratives. A common and perhaps quite unrealistic narrative of this sort is that of individual responsibility, e.g. that despite various economic or emotional stresses, and other pressures, a couple can "work things out" if only they try hard enough, or that "love can conquer all".

Preferred views of self are not simply idiosyncratic personal or even family beliefs; rather, they are soaked in the cultural expectations of what it is to be a "real" person, a valuable member of society. This view is typically coloured by patriarchal notions, so that to be a "real" person tends to imply being independent, logical, rational, not given to "excessive" emotionality, and self-sufficient. Similarly, at the relationship level, partners may expect to be close, sexually intimate, interested in each other, having fun when various factors such as inequalities and dependencies have arise as a result of one partner, usually the woman, becoming dependent and socially isolated following the birth of a child. Both may attempt to contort their relationship into this preferred view, partly because of pervasive cultural narratives that they can "work things out" if only they try hard enough and, if they cannot, perhaps they are "incompatible". These processes of self-blaming that may result from attempts to attain these preferred but sometimes unattainable states may fuel attempted solutions, which leads to a further sense of failure.

Such an analysis has implications for how therapists view themselves. On the one hand, it can make us more compassionate in recognizing the external factors that are operating, but it may also mean that we acknowledge that there is no real difference between us and our clients. It may be helpful if one can admit to having the same problems that everyone else has and not become duped into believing that it is possible to simply "rise above them". Many of us have experienced problematic marriages and relationships with our children, but this should not be seen as a disqualification to being a therapist; however, a therapist should not be seen to have experienced "too many", or he may be thought of as "indistinguishable" from the clients. A social constructionist view, then, can have the uncomfortable implication of narrowing the gap between clients and therapists. By emphasizing that both inevitably live in a socially constructed set of meanings, which includes structures, politics, games, deceptions, and so on, it thereby implies that it makes little sense to assign blame to families. On the contrary, the assigning of inadequacy or fault is one of the dominant discourses that operates in order to maintain the privileges of one group over others. If we recognize some of the games, manipulations, contradictions, and power struggles that make up the society we live in, why should we be surprised that such processes occur in families? Yet some therapists appear to suggest that it is, in fact, something about some families that is unusual and "different" to the therapist's way of being:

> As time went by, we realised even more clearly that these families were crack players, trained in a context that taught them to manipulate relationships, using set verbal ploys and craft moves refined and added to constantly over the years. Delving into this sophisticated bag of tools, we poor untutored beginners could only gradually recognise such tactics as simulation (falsities) or moves that were feints or warning threats. [Palazzoli et al., 1989, p. 78]

There may be some truth in Palazzoli's observation of these families. Alternatively, it could be suggested that the manipulations that go on in families are no more sinister, devious, underhand, or exploitative than those in the average boardroom, political meeting, or even hospital committee.

DISSOLVING PROBLEMS

Eron and Lund (1993) have suggested that a narrative approach to therapy is assisted by an understanding of how the problems have evolved. A significant part of this is to try to identify the beliefs that were in place and led to the particular solutions attempted. Secondly, it is necessary to consider how the results of these attempted actions were perceived and subsequently resulted in the difficulties turning into problems. Therapy is seen as initially requiring a careful historical analysis of the family's history and related system of beliefs. These are carefully explored with a family, and consideration is given to whether they are still in place, together with an analysis of how the beliefs may now be holding the problems in place. The aim of therapy is to generate some new narratives with the family that fit their existing stories but allow some possibilities for change:

We suggest . . . the therapist's strategy (that is, the alternative narrative that develops out of the therapeutic conversation) be informed by a careful consideration of family members' own stories and how they came to shape their predicament. In the absence of such an assessment, narrative therapists may well wind up doing what they accuse strategic therapists of doing: inventing their own realities and imposing them upon clients while positively reframing what they are doing as a co-creative venture. [Eron & Lund, 1993, p. 293]

Therapy can, in this way, be viewed as involving a set of conversations in which the therapist and the family are jointly engaging in co-constructing a new narrative. Nevertheless, such conversations inevitably contain strategic components: the therapist will consider whether it is appropriate to raise a particular issue at a given moment, whether to pursue a particular point, and so on. These can be seen as micro-strategies, moment-to-moment decisions about what is best said or not said, based on anticipation of how people might react. Adopting a co-constructive approach that starts from a position of acceptance is more likely to enable people to change their perceptions and narratives:

We would add that there is a strategic advantage to this non-impositional therapeutic position. By joining with [the person's] preferred view, the therapist becomes one important other who sees [him] in the way he would like. Once [he] sees the therapist seeing him in a way that fits his preferred view, he may be more open to reconsidering how intimate others see him. The assumption of this non-disjunctive position is an essential first step in building a problem-dissolving narrative. [Eron & Lund, 1993, p. 305]

This also indicates that a co-constructive framework advocated by narrative approaches (Anderson & Goolishian, 1988; Hoffman, 1993) contains the time-honoured concept of "joining". There is also a connection with many other forms of therapy, such as Roger's non-evaluative approach, which starts from a position of offering acceptance and unconditional positive regard.

To summarize: the evolution of a problem is seen to involve a course of actions or attempted solutions, based upon the family members' beliefs or narratives. These choices of action appear to be motivated by their attempts to maintain a positive view of themselves and their relationships. In turn, these preferred views appear to be shaped by socially acceptable and desirable narratives of self, e.g. to regard oneself, and be seen, as a sympathetic and caring person. Unfortunately, the desired outcomes do not invariably follow, and these "good intentions" may generate courses of actions that make the situation worse and, instead, result in a negative picture of self. As an example, attempts to cheer up, support, or do things for someone who seems apathetic and depressed following an illness can have the effect of making them feel inadequate, dependent, and a burden. This process may escalate, leaving all feeling hopeless, angry, ineffective, and frustrated. Ambivalent feelings of sympathy tinged with anger and resentment may develop, which make it all the harder for people to be able to "stand back" and try another approach to the problem.

One of the first steps in helping to dissolve the problems can be to consider an alternative pathway:

> Having charted the course of the problem, it is useful to consider how, given the same family and the same set of circumstances, a problem might *not* have developed. In a non-problem scenario, the parents might well respond with equivalent concern and involvement, but their construction of the event would be different. [Eron & Lund, 1993, p. 301]

If the precipitating events had been seen in a different way, then it is possible that a different set of actions might have been taken. The narratives that lead to a problem may contain ideas of a loss of control, that the situation is slipping away from the way people want them to be and everything is going badly wrong. It is likely not just that one predominant attempted solution emerges, but that the surrounding anxiety leads to an oscillation between attempted solutions. Frequently, this boils down to an alternation between solutions fuelled by caring and concern, as opposed to those fuelled by anger and resentment born from frustration and a sense of failure. The reactions to problems frequently demonstrate such oscillations between alternatives, leading to a sense of "stuckness", of "going round in circles", and a closing down of creative thinking.

White and Epston (1990) suggest that an important aspect of a narrative approach is to search for "unique outcomes", i.e. incidents in the recent or distant past where the difficulties were successfully dealt with or where the consequences were, at least, less severe. This is not dissimilar to the brief therapy approach of searching for successful previous solutions. In addition, a narrative approach focuses on how these emphasize narratives that portray the family members in a positive light, i.e. narratives that they prefer to hold about themselves. Karl Tomm's (1988) use of hypothetical questions also fits with such an approach, e.g. hypothetical scenarios can be explored in the past in addition to a consideration of alternatives possible in the future.

Narratives not only function by setting out a view of events —how events are defined and how things "should" be—but also contain a set of assumptions about contrasts and opposites. Kelly (1955) emphasized the bipolarity of beliefs and narratives and indicated that it is not just the premises of a particular narrative that shape actions, but the implied opposite. For example, most families would prefer to have a view of themselves as psychologically well, but this narrative takes its meaning from its perceived opposite. This opposite could be seen as temporary states of distress, the common "ups and downs" that people experience, or as a reaction to some conflict in the family. If the opposite state is rigidly seen as "mental illness", this may have implications for the range of solutions that might be generated when a member displays some distress: for example, they may become excessively anxious, feel helpless, and more readily seek medical assistance, with the consequence that ordinary "ups and downs" become pathologized and medically labelled.

The meanings given to actions in a family appear, therefore, to display a dynamic quality whereby they can become increasingly rigid or pre-emptive of any alternative narratives or ways of seeing the situation. Dissolving this rigidity may operate in terms of contemplating alternative narratives that fit with the family's belief system. However, since the family's belief system contains internalizations of dominant discourses that may be constraining and confusing, some critical discussion of these may be a necessary component of the sessions. There are various ways that this can be achieved. Tried and tested methods, such as family genograms, can be employed to consider how dominant ideas have changed or have remained the same over the generations, and what effects these have. A discussion of the life cycle of the family or the relationship can be oriented towards a discussion of what their initial expectations were, how these have altered over time, and the influence of social changes and movements, such as feminism or right-wing political views of family life. Families can also work together as "researchers" with the therapist, to gather information about how other families they know operate, what their beliefs appear to be, what identities and social positions they seem to be aspiring towards, and how these might be linked to their backgrounds: social class, race, religion, and so on.

THE MASTERS FAMILY

The extract presented below from a therapy session is intended to illustrate a narrative, co-constructional approach that also incorporates aspects of strategic thinking. Both the family and the therapist can be seen as having intentions, aims, and preferred stories of the "problems" and of themselves. For example, the therapist in this extract (the author) prefers to see problems from a social rather than an organic perspective. Both the therapist and the family prefer to view themselves as generally caring and helpful. However, at times they may have thought that the other(s) were going up the wrong path, pursuing a narrative that was unhelpful or a distortion or ignored some key facts. A constructional approach here is seen not as directionless but as at least to some extent strategic. It is sensitive to the family's position, including how they may react to certain alternative versions or narratives of events. However, the approach need not be "passive": for example, at times a version may be suggested that is provocative, and it is recognized that the family may not, at first anyway, like or accept a particular narrative. Likewise, family members may also present provocative or extreme versions of events, perhaps, in a sense, to get them out into the open, to "air them" as a prelude to "putting them away". The aim is not that any one view becomes imposed, but to allow both dominant and subjugated narratives to be aired. This enables therapy to proceed on the basis of continuous interpretations and synthesis of these alternatives—a co-construction of narratives.

The Masters family (also discussed earlier in chapter five) appeared to exemplify a common ambivalence about their son's "mental distress". On the one hand, they viewed him as "ill" and suffering from some form of medical or organic disturbance and, on the other, as disturbed, due to some social cause, perhaps as a result of something they had done wrong as a family. Their contact with various mental health professionals had appeared to reinforce these conflicting "voices", though these exist not just within the mental health profession but throughout the wider culture. As mentioned in chapter five, politics and the arts were important interests for all members of the family. Both parents were keen theatre-goers. Mr Masters had acted in some amateur productions, and his wife was an avid literary scholar and had been involved in the production and directing of plays. Tony and his sister Monica had both studied English and history at university. These literary interests were central to the family's life. These shared interests were underlined by a suggestion put to the family that, since they had a lot of interests in common, it might be pleasant for them to have some time devoted to these. They agreed to spend some time together in two different ways: once to meet to consider Tony's financial and other practical problems and, on a separate occasion, simply to go out and enjoy some activity together. The underlying strategy here was to disrupt the repetitive negative pattern of their contact being solely activated by Tony's disturbing confrontations. The suggestion also fitted with their shared interests, their preferred views of themselves, and the narrative they had articulated of previously having been a family that shared and enjoyed pursuing these interests together. It seemed that we all (therapist and the family) wanted to move towards a new narrative, or, in fact, a return to a narrative that was not saturated with a view of them, and of Tony as having mental health problems, but as caring for, needing, and enjoying each other's company, i.e. emphasizing the successes that they had experienced in the past rather than the failures.

The following extract is taken from the start of the third session:

Therapist: I seem to remember that last time we came up with the idea of you having two types of meetings, practical matters and some fun . . .

Mr M: Last week the three of us went and saw Ibsen's *Ghosts* . . . so we've had a bit of culture . . .

Therapist: That's the story about a family where someone is dying, isn't it?

Mrs M: You don't notice that until the end . . . the inherited syphilis . . . it's all about people's pasts being real . . .

Mr M: Not cheery really . . .

Mrs M: Not cheery . . . very well acted though.

Tony: Very well acted.

Therapist: Whose idea was it to go, who spotted it?

Mr M: I saw it advertised at the Art Centre and thought it might be quite a good evening . . . Tony agreed.

Therapist: Working with you has had an effect on me as well . . . I've been along to the Arts Centre twice since I saw you to watch films . . . *Presumed Innocent* with Harrison Ford . . .

Mrs M: It's a very powerful play . . . if you didn't know the play you would be a bit puzzled . . .

Apart from indicating that the therapist here had more middle-brow tastes than the family, this gives quite a powerful illustration of their shared beliefs about what counts as "fun". Furthermore, despite Tony's apparently serious problems, they attempt to get close as a family and to make him "feel better" by sharing literature and, in this case, going to watch what many would regard as an extremely painful play.

If we regard therapy as a collaborative exercise in which therapist and family jointly construct some new ways of looking at the world, then it follows that the therapist takes a genuine interest in the family's world and is prepared to learn from them. As an illustration of this stance, and consistent with the family's interests and knowledge, we were interested in what connections they had drawn between their own family life and families depicted in literature and drama. They were asked to think of a play that fitted their family situation:

Therapist: Have you thought of a play that fits your family?

Mrs M: *Hamlet*, maybe . . . not the Gertrude and Claudius bit . . . not the marrying your brother . . . not in that sense.

Mr M: (*laughing*) not unless he asks you . . .

Mrs M: Hamlet is a man in search of his identity. The audience doesn't know whether he is in a very confused state or whether he is pretending to be in order to confuse the court, and he is not sure of his own purpose or whether what the ghost tells him is right.

Mr M: I played Claudius in a version of *Hamlet* not very long ago and I got to know the play very well . . . though you [Mrs Masters] know it better than I do . . . but playing it doesn't make it any clearer.

Mrs M: The essence of the play is not knowing, and that says something about us . . . our relationship with you [Tony] . . . your relationship with yourself . . . but we have discussed it for over ten years . . . other people will come up with some simplistic theory, but when we have been with this problem for so long we know it is not as simple as that. All four of us are searching for a way to help you to clear the fog away. Its not going to be a magic wand . . .

Mr M: Hamlet is in a sense more in charge of his destiny than you are (*to Tony*). You were a patient, not an agent . . .

Mrs M: The problem is, Hamlet doesn't really know where

to go ... he tries to put things to various tests to see how people will react ...

Therapist: But he does make some discoveries, doesn't he, for example his uncles' misdeeds ... ?

Mrs M: Well, the king reacts very violently at the time and is obviously upset. The audience is aware that the king admits it, but it's not sure until right at the end whether Hamlet does ... though he has more proof than he had ...

Mr M: The evidence is fairly conclusive, but he can't do much about it because his nature doesn't allow him to do it ... he gets carried away by his actions ...

Therapist: Tony, how do you see it ... yourself in the role of Hamlet?

Tony: I think that Hamlet is stretching things a bit far ...

Therapist: I guess one of the themes I would like to pick up is that Hamlet is confused, but he is also in a very confusing situation ... nobody quite knows what is going on, so his confusion is in a sense real. In the end, his paranoia is actually justified, but everybody is denying it ... the confusion is wider than he is ... We can think of family life as a script, as something which runs along by itself ... but there is a difference in that in family life we are the authors of our own play ... we can write and rewrite the script ...

Mr M: It can become more script and less improvisation.

Tony: It's like saying, "I don't want it to happen like that, I want it to happen like this."

Mr M: As long as feel you are given a script but can be involved in the rewrite.

Therapist: I find myself in an interesting position with dramatists ... they can leave people in wretched despair and that's a masterpiece, but that's where we come ... (*laughter*) ... enter stage left the therapist ...

Mr M: Dramatists don't have to sort it out, they can walk away ... the messenger nearly always gets killed in Shakespeare ...

Mrs M: It all began halfway through your exams. It must

have begun earlier for you and became visible to us . . . did it come earlier for you? You were compulsively writing notes for your history essay.

Tony: I don't think so. I couldn't get anywhere, I didn't actually do any work . . .

CONSTRUCTING NEW NARRATIVES AND CHOICES

The family, in this extract, were encouraged to explore a hypothetical narrative of themselves as a play. This fits with their interests and preferred picture of themselves as interesting, thoughtful, creative, and cultured people. They chose to discuss the play *Hamlet,* and in the discussion each person seems to be allotted a different role: for example, the mother appears to be regarded as the director of the play, the father the actor who, although he knows the lines and can act the play, nevertheless doesn't understand it as well as his wife—"I played Claudius . . . and I got to know the play very well, though you [Mrs Masters] know it better than I do". Embedded in this remark we could also see a narrative which is of Mr Masters' sense of failure in the family. This reinforced our perception—based upon remarks he had made in earlier sessions about his sense of failure as a counsellor in not having been able to help Tony— that he felt generally powerless and inadequate. Many families experience a sense of failure at "having to" attend for help, that they have failed, and we wondered whether this sense was more acute for Mr Masters. Some of this seemed to emerge in what seemed at times like veiled attacks towards the therapist: for example, he remarked that they have all been searching for a way to help, but "we know it is not as simple as that". Perhaps a more amusing dig was Mr Masters' observation that in Shakespeare's plays, "the messenger nearly always gets killed". Was the therapist being regarded here as like the messenger who sometimes brings bad or unwanted news?

Tony's role, on the other hand, is less clear. Is he in the play or not; is he pretending to be mad as Hamlet is perhaps; or is Tony genuinely ill? Interestingly, Tony appears to make a most "sensible" comment in saying that thinking of his family and himself as *Hamlet* is "stretching things a bit far". Perhaps a narrative of his condition as similar to Hamlet's was perceived by him to be too far removed from their family situation—they did not live in Denmark, for one thing! However, Tony does show acceptance of the implicit suggestion within the metaphor of the play that families can write and rewrite their own script when he comments: "I'ts like saying, 'I don't want it to happen like that, I want it to happen like this'."

Through the metaphor of the play, both the family's confusions and ambivalent ways of regarding Tony become clear, but we can also see how this ambivalence is embedded in our cultural heritage. By drawing out some of the differences between drama and therapy, an attempt here is made to suggest that, unlike actors in a play, they as a family can—to some extent, at least—write their own script, i.e. take charge of their own destinies, create some new options, and make some new choices. Yet, at the same time, we can see that the wider social discourses, as embodied in the play, serve to restrict the choices that families can create. Outside the confines of the therapy suite, the family will almost certainly encounter the medical model of mental disturbance and the view that, apart from medication, there is little they can do.

As the family alternate their attention from the story of *Hamlet* to themselves, there is an exploration of alternative narratives: mad–pretending, confused–testing reality, patient–agent, reality–illusion, actors–authors. The ambivalences and dilemmas in the Masters family are common to us all and have implications for how we treat mental disturbance: if the person is seen as "genuinely" ill, he or she is more likely to receive sympathy, some kindness, but also a disconfirmation—the person loses his or her status as a "real" responsible person who is capable of and entitled to make his or her own choices. On the other hand, if the person is seen as not genuinely ill, "malingering", or pretending, then irritation and anger is likely to result. In the Masters family, this dilemma was all the sharper because of the reluctance they had in expressing feelings and their apparent tendency to intellectualize. Mr Masters remarked that he found it difficult to express his feelings, and they all agreed that they preferred to take a rational, intellectual approach to problems.

Change here is seen to have occurred through, firstly, establishing a positive relationship with the family which fosters some creative exploration, and some new, jointly constructed ways of seeing themselves and their problems. The therapist and family start to agree to employ some new narratives, or to emphasize differently some established ones that allow differentiations to develop, leading to some new ways of interpreting and explaining events. The metaphor of the play *Hamlet* serves to promote a conversation with the family which reveals their beliefs, interests, and explanations. This conversation with the family starts to reveal some of the stories, narratives, and metaphors that exist in our culture and also the part that these play in shaping their thinking and feelings. The language, metaphors, and visual references that families employ with each other contains, as Foucault (1967) suggests, the history of ideas and prevalent concerns, beliefs, and understandings in our society.

The consideration of alternative narratives reveals the different choices of actions that these allow. An emphasis on bipolarity, regarding meaning, as inevitably concerned with difference and contrasts can serve as a reminder that "ambivalence" and "inconsistency" are inevitable aspects of perceptions and thinking about problems (Bateson, 1972; Kelly, 1955). This can be a useful antidote to some aspects of constructional approaches that focus, for example, on narratives and stories without emphasizing that a narrative implies a contrast (Sluzki, 1992). Simply, a choice of a narrative requires some evaluation—i.e. assumptions that it is a "good" one or that it is "accurate", as opposed to "bad" or "inaccurate". When a family's experience is discussed in terms of a story, it can be helpful to bear in mind that a contrasting story might therefore also suggest itself. In addition, the focus on personal as well as shared meanings alerts us to the possibility that each person in the family is likely to interpret and react to the narratives in different ways (Palazzoli et al., 1989).

SUMMARY

Systemic family therapy appears to have gone through a number of stages: from an initial fascination with patterns and processes in families, to an exploration of family members' constructions and beliefs, and, most recently, to an analysis of how these beliefs are, in turn, shaped by the wider social world in which each family is engaged. This is, of course, a gross simplification. Arguably, the roots of constructivist thinking were evident in the original pioneering studies. Also, the emphasis on systemic thinking as offering a new epistemology—and, in fact, the consideration of epistemology at all—contained a critical consideration of the prevailing models, especially the individualistic and pathologizing views of problems. Likewise, systemic perspectives can appear to imply a shifting of pathologizing up a level—instead of the individual as pathological, it is the family.

Yet family relationships can be seen to contain patterns and processes that encapsulate problems: abuses and injustices are real. Tellingly, the victims of abuse usually have few uncertainties about seeing this as a real and negative experience. It is usually the more powerful and privileged who question this reality. Systemic approaches alert us to look for real, recurring patterns as well as meanings, and to lose sight of the importance of actual events and behaviours in families may be a mistake. These patterns, as well as narratives, regulate family members' actions, and they shape and constrain their experiences, their identities, and the meanings they can generate. At the extreme, physical violence and sexual abuse may permit some alternative narratives, but not many. It is hard to imagine, for example, how being regularly beaten can be construed as a positive experience. Therapeutic change must therefore involve a change both in how problems are seen and also in the process of how family members act with each other. These two facets of family life—action and construing—are inextricably and dialectically interwoven. Furthermore, both these facets exist in a dynamic state over time. All aspects of family experience—actions, emotions, and beliefs—may display patterning, escalations, polarizations, and stability over time.

Finally, one of the aims of this book has been to suggest that a view of people in families and other relationships as actively making choices, attempting solutions to their difficulties, and acting in a strategic manner is compatible with a social constructionist view. The beliefs that people hold are potentially unlimited—there may be no borders in the imagination—but, nevertheless, what we see to be possible and permissible may be shaped by the dominant narratives that surround us. A necessary first step in a therapeutic encounter may be like that in a revolutionary process—a realization of how our imagination may have become oppressed and contained in various ways. In recognizing that the dominance of ideas is linked to the dominance of power, therapy must therefore inevitably be a political activity. Emotionally distressed people who have come to be labelled as mentally ill have been, and continue to be, amongst the most abused, powerless, and oppressed people in the world. Prevalent narratives featuring ideas of individual or family inadequacy may play a considerable part in maintaining an ecology of ideas, a system of beliefs, that encourages not only us as therapists, but also the families we encounter, to maintain such oppression.

REFERENCES

Anderson, H., & Goolishian, H. (1988). "Human systems as linguistic systems." *Family Process, 27,* 371–393.

Anderson, H., Goolishian, H.A., & Winderman, L. (1986). "Problem determined systems: toward transformation in family therapy." *Journal of Strategic and Family Therapy, 4,* 1–13.

Antaki, C. (Ed.) (1989). *Analysing Everyday Explanation.* London: Sage.

Ashby, W. R. (1956). *An Introduction to Cybernetics.* London: Chapman & Hall.

Austin, J. (1962). *How to Do Things with Words.* London: Oxford University Press.

Averill, J. R. (1985). "The social construction of emotion: with special reference to love." In: K. J. Gergen & K. E. Davis (Eds.), *The Social Construction of the Person.* New York: Springer.

Bahktin, M. M. (1981). *The Dialogical Imagination* (trans. C. Emerson & M. Holquist). Austin, TX: University of Texas.

Bannister, D. (1960). "Conceptual structure in thought disordered schizophrenics." *Journal of Acta Psychologia, 20,* 104–120.

Bateson, G. (1958). *Naven* (2nd edition). Stanford, CT: Stanford University Press.

Bateson, G. (1972). *Steps to an Ecology of Mind.* New York: Ballantine.

Bateson, G. (1980). *Mind and Natures: A Necessary Unity.* London: Fontana/Collins.

Bateson, G., Jackson, D. D., Haley, J., & Weakland, J. H. (1956). "Towards a theory of schizophrenia." *Behavioural Science, 1* (4), 251–264.

Beck, A. T. (1967). *Depression: Clinical, Experiential and Theoretical Aspects.* New York: Harper & Row.

Becker, H. S. (1974). "Labelling theory reconsidered." In: P. Rock & M. McIntosh (Eds.), *Deviance and Social Control.* London: Tavistock.

221

Black, D. (1987). "Handicap and family therapy." In: A. Bentovim, G. C. Barnes, & A. Cochlin (Eds.), *Family Therapy: Complementary Frameworks of Theory and Practice.* London: Academic Press.

Bogdan, J. L. (1984). "Family organization as an ecology of ideas: an alternative to the reification of family systems." *Family Process, 23,* 375–388.

Bogdan, J. L. (1986). "Do families really need problems? Why I am not a functionalist." *Family Therapy Networker, 10* (4), 30–35.

Boyle, M. (1990). *Schizophrenia: A Scientific Delusion?* London: Routledge.

Brazelton, T. B., & Cramer, B. G. (1991). *The Earliest Relationship: Parents, Infants and the Drama of Early Attachment.* London: Karnac Books.

Brown, G. W., & Harris, T. (1989). *The Social Origins of Depression.* London: Routledge.

Bruner, J. S. (1977). "Early social interaction and language acquisition." In: H. R. Schaffer (Ed.), *Studies in Mother-Infant Interaction* (pp. 271–289). London: Academic Press.

Bruner, J. S. (1990). *Acts of Meaning.* Cambridge, MA: Harvard University Press.

Campbell, D., & Draper, R. (Eds.) (1985). *Applications of Systemic Family Therapy.* London: Grune & Stratton.

Campbell, D., Draper, R., & Huffington, C. (1989). *Second Thoughts on the Theory and Practice of the Milan Approach to Family Therapy.* London: Karnac Books.

Carter, E., & McGoldrick, M. (1988). *The Changing Family Life Cycle: A Framework for Family Therapy* (2nd edition). New York: Gardner.

Cecchin, G. (1987). "Hypothesizing, circularity and neutrality revisited: an invitation to curiosity." *Family Process, 26* (4), 405–413.

Chodorow, N. (1978). *The Reproduction of Mothering.* Berkeley, CA: University of California Press.

Cooper, D. (1970). *The Death of the Family.* New York: Pantheon.

Cronen, V. E., Pearce, W. B., & Tomm, K. (1985). "A dialectical view of personal change." In: K. J. Gergen & K. E. Davis (Eds.), *The Social Construction of the Person.* New York: Springer-Verlag.

Dallos, R. (1991). *Family Belief Systems, Therapy and Change.* Milton Keynes: Open University Press.

Dallos, R., Neill, A., & Strouthos, M. (in press). "Pathways to pathology." *Journal of Family Therapy.*

Dallos, R., & Procter, H. G. (1984). *Family Processes* (Unit 2, D307, Social Psychology). Milton Keynes: Open University.

Dell, P. F. (1982). "Beyond homeostasis: toward a concept of coherence." *Family Process, 1*, 21–41.

De Shazer, S. (1982). *Patterns of Brief Therapy: An Ecosystemic Approach*. New York: Guilford Press.

Devine, P. H. (1989). "Stereotypes and prejudice: their automatic and controlled components." *Journal of Personality and Social Psychology, 56*, 5–18.

Duck, S. (1994). *Meaningful Relationships*. London: Sage.

Edwards, D., & Middleton, D. (1988). " Conversational remembering and family relations: how children learn to remember." *Journal of Social and Personal Relations, 5*, 3–25.

Efran, J. S., Lukens, R. J., & Lukens, M. D. (1988). "Constructivism: what's in it for you?" *Family Therapy Networker, 12* (5), 27–37.

Epstein, E. S., & Loos, V. E. (1989). "Some irreverent thoughts on the limitations of family therapy: toward a language based explanation of human systems." *Journal of Family Psychology, 3*, 405–421.

Eron, J. B., & Lund, T. W. (1993). "'How problems evolve and disolve': integrating narrative and strategic concepts." *Family Process, 32*, 291–309.

Ferreira, A. J. (1963)."Family myths and homeostasis." *Archives of General Psychiatry, 9*, 457–463.

Fisch, R., Weakland, J. H., & Segal, L. (1982). *The Tactics of Change*. San Fransisco, CA: Jossey-Bass.

Foreman, S. (1995). "Inequalities of power, strategies of influence and sexual problems in couples." Unpublished Ph.D. thesis, Open University, Milton Keynes.

Foreman, S., & Dallos, R. (1996). *Couples, Power and Sex: The Politics of Desire*. Milton Keynes: Open University Press.

Foucault, M. (1967). *Madness and Civilisation*. London: Tavistock.

Foucault, M. (1975). *The Archeology of Knowledge*. London: Tavistock.

Framo, J. L. (1965). "Rationale and techniques of intensive family therapy." In: I. Boszormenyi-Nagy & J. L. Framo (Eds.), *Intensive Family Therapy*. New York: Harper.

Freud, S. (1905). *Three Essays on the Theory of Sexuality. S.E, 7.*

Freud, S. (1914)."On the history of the psycho-analytic movement." *S.E., 14.*

Gergen, K. J. (1985). "The social constructionist movement in modern psychology." *American Psychologist* (March).

Goffman, I. (1975). *Frame Analysis*. Harmondsworth: Penguin.

Goldberg, D., & Huxley, P. (1980). *Mental Illness in the Community: The Pathway to Psychiatric Care*. London: Tavistock.

Goldberg, D., & Huxley, P. (1992). *Common Mental Disorders*. London: Routledge.

Goldner, V. (1991). "Sex, power and gender: a feminist systemic analysis of the politics of passion." *Journal of Feminist Family Therapy, 3* (1/2).

Goldner, V., Penn, P., Sheinberg, M., & Walker, G. A. (1990). "Love and violence: paradoxes of volatile attachments." *Family Process, 29*, 343–364.

Goolishian, H. (1988). "Constructivism, autopoiesis and problem determined systems." *Irish Journal of Psychology, 9* (1), 130–143.

Goolishian, H., & Anderson, H. (1987). "Language systems and therapy: an evolving idea." *Psychotherapy, 24*, 529–538.

Gottman, J. M. (1982). Emotional responsiveness in marital conversations. *Journal of Communication, 16*, 108–119.

Haley, J. (1963). *Strategies of Psychotherapy*. New York: Grune & Stratton.

Haley, J. (1976a). "Development of a theory: a history of a research project." In: C. E. Sluzki & D. C. Ransom (Eds.), *Double Bind: The Foundation of the Communicational Approach to the Family*. New York: Grune & Stratton.

Haley, J. (1976b). *Problem Solving Therapy* (2nd edition). San Fransisco, CA: Jossey Bass, 1987.

Haley, J. (1981). *Uncommon Therapy*. New York: W. W. Norton.

Hall, S. (1992). "The West and the rest." In: S. Hall & B. Grieben (Eds.), *Foundations of Modernity*. Cambridge: Polity Press.

Harre-Mustin, R. T. (1991). "Sex, lies and headaches: the problem is power." *Journal of Feminist Family Therapy, 3*, 39–61.

Harvey, J. H., Orbuch, T. L., & Weber, A. L. (Eds.) (1992). *Attributions, Accounts and Close Relationships*. London: Springer-Verlag.

Heider, F. (1946). "Attitudes and cognitive organisation." *Journal of Psychology, 21*, 107–112.

Heider, F., & Simmel, M. (1944). "An experimental study of apparent behaviour." *American Journal of Psychology, 57*, 243–259.

Hendrick, C., & Hendrick, S. S. (1988). "Lovers wear rose-coloured glasses." *Journal of Social and Personal Relations, 5*, 161–183.

Hoffman, L. (1976). "Breaking the homeostatic cycle." In: P. Guerin (Ed.), *Family Therapy: Theory and Practice*. New York: Gardner Press.

Hoffman, L. (1988). "A constructivist position for family therapy." *Irish Journal of Psychology, 9* (1), 110–129. Also in: *Exchanging Voices*. London: Karnac Books, 1993.

Hoffman, L. (1990). "Constructing realities: the art of lenses." *Family Process, 19* (1), 1–13. Also in: *Exchanging Voices*. London: Karnac Books, 1993.

Hoffman, L. (1993). *Exchanging Voices*. London: Karnac Books.

Jackson, D. D. (1957). "The question of family homeostasis." *Psychiatry Quarterly Supplement, 31*, 79–99.

Jackson, D. D. (1965). "The study of the family." *Family Process, 4*, 1–20.

Jacoby, R. (1975). *Social Amnesia: A Critique of Conformist Psychology from Adler to Laing*. Hassocks: Harvester Press.

James, K., & McIntyre, D. (1983). "The reproduction of families: the social role of family therapy?" *Journal of Marital and Family Therapy, 9* (2), 119–129.

Jones, E. E., & Nisbett, R. G. (1972). The actor and observer: divergent perceptions of the causes of behaviour. In: E. E. Jones et al. (Eds.), *Attributions*. New York: General Learning Press.

Jost, J. T., & Banaji, M. R. (1994). "The role of stereotyping in system-justification and the production of false-consciousness." *British Journal of Social Psychology, 33* (1), 1–29.

Keeney, R. (1983). *Aesthetic of Change*. New York: Guilford.

Kelley, H. H. (1967). "Attribution theory in social psychology." *Nebraska Symposium on Motivation, 15*, 192–238.

Kelly, G. A. (1955). *The Psychology of Personal Constructs, Vols. 1 and 2*. New York: W. W. Norton.

Kelly, G. A. (1963). *A Theory of Personality: The Psychology of Personal Constructs*. New York: W. W. Norton.

Laing, R. D. (1966). *The Politics of the Family and Other Essays*. London: Tavistock.

Laing, R. D., Philipson, H., & Lee, A. P. (1966). *Interpersonal Perception*. New York: Harper & Row.

La Rossa, R. (1986). *Becoming a Parent*. Beverley Hills, CA: Sage.

La Rossa, R. (1995). "Stories and relationships." *Journal of Social and Personal Relationships, 12* (4), 555–558.

Lau, A. (1984). "Transcultural issues in family therapy." *Journal of Family Therapy, 6*, 91–112.

Lavin, T. J. (1987). "Divergence and convergence in the causal attributions of married couples." *Journal of Marriage and the Family, 49*, 71–80.

Littlewood, R., & Lipsedge, M. (1989). *Aliens and Alienists: Ethnic Minorities and Psychiatry*. London: Unwin Hyman.

Lukes, S. (1974). *Power: A Radical View*. London: Macmillan.

Madanes, C. (1981). *Strategic Family Therapy*. London: Jossey-Bass.

Marx, K., & Engels, F. (1846). *The German Ideology* (edited by C. J. Arthur). New York: International Publishers, 1970.

Maturana, H. R., & Varela, F. J. (1980). *Autopoiesis and Cognition*. Dordrecht: D. Reidel.

McKinnon, L., & Miller, D. (1987). "The new epistemology and the Milan approach: feminist and socio-political consideration." *Journal of Marital and Family Therapy, 13*, 139–155.

Mead, M. (1949). *Male and Female*. Harmondsworth: Penguin.

Millet, K. (1970). *Sexual Politics*. New York: Avon Books.

Minuchin, S. (1974). *Families and Family Therapy*. Cambridge, MA: Harvard University Press.

Palazzoli, M. S., Anolli, L., DiBliaso, P., Giossi, L., Pisano, I., Sacchi, C., & Ugazio, V. (1987). *The Hidden Games in Organisations*. New York: Pantheon.

Palazzoli, M. S., Boscolo, L., Cecchin, G., & Prata, G. (1980). "Hypothesising—circularity—neutrality: three guidelines for the conductor of the session." *Family Process, 19*, 3–12.

Palazzoli, M. S., Cecchin, G., Prata, G., & Boscolo, L. (1978). *Paradox and Counter-Paradox*. New York: Jason Aronson.

Palazzoli, M. S., Cirillo, S., Selvini, M., & Sorrentino, A. M. (1989). *Family Games: General Models of Psychotic Processes in the Family*. London: Karnac Books.

Panalp, S., & Surra, C. A. (1992). "The role of account-making in the growth and deterioration of close relationships." In: J. H. Harvey, T. L. Orbuch, & A. L. Weber (Eds.), *Attributions, Accounts and Close Relationships*. London: Springer-Verlag.

Pearce, W. B., & Cronen, V. E. (1980). *Communication, Action and Meaning*. New York: Praeger.

Penfold, P. S., & Walker, G. A. (1984). "The psychiatric paradox of women." *Canadian Journal of Community Mental Health, 5* (2): 9–15.

Penn, P., & Frankfurt, M. (1994). "Creating a participatant text: writing, multiple voices, narrative multiplicity." *Family Process, 33* (3), 217–231.

Piaget, J. (1955). *The Child's Construction of Reality*. London: Routledge & Kegan Paul.

Pollner, M., & Wikler, L. (1985). "The social construction of unreality." *Family Process, 24* (2), 241–259.

Procter, H. G. (1981)."Family construct psychology." In: S. Walrond-Skinner (Ed.), *Family Therapy and Approaches*. London: Routledge & Kegan Paul.

Procter, H. G. (1985). "A personal construct approach to family therapy and systems intervention." In: E. Button (Ed.), *Personal Construct Theory and Mental Health*. London: Croom Helm.

Reimers, S., & Treacher, A. (1995). *Introducing User-friendly Family Therapy*. London: Routledge.

Rosaldo, M. Z. (1984). "Toward an anthropology of the self and feeling." In: R. Schweder & R. LeVine (Eds.), *Culture Theory: Essays in Mind, Self, and Emotions*. Cambridge/New York: Cambridge University Press.

Rosenhan, D. L. (1973). " On being sane in insane places." *Science, 179*, 250–268.

Ross, M., Amabile, T. M., & Steimetz, J. L. (1977). "Social role, social control, and biases in social-perception processes." *Journal of Personality and Social Psychology, 35*, 485-494.

Sandler, J. (1993). "On communication from patient to analyst: not everything is projective identification." *International Journal of Psycho-Analysis, 74*, 1097–1107.

Selvini, M. (1992). " Schizophrenia as a family game." *Networker* (May/June), 81–83.

Shotter, J. (1987). "The social construction of an 'us', problems of accountability and narratology." In: R. Burnett, P. McGhee, & D. D. Clarke (Eds.), *Accounting for Relationships* (pp. 225–247). London: Methuen.

Shotter, J. (1992). "What is a 'personal' relationship? A rhetorical–responsive account of 'unfinished' business." In: J. H. Harvey, T. L. Orbuch, & A. L. Weber (Eds.), *Attributions, Accounts, Close Relationships*. New York: Springer-Verlag.

Sluzki, C. E. (1992). "Transformations: a blueprint for narrative changes in therapy." *Family Process, 31*, 217–230.

Sluzki, C. E., & Ransom, D. D. (Eds.) (1976). *Double Bind: The Foundation of the Communicational Approach to the Family*. New York: Grune & Stratton.

Speed, B. (1984). "How really real is real?" *Family Process, 23*, 511–520.

Speed, B. (1991). " Reality exists O.K. An argument against constructivism and social constructionsism." *Journal of Family Therapy, 13* (4), 395–411.

Storms, M. D. (1973). "Videotape and the attribution process: reversing actors' and observers' point of view." *Journal of Personality and Social Psychology, 27*, 165–175.

Szasz, T. (1962). *The Myth of Mental Illness*. London: Secker & Warburg.

Tomm, K. (1988). "Interventive interviewing, Part 3: Intending to ask circular, strategic or reflexive questions." *Family Process, 27* (1), 1–17.

Trevarthen, C. (1992). "The function of emotions in early infant communication and development." In: J. Nadel & L. Camioni (Eds.), *New Perspectives in Early Communicative Development.* London: Routledge.

Veroff, J., Sutherland, L., Chadrha, L., & Ortega, R. M. (1993). Newlyweds tell their stories: a narrative method for assessing marital experiences. *Journal of Social and Personal Relationships, 10,* 437–457.

von Bertalanffy, L. (1962). "General Systems Theory: a critical review." *General Systems Yearbook, 7,* 1–20.

Von Glasersfeld, E. (1979). "The control of perception and the construction of reality." *Dialectica, 33,* 37–50.

Vygotsky, L. S. (1978a). *Mind in Society.* Cambridge, MA: Harvard University Press.

Vygotsky, L. S. (1978b). *Thought and Language* (2nd edition). Cambridge, MA: MIT Press.

Watzlawick, P. (1963)."A review of the double-bind theory." *Family Process, 2* (1), 132–153.

Watzlawick, P. (1984). *The Invented Reality.* New York: W. W. Norton.

Watzlawick, P., Beavin, J., & Jackson, D. D. (1967). *Pragmatics of Human Communication.* New York: W. W. Norton.

Watzlawick, P., Weakland, J. H., & Fisch, R. (1974). *Change: Principles of Problem Formation and Problem Resolution.* New York: W. W. Norton.

Weakland, J. H. (1976). "Toward a theory of schizophrenia." In: C. E. Sluzki & D. D. Ransom (Eds.) (1976). *Double Bind: The Foundation of the Communicational Approach to the Family.* New York: Grune & Stratton.

Weakland, J. H. (1982). *The Tactics of Change.* San Fransisco, CA: Jossey-Bass.

Weber, A. L. (1992). "The account-making process: a phenomenological approach." In: T. L. Orbuch (Ed.), *Relationship Loss.* New York: Springer Verlag.

White, M. (1995). *Re-Authoring Lives: Interviews and Essays.* Dulwich, Australia: Dulwich Centre Publications.

White, M., & Epston, D. (1990). *Narrative Means to Therapeutic Ends.* New York: W. W. Norton.

Whitehead, A. N., & Russell, B. (1910). *Principia Mathematica.* Cambridge: Cambridge University Press.

Wiener, N. (1954). *The Human Use of Human Beings* (2nd edition). New York: Avon, 1967.

Wiener, N. (1961). *Cybernetics.* Cambridge, MA: MIT. Press.

Wile, D. B. (1981). *Couples Therapy.* New York: John Wiley.

Williams, J., & Watson, G. (1988). "Sexual inequality, family life and family therapy." In: E. Street & W. Dryden (Eds.), *Family Therapy in Britain.* Buckingham: Open University Press.

Wortis, J. (1974). *Fragments of an Analysis with Freud.* New York.

Wynne, L., Ryckoff, I., Day, J., & Hirsch, S. (1958). "Pseudo-mutuality in the family relations of schizophrenics." *Psychiatry, 21,* 205–220.

INDEX